Pilaf, Risotto, and
Other Ways with Rice

❧

Pilaf, Risotto, and Other Ways with Rice

SADA FRETZ

LITTLE, BROWN AND COMPANY

BOSTON   NEW YORK   TORONTO   LONDON

First Edition

Library of Congress Cataloging-in-Publicaton Data

Fretz, Sada.
    Pilaf, risotto, and other ways with rice / Sada Fretz.
        p.   cm.
    Includes index.
    ISBN 0-316-29416-0
    1. Cookery (Rice)   2. Rice.   I. Title.
TX809.R5F74   1995
641.6'318—dc20   94-17683

10 9 8 7 6 5 4 3 2 1

RRD-VA

*Published simultaneously in Canada
by Little, Brown & Company (Canada) Limited*

Printed in the United States of America

Contents

❧

Pilaf, Risotto, and Other Ways with Rice

✤

ONE

About Rice and How to Cook It

✧

RICE is the sustaining grain for roughly half the people of the world. For many it anchors every meal, an abiding presence identified in myth and ritual with life itself. In many Asian languages the word for rice is the same as the word for food, and the words for "come eat rice" serve as both an invitation to dinner and a summons to the table comparable to our "dinner's ready." In parts of Asia, food *is* rice, and all other edibles — vegetables, beans, fish, meat — are considered extras: merely relishes or toppings for the rice. The anthropologist E. N. Anderson reports in his book *The Food of China* that people in southern China will insist they haven't eaten all day if they haven't had their rice, even though they might have filled themselves with "snacks."

No one knows how long rice has grown wild. I. I. Chang of the International Rice Research Institute in the Philippines has suggested that it goes back to Gondwanaland before that ancient supercontinent broke up into the earth's present configurations. How long humans have been gathering and cooking the wild grain or even how long people have been cultivating rice is also lost in the distant past; but the earliest evidence of rice cultivation, unearthed in China's Yangtze Delta, is more than seven thousand years old. Other sites in central and southern China and in northern Thailand are almost as old. By 3000 B.C., according to Anderson, rice-farming communities were well established from Taiwan to India.

Asia still grows and consumes 90 percent of the world's rice crop. But rice is cultivated on every continent except Antarctica and is daily fare in much of the Middle East, West Africa, and Central and South America, on Caribbean and Pacific islands, and in our own state of South Carolina.

Today rice grows in tropical and in temperate climates, in flooded lowland paddy fields and on rain-fed hillsides. It is farmed laboriously by stooping peasants calf deep in water, as is still the case in much of Asia, or with planes, combines, and chemicals, as in the United States today, where its highly mechanized production is concentrated in Arkansas, Texas, Louisiana, and California.

The United States is now the world's second leading rice exporter, after Thailand, though we grow less than 1.5 percent of the world's crop, a clear reflection on our relatively limited domestic consumption. In 1991, when the average Burmese ate 416 pounds of rice, the average Thai 329, and the average Chinese (including wheat-eating northern Chinese) 243, the figure for Americans was 22. But that is more than triple what it was two decades earlier — and it is growing.

Since 1987 Americans have been putting away more rice than pasta. In fact, the pasta frenzy of the 1980s that helped wean us from our meat-and-potatoes habit might be credited with preparing us for rice. Most immediately, it was a natural progression from Italian pasta to northern Italy's risotto. Then other ways with rice came in with the newest wave of immigrants: about 85 percent of those arriving in the 1980s were from rice-eating cultures, and their restaurants and food stores have been educating the rest of us. At the same time air freight costs have fallen and flying food importers have been enticing us with formerly exotic ingredients used in rice-based cuisines around the globe.

Even our medical advisers are encouraging our interest in rice. Doctors are telling us to eat more complex carbohydrates (starches), and rice (except for its water content) is about 90 percent starch. For people who eat large amounts of rice, it is an adequate source of protein, especially when the protein is complemented by dashes of soy products and fish sauce, as it is in eastern and southeastern Asia, or paired with beans, as it is almost anywhere. Whole grain (brown) rice is also a good source of fiber and of several vitamins and minerals.

Brown or white, rice has considerable negative nutrition value: It is cholesterol free, virtually fat free, and consequently low in calories, as well as low in salt. It is easy to digest and nonallergenic and so a perfect food for the sizable minority of people who have problems with wheat. It is often eaten plain or mixed with other nutritious nonfat or lowfat food, so that a rice meal is more likely than a plate of dressed spaghetti to conform to current dietary guidelines. And when similarly boiled, rice is almost as fast cooking as spaghetti.

But rice's chief appeal to restless North Americans might lie in the ease with which it can accommodate an endless variety of tastes and treatments. A rice dish can be as pristine or as rococo as the cook chooses to make it; and in preparing it today's cooks can draw on a world of cooking styles.

About This Book

During the 1980s and early 1990s, with new ethnic markets sprouting up around us and once exotic ingredients showing up on supermarket shelves, there was a rush to acquire whatever herb or spice or sausage or chile pepper was required for a Thai curry or an Indian biryani, a paella Valenciana or an arroz a la Mexicana. But too many home cooks and recipe writers appeared not to know or not to care that the *way* these and other traditional dishes are prepared is as important as what goes into them, and that the most important ingredient for many if not all of them is the appropriate rice.

A major emphasis in this book is on the different ways in which rice is cooked in different rice-cooking cultures. Many of the recipes are original, and few if any pretend to be authentic reconstructions of particular dishes prepared in obscure villages exactly as long custom has decreed. I leave that worthy function to authors who are natives or longtime residents of the particular places whose cuisines they are transmitting to the world. But when one of these recipes or groups of recipes claim to represent, for example, a Persian, Mexican, Spanish, Japanese, or South Carolina tradition or dish or cooking style, it follows procedures used by that country's (or region's) cooks and calls for the type of rice (or the closest available approximation) that is traditional there.

Many of the recipes included here are for traditional dishes learned from cooks whose foremothers have been making them for generations, if not centuries. Others, for common ethnic specialties, are my syntheses of several versions acquired from different printed and living sources. (When a recipe owes much to a specific source, encountered either in person or in print, that is acknowledged in the headnote to the recipe.) Still others are for original variations created within traditional modes.

Then there are freer inventions or departures, with no claims to pedigree, that might blithely combine ingredients from different climes and techniques from different cultures. If they encourage readers to create their own improvisations, so much the better. My point in emphasizing traditional ways of cooking is not to fossilize a living art; it's just that even if you only want to produce something tasty and presentable for family or friends, you are more likely to succeed — and you will surely have more choices — if you understand some of the techniques and principles that have been honed and handed down by centuries of rice cooks in scattered corners of the world.

In keeping with this emphasis on traditional ways of rice cooking, I've divided the rice recipes into three broad groups: on pilaf and its extended family, almost exclusively prepared with long-grain rice; on distinctive Spanish and Italian ways with their own medium-grain rice; and on a sampling of East Asian and Asian-inspired dishes, which employ a variety of rices. Since reality is never as tidy as our cataloging instincts would like, and since readers' convenience in finding and using recipes doesn't always jibe with culinary genealogy, this arrangement has involved some liberties and perhaps some gerrymandering of culinary territories. These will be explained as they occur.

Kinds of Rice

Of at least twenty species of rice known to grow wild on earth, only two have been cultivated by humans. These are *Oryza glaberrima,* native to West Africa and unknown elsewhere, and the Asian *Oryza sativa,* which includes all the rices grown and eaten in the rest of the world. The cultivated varieties of these species are still being counted. A few years ago officials of the International Rice Research Institute in the Philippines estimated their number at close to 120,000. Some Asian markets carry dozens of varieties, and their customers are discerning mavens, literally sniffing out the different kinds and qualities among them.

Various as they are, all *Oryza sativa* varieties fall into one of two categories, based on the shape of the grain. In the 1920s a team of Japanese rice scientists assigned these categories the labels that we use today. The short-grain rices grown and eaten in Japan, though originally from China, became *Oryza sativa japonica.* Long-grain rice, grown in India but also native to China and Southeast Asia, is known as *Oryza sativa indica. Javonica,* named later and sometimes classified as a third type, evolved in Indonesia from rice native to Southeast Asia but is not grown or used elsewhere.

The long-grain *indica* rices tend to be less starchy than the *japonica* grains and are thus preferred for pilaf cooking, which aims for separate, dry grains. Actually, long-grain rices tend to have more of one type of starch, amylose, and less of amylopectin, the stickier starch, than do the short-grain varieties. But this is just a usual association, reinforced by breeding, not an invariable link. For example, jasmine rice from Thailand, a lovely long-grain rice prized for its fragrance, has a little more of the sticky starch than is typical for its shape. Commonly used in coconut rice dishes, Thai jasmine rice is now widely available here and well worth adding to your rice cupboard.

Another aromatic long-grain rice, the most exquisite available today, is northern India's basmati, a long, thin, delicate grain that stretches lengthwise when cooked and whose texture takes beautifully to light, dry rice preparation. Dehradun basmati, named for the northern Indian location where it grows, is a favorite with Indian and Iranian rice cooks and is by far the best basmati I've sampled. (There are also different grades of dehradun basmati, which is evident in their performance, but I don't know that the grades are labeled on the bags sold here.) Because Indian basmati calls for washing and soaking and costs more than other rices, it is usually reserved for special dishes and special occasions. On the other hand, a plain basmati side dish on an ordinary Wednesday can do much to lift the midweek spirits.

American basmati-type rices, such as Texmati, are also very good but can't match Indian basmati in fragrance or texture. The brown basmati in bins at natural-food stores and almost all unspecified bulk basmati sold here is American and not true basmati, though often possessed of some basmati qualities. By the time this book is published, the Texmati company, RiceTec, which also puts out a jasmine-type rice called Jasmati, will be marketing its new Kasmati rice, said to be developed from Indian varieties and more like real basmati.

Popcorn rice, cultivated in small quantities by a few Louisiana growers, is a superior American aromatic rice, delicious with just a little salt or butter. According to grower Paul Guillory, popcorn rice (so named because "someone said it smells like popcorn") has been cultivated from a strain thought to descend from Indian basmati and found in a mixed-seed sample that the Louisiana Agriculture Experiment Station imported from France in 1906. Not widely available, popcorn rice can be ordered in amounts as small as two pounds from Mr. Guillory, Route 3, Box 55, Welsh, LA 70591, phone 318-734-4440, or from Ellis Stansel (who sets a ten-pound minimum), P.O. Box 206, Gueydan, LA 70542, phone 318-536-6140.

The standard American rice brand that I used for many of the generic long-grain rice recipes in this book is Carolina brand extra-long-grain rice. Other brands are favored in different parts of the country.

Today the most commonly used of the short-grain *japonica* category are the slightly longer varieties labeled medium-grain. Short- or medium-grain rice is used in some Chinese regions and some Chinese preparations and is virtually the only rice grown and used in Korea and Japan. Japanese Americans are happy with good California brands of medium-grain rice such as Kokuho Rose and Tamaki, though in blind tastings reported in the *Wall Street Journal*, rice connoisseurs in Japan preferred their own expensive (and heavily subsidized) traditionally grown rice. It is not exported. Traditional Puerto Rican rice cooks also use short- or medium-grain rice; my most exacting adviser uses the California brands mentioned above.

Some call all short-grain rice "sticky rice," because it tends to be more clingy than the long-grain kind, but that term should be reserved for the truly sticky short-grain rice usually labeled "sweet rice" (though it is not sugary-sweet) and often referred to in print as "glutinous rice" (though no rice contains any gluten). Sticky rice (as its users call it) is daily fare in a small mountainous area of southeastern China and northern Thailand, Laos, and Vietnam, where there are also sticky long-grain varieties; but sticky rice is used elsewhere in Asia chiefly for porridge, stuffings, and sweets, as well as in brewing and commercial thickeners. For eating it is usually steamed, because it becomes gluey when cooked in water.

Coastal Spain and northern Italy, the only significant ricelands of Western Europe, grow their own varieties of medium-grain *japonica* rice. Italian rice is distinguished by its firm center and absorbent, translucent coating, good for achieving the creamy, clingy texture desired in risotto while retaining a chewy core. Spanish rice, grown chiefly in Valencia, has a medium grain suited to Spain's paella cooking. Italian rice is the best substitute.

White, Brown, and Converted Rice

Besides genetic types, rice can be categorized by the kind and degree of processing it has undergone. Almost all rice consumed throughout the world is refined white rice that has had its germ and outer bran layer stripped away. Refining rice can have disastrous consequences, as the often-told story of the discovery of vitamins dramatically reveals. In the nineteenth century, after advances in milling technology made polished rice whiter and cheaper than ever, a mysterious disease called beriberi became endemic among the poor of Indonesia, then a colony of the Netherlands. A Dutch doctor sent to investigate noticed that even the hospital chickens were ailing and dying; but when the kitchen staff began to throw the discarded rice bran to the chickens, they recovered. In a flash, the doctor realized that some unknown substance in the millings was essential to the chickens' and the humans' health.

Now thiamine, or B_1, the anti-beriberi vitamin required for metabolizing carbohydrates, is added back, along with some other nutrients lost in the milling, to "enrich" refined white rice and white flour. But as natural-food shoppers know, enriched white rice still has less of many vitamins and minerals than it started out with and far less of the fiber present in whole-grain brown rice. Just how important this is to a well-fed American with other sources of these nutrients is another question; but without some whole grains, most of us don't get the fiber that current nutrition guidelines recommend.

Besides, brown rice has a pleasant, nutty taste and enough heft to satisfy, especially in a meatless meal. It's good in stuffings and in summer salads, and it's delicious toasted. It's less suitable for risotto or for fried rice or with a delicate or subtle sauce. Another possible disadvantage is that it takes twice as long to cook; and it can become rancid if kept unrefrigerated for months, especially in hot weather.

Although not traditional in any culture, pilafs made with brown rice are included in Chapter Three of this book (and listed in the index), and brown rice is used in the East-West recipes in Chapter Five.

Converted Rice, a trademark of the Uncle Ben's rice brand, has been parboiled before refining, a steaming process that forces some of the outer vitamins and minerals into the kernel. Hence it is more nutritious than regular white rice but less so than brown rice. Many Americans like Uncle Ben's long-grain converted rice because it always cooks up in separate, intact grains. In 1990 *Consumer Reports* rated it number one for taste and texture, though the testers noted that the directions call for too much water. However, many rice mavens who appreciate the special qualities of different grains are less impressed with converted rice. According to John and Matt Thorne, who tested rices for the spring 1993 issue of their highly independent food letter *Simple Cooking,* "Even bargain-basement ordinary rice has a noticeably sweeter, brighter taste. . . . Like frozen vegetables, converted rice has a vague 'cooked' taste; all its flavor edges have been rubbed away in some distant processing plant."

Though I tend to agree with the Thornes, I'll allow some difference of opinion about converted rice. But instant, or minute, rice is indisputably funny stuff with no taste and a very unricelike texture. Partially precooked in the factory, it's not worth the time it takes to finish the job. Have a sandwich instead.

Wild Rice

As everyone who writes about it seems compelled to point out, the North American aquatic grass that early European explorers named "wild rice" isn't really a rice. Both are members of the grass family, but wild rice (botanically, *Zizania aquatica*) is not closely related to the genus *Oryza,* the classification that includes all the true rice types and varieties described above. Still, it is called rice and is cooked like rice, often mixed with real rice, and so cookbooks customarily include it in their rice recipe pages.

If not real rice, until recently all wild rice was at least wild, growing mostly in the lakes and marshes of the northern Great Lakes region of the United States and Canada. For centuries it has been an important source of food and income for the Native American people of that region, who harvest it laboriously by hand. The Ojibway (or Chippewa) people still gather annually at harvest camps to perform the almost sacred task of hand-picking and hand-processing the grain that they call *manoomin.* (It is said that the Menominee Indians take their name from the wild rice plant.) But for the past three decades the cultivation of *Zizania aquatica* has fallen increasingly into white and corporate hands. By the late 1980s, 95 percent of all commercial wild rice was grown in artificially created paddies, most of them in California, and then mechanically harvested and processed. The rice is far cheaper to prepare that way, though the cost to consumers is still high. The cost to Ojibway ricers, financial and cultural, is far higher.

As described in Thomas Vennum's book *Wild Rice and the Ojibway People,* in a traditional wild rice harvest pairs of ricers set out in two-person canoes, one partner poling the canoe while the other bends the stalks and beats them with a rice stick, knocking the grains off and into the canoe. Later, boatloads of rice are dumped to air-dry in the sun, then parched on an open fire. Thus prepared, the grains are poured into big tubs, where they are hulled by men in special "jigging" moccasins who tramp on them vigorously in a prescribed circular motion. Finally the jigged rice is tossed to winnow off the chaff. By each day's end the ricers are dancing in celebration and feasting on new rice.

In bad times past the Ojibway have lived through winter stretches on wild rice alone. In better times they added bear or buffalo fat to the cooking pot or mixed the rice with maple syrup or blueberries. Sometimes they popped it like popcorn or puffed it by soaking it overnight, then roasting it over a fire. In happy times they used it, and still do on occasion, as stuffing for roast venison or for fresh-caught fish or duck. It's not hard to understand why some Ojibway old-timers still shun whites' store food. Wild mallard ducks who have fed on wild rice, a remembered blessing of my own childhood in Michigan's Upper Peninsula, are not lightly exchanged for conveniently packaged sawdust.

To cook wild rice I follow the Ojibway method of putting it in a pot with twice its volume of boiling broth or water. Add fat (I put a spoonful of butter, having neither the resources nor the inclination to acquire bear grease), then adjust the heat to a low boil, just a little stronger than the low simmer that cooks regular rice. It's done in forty or fifty minutes, when the liquid is absorbed.

Many cookbooks call for far more liquid and longer cooking time, so that the grains burst and soften. The Ojibway sometimes cook it this way for a kind of fluffy porridge that can be stretched to fill more stomachs; but for most purposes wild rice should be fairly chewy, cooked just short of bursting. It's delicious cooked in duck broth or a good turkey or chicken broth, seasoned with sage and thyme. It can also be boiled in water like spaghetti, then drained through a sieve and seasoned with salt and butter.

Because of its high price and firm texture, wild rice is often mixed with brown or white rice for stuffings, salads, and side dishes. This is fine, if you do the mixing yourself. Premixed packages are long on the cheaper rices, short on wild rice, and thus outrageously overpriced.

A Dozen One-and-Only Ways to Cook Plain Rice

While gathering recipes for this book, I spoke with dozens if not hundreds of rice cooks, many of whom found me pretty ignorant. Repeatedly, conversations took this turn:

SOURCE: . . . And then you cook the rice.

ME: How do you do that?

SOURCE: Oh, just the regular way.

ME: What is that?

SOURCE (incredulous): Surely you have directions in your book for how to cook plain rice!

Only the instructions that followed this exchange departed from the script; but they took off in all directions. So do the often dogmatic rules and assertions found in leading cookbooks. Here are a few bits of advice encountered in my field research and kitchen library:

"Don't salt the water; it distracts the rice."

"Add three tablespoons of salt to keep the rice from breaking."

"You must never lift the lid until the rice is done."

"Uncover and turn the rice up from the bottom every ten minutes."

"Boil rapidly for seven minutes exactly."

"Steam slowly for an hour."

"The rice in American stores is old and dry. Young rice from a fresh harvest is best."

"The best rice has been aged for years to seal in its fragrance."

"Drop the rice into boiling water."

"Always start the rice in cold water."

"Cook until the water disappears before covering the pot."

"Bring rice and water to a boil in a covered pot."

On one point there seems to be near unanimity: When combining rice with water for absorption, the water should rise one knuckle (of an extended finger) above the surface of the rice. I've been given this solemn and identical advice by Asians, Cajuns, and countless others, including a salesman of electric rice cookers and other modern appliances. But when the proportions are measured in cups, confusion returns. Cubans say that the key to perfect rice is equal amounts of rice and water. A Greek cookbook decrees that "exactly" 2 cups of water and 1 cup of rice "must be measured very carefully." Mexican cooks add a full $2\frac{1}{2}$ cups of water for every cup of rice. One Vietnamese cookbook in my kitchen calls for $2\frac{1}{2}$ cups of water for a full 3 cups of rice. Yet another from the same country wants $3\frac{1}{4}$ cups of water for 2 cups of rice.

Some of the differences can be explained. Long-grain rice needs more water than short-grain varieties. New rice uses less than old, dry rice (whichever age you prefer). Rice that has been washed or soaked needs a little less than rice that starts out dry. More water will escape from rice that's cooked uncovered. In humid weather I use less water to avoid soggy rice. Still, it's hard not to conclude from this babel of commandments that there is more than one path to perfect rice.

Preparing Rice for Cooking

My purpose in the following paragraphs is not to make a simple task more complicated. Pouring rice straight from a box into a pot of water is a perfectly respectable way to begin. But certain rices call for special preparation to realize their full potential; and certain dishes benefit from rice that has been so prepared.

Washing Rice

Washing rice is traditional in Asia, almost always called for with Indian basmati, and important in pilaf cooking, because the water rinses away the surface starch so that the rice grains will cook up separate and dry.

There are two ways to wash rice. Indian cooks put the rice in a large bowl, cover with water, swish around, then tip off the water. (This is most easily done if the water is poured off through a sieve to catch any rice that goes along.) Then more water is added and drained off. After eight or nine such rinses, the poured-off water should be running clear of starch and the rice can be drained or put to soak.

Another, faster but less thorough way to wash rice is to put it in a large strainer under cold running water. Rake with your fingers and rinse until the water runs clear. If not soaking the rice, shake the sieve to drain off residual water.

Many say that it is not necessary to wash American rice. In fact, it is not necessary to wash basmati, except to clean it, which imported basmati sometimes requires. Basmati performs well when treated just like American rice but better when treated with respect. Similarly, American rice is usually not washed, but it can benefit from a starch rinse for certain preparations. Traditional cooks from several cultures wash American rice.

Washing rice has fallen out of favor because it rinses off the vitamins and minerals that have been added back to American white rice in the enrichment process. This doesn't bother me, since the only vitamins added to my Carolina rice, the B vitamins thiamine and niacin, are common in all sorts of foods, and a serving of rice contains only a small percentage of the daily allowance. Iron, the only mineral added back, could be of value to some women, but even where this is significant I don't think washing rice for special occasions is an invitation to anemia, let alone beriberi or the niacin-deficiency disease, pellagra.

Soaking Rice

Several recipes in this book, especially those from Persian, Indian, and Mexican cooks, call for soaking washed rice before cooking. Overnight soaks were once the rule, but changes in rices and lifestyles have shortened the duration to 2 hours in Persian cooking, 30 minutes in India, and 10 to 15 minutes in Mexico.

To soak, put washed rice in a bowl with cool water to cover by an inch or so. When specified soaking time is up, drain through a sieve. Rice should always be rinsed of starch before soaking, but not all washed rice has to be soaked. Washed and, especially, soaked rice requires less water when cooked by the total absorption method described below.

Cooking Rice

There are three ways of swelling the rice grains with hot liquid to tenderize and cook: boiling the rice like spaghetti; combining rice with just enough liquid in what Tom Stobart's *Cooks Encyclopedia* has awkwardly but most accurately described as the "total absorption" method; and steaming it over boiling water. Here is an outline of each, with descriptions of the major variations employed in the recipes to come. Timing and proportions are for refined white rice unless brown rice is specified.

Boiling Rice

Pour the rice into rapidly boiling salted water ($3\frac{1}{2}$ to 4 quarts of water for 1 or 2 cups of rice). Stir once and return to a boil. When tender but not mushy, drain through a strainer. Boiling time differs with the type and condition of the rice. Roughly, basmati that has been presoaked should be done after 6 or 7 minutes in the water. Unsoaked basmati will take 10 or 12 minutes. American brown basmati might take 30 minutes. Carolina or similar American rice, unsoaked, takes 18 minutes. Regular brown rice takes 35 to 40 minutes. Italian rice such as arborio, which is never soaked, takes 15 to 18 minutes, less if it will then be baked or deep-fried as in rice balls.

After boiling, rice can be tossed with fat (usually butter), seasoned, and served as is. In Persian chelo and pilau (page 61), boiled rice is cooked over oil or butter in a covered pan over very low heat until "dry"; this is sometimes called "steaming" or "soaking." Boiled rice can be finished in the oven with some fat and seasoning for the same effect, or baked with other foods and seasonings as in any number of special preparations.

Total Absorption

In this method the rice is put in a heavy-bottomed pot with water, usually about 2 cups of water for 1 cup of rice, and cooked until it absorbs all the water. This can be done in several ways, all subject to adjustment to suit your preference, conditions, and rice at hand.

The back-of-the-box way. Most packaged American rices come with directions like these: Drop the rice into rapidly boiling water with $\frac{1}{2}$ teaspoon salt and 1 teaspoon to 1 tablespoon oil or butter for every cup of rice. (The fat is important, because it coats the grains and helps prevent sticking and clumping.) Return to a boil. Then cover the pot, reduce heat, and simmer white rice 20 minutes, brown rice 40 minutes. Remove from heat and let stand, still covered, another 5 or 10 minutes. Though some boxes call for more liquid, $1\frac{3}{4}$ cups water (2 cups for converted rice) is plenty with 1 cup of American rice to be cooked covered, as here. In humid weather or with soaked rice $1\frac{1}{2}$ cups of water is better. For larger quantities of rice, use proportionately less water: $2\frac{1}{2}$ cups of water for $1\frac{1}{2}$ cups raw rice, or 3 cups water for 2 cups raw rice.

The cold start. In *Vibration Cooking; Memoirs of a Geechee Girl,* Vertamae Smart-Grosvenor tells of growing up in the unique "Geechee" (or Gullah) community of slaves' descendants in South Carolina rice country. She remembers her pride in learning early to cook rice so that "every grain stands by itself." John Martin Taylor, another coastal South Carolina cookbook author and food authority, swears that her method is foolproof. As she points out, the Chinese wash and cook rice the same way.

In a recent phone conversation, Verta elaborated on the instructions in her book. Her entire procedure is worth repeating, though the washing is an option and not necessarily linked with the cold-start method.

"First, wash the rice. Put it in water, drain it, and then rub it between the palms of your hands. Rub all the rice. Do this three times. Or just let water run through it, then shake it dry and rub it. Then put it in cold water with a little salt and a little oil. Use a little less than 2 cups of water for 1 cup of rice because the rice will still be a little wet from washing. Put on the lid, but keep it a little bit off, and heat over high heat (but not too high) until the water boils. Then shake the pan — don't stir — and turn down the heat to simmer. Put the top on tight and cook the rice for exactly 13 minutes. Then cut off the heat, but don't take off the cover. Let it stand 12 minutes. When you take off the cover, every grain will stand by itself." Double Verta's times if cooking brown rice the cold-start way and reduce the proportion of liquid, as specified for the back-of-the-box way (above), when cooking more than 1 cup of rice.

The initial sauté. This is common in the pilaf cooking of Turkey, Greece, and Egypt, and in other rice preparations. Instead of beginning in cold or hot water, heat 2 tablespoons oil or butter in a heavy saucepan, then add the rice and sauté until coated with oil. Some continue until the grains have turned translucent, then chalky white. Mexican cooks continue until the grains are scorched a light gold color. The sauté helps to keep the grains separate and intact. Hot or boiling liquid in the proportions given above is then added to the sautéed grains.

Partial cooking uncovered. Sautéed or not sautéed, once the rice and liquid have come to a boil, the temperature can be adjusted to bubble gently uncovered for about 10 minutes, until the surface liquid disappears and little steam holes appear on top of the rice. Then the pot is covered to cook another 10 minutes over very low heat. (Brown rice needs a total cooking time of 40 to 45 minutes and takes longer to absorb the water.) This step helps to prevent soggy rice and to achieve the "dry" effect desired in pilaf cooking. With this method timid cooks can use a full 2 cups of water for 1 cup of rice (or $3\frac{1}{2}$ cups liquid for 2 cups rice); but the proportions given for the back-of-the-box way, above, also work here when a drier rice is preferred.

Wrapping the lid. Whether steaming a Persian chelo or executing any variation of the total absorption method, wrapping the pot lid in a cloth dish towel is a huge help in achieving fluffy rice. The cloth absorbs the moisture that rises from the rice during the steaming period so that it doesn't drip back down and dampen the rice. Some wrap the lid only for the final rest period after cooking, but a wrapped lid can be used (and is, in Persian chelo and pilau, for example) for the entire period of covered cooking over low heat. In this book some special recipes call specifically for wrapping the lid, but it can be done for any rice dish cooked by the total absorption method or set to steam dry in a covered pot after boiling.

To wrap the pot lid, spread out a cloth dish towel and put the lid down on the towel, top up. Fold the edges of the towel up over the top of the lid. Cover the pot with the towel-wrapped lid, securing towel corners on top by pinning, tying, or weighting down if necessary. (I don't find this necessary.)

The Japanese way with short- and medium-grain rice. Short- or medium-grain rice can be cooked just like long-grain rice, except that when cooked by the total absorption method it requires less water, a little more than 1 cup of water to 1 cup of rice. But Japanese and Koreans, who cook this rice every day, have developed their own methods using plain water with no salt or fat. The result should be slightly clingy but not sticky and never mushy.

Put the rice in a sieve and rinse under running water, raking with your fingers, until the water runs clear or almost clear. Shake the sieve and hang it over a bowl to allow the rice to drain for 30 to 60 minutes. Then put the rice in a saucepan with 1 cup plus 2 tablespoons of cool water for 1 cup of rice or $2\frac{1}{4}$ cups of water for 2 cups of rice. Cover and bring to a boil. When you hear it boiling, reduce the heat to low and cook 15 minutes. Remove from heat and let rest, still covered, another 10 to 15 minutes. (If you find it easier, bring the rice and water to a boil uncovered, then cover and proceed.)

Some Japanese, instead of letting the washed rice drain for 30 to 60 minutes, put it directly into the saucepan with the cooking water and let it soak in the pan for 30 to 60 minutes before bringing to a boil and cooking as directed above.

Skillet cooking and slow steaming. Many main-dish recipes in the pilaf section, Chapter Three, and in the Spanish section of Chapter Four call for cooking rice with other foods in a large skillet. When cooking on a gas stove without large burners, as I do, you might have to move the skillet now and then (1 or 2 inches in a different direction each time) to ensure even cooking. Skillet cooking or slow cooking on an electric stove might require some kind of heat diffuser to prevent a pattern of burned and undercooked rings. (Flame tamers don't work for paella, which needs high heat; instructions on paella cooking in Chapter Four suggest oven cooking for electric stove owners.) When reducing heat for slow cooking on a slow-responding electric stove, it is best to switch the pot to another burner already set for very low heat.

For the final steaming of Persian pilau and chelo and for some Indian dishes, some cookbooks call for raising the pot on a wok ring or other device to avoid overheating. Mrs. Kathryn Lotson of lowlands Georgia uses a lid from an old black woodstove — a perfect solution for those who had the opportunity and the foresight to save them. I find, however, that the single-ring flame on my minimal gas stove can be turned down sufficiently to achieve excellent results without props or pads.

Steaming Rice

Sticky rice (also called glutinous or sweet rice) is almost always steamed, because it can become gluey when cooked in water. Steaming results in an inviting glistening surface that is definitely sticky but not gloppy.

The process for steaming sticky rice begins several hours or a day before the steaming. First, put the rice in a sieve and rinse under cool running water, raking with your fingers, until the water runs clear or almost clear. (Or wash it in a bowl with several changes of water, as in the Indian method described on page 13.) Then put the rice in a bowl with water to cover and soak several hours or overnight. Drain through a sieve, shaking to get rid of excess water.

The Chinese traditionally steam rice in a slatted bamboo steamer set in a wok with water in the bottom. The Japanese have their own device. A cheesecloth-lined couscous steamer works fine, as does my everyday vegetable steamer, essentially a covered saucepan with a perforated bottom that fits over another saucepan containing the water. (This also requires a cheesecloth lining.) You can improvise a steamer by putting a rack in a wok over boiling water. Put the rice in a bowl on the rack, then cover the wok for the steaming period. If you don't have a wok or steamer, use a cheesecloth-lined colander set into a big spaghetti pot over boiling water, with the pot lid over the colander. You might have to tie a twisted dish towel or more cheesecloth around the outside where the pot and colander meet to prevent steam from escaping through the seam.

Whatever the device, once it is sealed tight, let the rice steam for 30 minutes, then uncover and sprinkle 4 tablespoons of cool water over the rice. Replace cover and steam for another 10 to 15 minutes, making sure that the water does not boil away.

Machine Cooking

Rice cookers. Today cooks in rice country from Carolina to Korea cook their plain rice in electric rice cookers (or rice steamers) that turn off automatically when the rice is done. In some the rice and water are combined in one bowl to cook by the total absorption method described earlier. Others steam the rice in a separate bowl placed over a tray of water. Still others mix rice with water for absorption but also employ steam from a separate chamber of water below. Good rice cooks everywhere swear by these devices, although my Korean contacts, who use them daily, tell me that their mothers make better rice the old way.

Microwave ovens. These devices save no time over the conventional stovetop method. However, for microwave enthusiasts or for those who might want to get the rice pot off a crowded stove, the American Rice Council offers these guidelines:

Put a cup of rice and an optional teaspoon of salt and tablespoon of butter or margarine in a deep 2- to 3-quart microproof dish. Add water. For long-grain white rice, use $1\frac{3}{4}$ to 2 cups water. For medium- or short-grain white rice, use $1\frac{1}{2}$ cups water. Cook 5 minutes on high, 15 minutes on medium (50 percent power). Brown rice takes 2 to $2\frac{1}{2}$ cups water and an extra 15 minutes on medium. For converted rice, use 2 to $2\frac{1}{2}$ cups water and cook 5 minutes on high, 20 minutes on medium.

Pressure cookers. Devotees of pressure cookery, who tend to be of the whole foods persuasion, laud the way these machines cook rice, though the outcome is not dry and fluffy as traditional pilaf cooks desire. Owners of these devices will no doubt use their manuals for basic rice cooking instructions and turn to pressure-cooking cookbooks for others. Lorna Sass's three health-oriented books about pressure cookery (*Cooking Under Pressure* is her first title) contain several rice recipes, including her own unorthodox interpretations of risotto, paella, and sushi rice. Most (but not all) of her recipes call for brown rice and most but not all save some time over conventional stovetop and oven cooking methods.

Caveat: As an aging eccentric surviving cheerfully without a car or a dishwasher, let alone a microwave (I do have a food processor and use it occasionally), I own none of these machines and only pass along the word of others deemed reliable. All the recipes in this book call for conventional stovetop or, occasionally, oven methods.

Roasted Rice

I first encountered roasted rice in *The Art of Just Cooking*, by Lima Ohsawa, wife of macrobiotic guru George Ohsawa. Ohsawa roasted brown rice in a dry pressure cooker, then added water and proceeded to cook the rice as usual. I use an oven or skillet but still choose brown rice for roasting because of its deeper, nuttier flavor. White rice can also be roasted to good effect.

To oven-roast brown or white rice, spread the rice on a baking sheet and put it in a preheated 400°F oven for 10 minutes or until toasty but not dark brown, checking now and then to reposition if the grains around the edges are browning faster than the ones in the center.

For a skillet alternative, which has the advantage of being easily watched, spread the rice on a large, heavy, unoiled skillet over moderately high heat. Roast 10 to 15 minutes, stirring or shifting the grains once or twice as needed to keep them cooking evenly. Remove to a plate or bowl when golden or toasty brown.

Once roasted, the rice can be cooked as usual on the stove or in the oven. Have it slightly chewy and deliciously nutty, as I prefer, or cook it in a bit more water until the grains burst open and become curved and fluffy like well-cooked wild rice.

Thai and Vietnamese cooks roast long-grain white rice in a dry wok, stirring constantly as if stir-frying. When golden or toasty brown, the rice is removed from the hot wok, cooled, then ground to a coarse powder. This can be done in a spice or coffee grinder. The powder is used to thicken and flavor soups.

Stuck Rice and Golden Crusts

Growing up in a North American meat-and-potatoes family, I would have considered rice stuck to the bottom of the pot a sign of careless cooking. But cooking rice deliberately to form a crust is a venerable practice among rice cooks as far apart as Japan and Louisiana.

Japan is just one of several eastern Asian countries where a crisp golden brown rice "cake" is cultivated on the bottom of a pot of cooking rice. The Japanese call it okoge, or scorch, and have it as a treat with pickled condiments, sometimes moistened with green tea, after they've finished off the soft rice on top. Or they'll pour boiling water over the okoge to make a sort of rice tea. Koreans do the same. The Chinese cultivate a crust by leaving a bottom layer of cooked rice in the pot after scooping out the rest of the rice for a meal. Once browned, this bottom cake is lifted from the pot (as on page 63) and left to dry, then eaten as is or deep-fried in oil and dropped into a hot "sizzling soup," as on page 209.

The late Louisiana food enthusiast Leon Soniat recalls the pleasures of the crust in his cookbook-cum-food-memoir *La Bouche Creole.* He explains how his mother used to cook her rice for the standard 20 minutes, then add a tablespoon or so of lard and continue cooking it another 20 minutes for a crisp golden bottom. "As children," he wrote, "we always fought for the crust."

Traditional Puerto Rican cooks also rely on lard and longer cooking to achieve what they call the pegao (from the Spanish word *pegado,* meaning "stuck to"). Like the Louisiana Creole version, the Puerto Rican pegao is usually scraped up in pieces and served separately beside the rice. Today Puerto Rico's pegao and its Cuban counterpart, called the raspa, are more likely made with oil, as in my neighbor Geri Wasserman Hernandez's Puerto Rican Arroz con Gandulez on page 105. Cuban and Puerto Rican cookbooks don't mention the crust, Geri explains, because "everyone takes it for granted."

In Valencia, the rice center of Spain and the proud home of paella, a rice dish is scarcely finished without a crust. Most admired is the soccarrat that forms when paella is cooked the traditional way, outdoors over a wood-burning fire (page 151). Fishermen relish the quemada (literally, but not actually, "burned") on their arroz abanda, rice cooked in fish stock. Another Valencian dish, arroz con costra, has beaten eggs poured over baked rice near the end of the cooking time to form a rich top crust.

As in other matters of rice cooking, everywhere a crust is cultivated there are different but equally adamant rules for its achievement. "It's important to have the right pot," I've been told over and over. But whereas the right pot in Spain is a wide, shallow cast-iron or cast-aluminum paella pan, my Puerto Rican advisers swear by a stainless steel kettle called a caldero. Azerbaijani, I learned from Anya von Bremzen and John Welchman's Soviet cookbook *Please to the Table,* insist on a copper pot to create the crust known there as a kazmag.

One dish popular in coastal South Carolina's heyday of rice glory was a sort of pie shell made of cooked rice, baked to a crust all around. A Carolina recipe from 1770 calls for pressing overcooked boiled rice against the bottom and sides of a buttered pan, then baking it until "a good light brown" and using it as an edible container for "a rich fill . . . of beef or veal or any thing you please." Carolina food authority John Martin Taylor created a modern vegetable version for his book *Hoppin' John's Lowcountry Cooking.*

Karen Hess, the authority on Carolina rice cooking, has traced these charming rice "pyes" to France, where they reached some kind of pinnacle in an elaborately patterned crusted casserole set down in 1815 by the great French chef and culinary force Carème. Hess has found other rice casserole recipes in English and American cookbooks from the same period, and she notes their similarity to the older Persian version, kateh.

But it's always hard to talk about rice crusts without returning to the Persians, who pioneered baked crusts and bottom crusts (called tadig, pronounced *tahdeeg*) and have made an art form of the latter, creating eggy crusts and yogurty crusts and even crusts made of other foods such as flat bread and sliced potatoes, set down over melted fat below the steaming rice. (See recipes for tadig on pages 62–65.) The most unusual in this last category might be the pumpkin crust that turns up in *Please to the Table* among the Persian-style pilafs of Azerbaijan.

If the Persians have perfected bottom crusts, northern Italians might be the masters of the crusted "pye": Their version, best known as *timballo di riso* (see variations on pages 192–197), is a versatile and festive casserole, rich in flavor and easily turned out for an impressive presentation.

To achieve a bottom crust on everyday rice cooked by the total absorption method with a little fat, instead of turning the heat off for the final resting period, turn it down as low as possible and leave the pot on heat for another 20 minutes. Scrape up the crust and serve it separately or over the rice. As with any rice dish cooked by the total absorption method, a heavy-bottomed pot is essential.

Molded Rice

From Thailand to Italy, cooked rice is sometimes molded before serving. The shape crumbles as soon as it is cut into with a spoon or fork, but it makes a pretty presentation.

To mold individual portions, gently press the required amount of rice into a cup, small bowl, or other container. Then turn the cup upside down on the plate. Lift off the cup and the rice should remain behind. (If it doesn't, try again and give the cup a few taps.) Drizzle with an attractive sauce, such as a red pepper puree, or top with a few mint leaves or other herbs.

For serving at table, a risotto or other rice dish can be pressed into a ring mold and turned out onto a serving platter. To ensure a smooth turnout with risotto, lightly butter the inside of the mold before pressing in the rice. Once the molded rice is turned onto the platter, the center can be filled with any attractive edible that might complement the rice.

For more serious dishes in which rice is baked in a mold, see the recipes for Persian kateh and Italian timballo in Chapters Three and Four.

TWO

The Flavor Factor

❧

HOW is it that literally billions of people can enjoy eating so bland a food as rice day after day, meal after meal? One reason is just that rice *is* bland, thus both easy to take and able to absorb or offset the more assertive flavors of foods that are cooked or served with it. Many who eat rice every day enjoy it plain and add their choice of condiments and sauces at the table. Others flavor the rice itself by adding to the cooking pot some combination of accents drawn from an almost infinite variety of fats, sautéed vegetables, herbs, spices, broths and other cooking liquids, dried fruits, citrus juice or zest, and nuts. The recipes in this section are for stocks, toppings, and other trimmings that add flavor to plain rice or to more elaborate rice dishes.

A Note on Salt

The amount of salt used in American kitchens today ranges from none, among those concerned about high blood pressure, to staggering amounts by people who reject as tasteless any dish not seasoned with their accustomed profusion. For this reason I usually call for "salt to taste" and let each cook decide how much to use. Where amounts are specified, it is usually in recipes where only a dash is called for or where the salt has functions other than enhancing flavor.

Fats in Rice Cooking

"A lump of lard dropped into plain white rice makes a delicious side dish," says my Puerto Rican rice-cooking adviser Eduard Miranda, a traditionalist who still renders fat to make lard at home but concedes that even his mother has now switched to oil for her family's hearts' sake. In Central Asia and the Middle East, fat from the tails of a special breed of fat-tailed sheep has been a prized ingredient from the birth of pilaf to the present day. Italians like to say that rice is born in water and dies in wine; but a traditional risotto begins and ends with butter. A typical nineteenth-century recipe for hoppin' John, the New Year's Day good-luck dish of the American South, calls for "1 pint of red peas, 1 pint of rice, 1 pound of bacon" — a [w]hoppin' proportion of pork to peas and rice!

For every Western rice bowl awash in saturated fat, there are several Asian ones of plain rice, served with lowfat or nonfat flavorings on the side. But let's face it, butter, bacon, or other animal fat is essential to some traditional rice dishes. Others throughout the tropics, East and West, are always cooked in coconut milk. As both coconut and animal fats are made up largely of saturated fatty acids, the kind associated with high blood cholesterol levels and increased risk of heart disease, these rice dishes are not for everyday eating. According to official guidelines, no more than 10 percent of calories should be from saturated fat. But rather than eliminate or mutilate whole categories of venerable and highly prized rice specialties, I include some here as worthy candidates for that 10 percent.

Of the recipes in this book, some of the Asian dishes in Chapter Five contain no fat, and later in this section there are recipes for lowfat and nonfat Asian toppings to use with plain rice, a good choice for everyday eating. Most of the recipes in Chapters Three and Four use olive oil or other oils high in mono-unsaturated fat, the heart-healthy kind that the guidelines recommend because it reduces total blood cholesterol, a factor in heart disease, without lowering the amounts of "good" cholesterol, or HDLs (high density lipoproteins), that protect against heart disease.

Small amounts of pork fat are called for in a very few traditional dishes (five in all) where I feel the flavor is essential. I'm convinced that if you cook hoppin' John for New Year's Day in the proportions called for here, it is bound to bring you more good luck than bad. A few more main-dish recipes include red meat, sometimes as an option, almost always with several other ingredients and in very small amounts. A leading heart researcher once recommended that Americans treat meat not as the center of a meal but as a condiment. Arteries aside, I find meat far more palatable that way.

The coconut milk used in these recipes is usually diluted but is still highly saturated and best reserved for occasional indulgence.

Then there is butter, used lavishly in some rice cooking traditions. In my recipes from these traditions I sometimes reduce the amount of butter and sometimes substitute olive oil or mix the two or offer a choice. But I have retained a few that soak up scandalous amounts of butter. To me these are worth the occasional indulgence and the painless penance of fat-free meals to right the balance.

In the spirit of moderation without deprivation, then, here are a few suggestions for controlling fat intake while enjoying rice as an everyday staple and in an occasional splurge:

• If other food on the day's menu contains fat, cook the rice plain and flavor it with a nonfat Asian topping such as Guam's tasty and very simple finadene (page 41). This needn't be accompanied by an entire Asian or Guamanian meal.

• Have vinegar-flavored sushi rice (page 204) with a few of the taste-intensive Japanese toppings in this chapter.

• Use nonfat yogurt for the yogurt toppings later in this chapter. Serve melted butter toppings separately so that every diner can take as little as he or she chooses.

• Cook rice in defatted stock, whether homemade or canned. Even canned chicken broth is now available with almost no fat, and even canned broth can be put in the refrigerator to bring the fat to the top for skimming. The soaking liquid from dried mushrooms to be used in a rice dish also contributes intense flavor without fat.

• When cooking rice in defatted stock or water, add flavor with fresh herbs, spices, lemon juice and fresh raw ginger, or grated lemon or orange zest.

• As an alternative to sautéed vegetables in pilaf, steam chopped vegetables over the liquid that will be used to cook the rice, then add them to the rice and liquid. Ginger and garlic can be peeled and sliced and dropped in raw with the rice or liquid. Or roast a red pepper as directed on page 49 and cut it into strips to top the cooked rice.

• Cook pilaf dishes in nonstick pans and reduce the amount of oil or butter for the sauté. Risotto seems to need a certain amount of fat; still, when divided among several as a first course or when served with Italian bread and salad for a meatless main course, a risotto meal need not be high in fat.

• If using rice as a side dish with red meat, reconsider proportions. Cook large quantities of interesting rice, salad, and vegetable dishes, smaller portions of meat. Better yet, forget about "side" and "main" dishes and serve rice as an equal partner with chicken, fish, beans, or a substantial vegetable.

• Take heart. In 1993 the Center for Science in the Public Interest, a well-known progressive nutrition research center, shocked customers and owners of Chinese restaurants by announcing that their food, especially in take-out establishments, had an unhealthfully high fat content. But before the shock waves subsided, the group came out with a partial retraction: When the plain rice that comes with the orders is figured in, the meal's fat content is well within recommended limits.

Stocks

What's the difference between a stock and a broth? According to *The New Professional Chef,* a cooking manual from the Culinary Institute of America, "The major distinction is that broths are intended to be served 'as is,' whereas stocks are a base preparation used in the production of other dishes." Since these preparations are to be used for cooking rice, then, I'll call them stocks — though other authorities might disagree and most cookbooks seem to use the terms interchangeably.

It can't be said too often that homemade stocks or broths make any dish taste better, though contemporary reality is such that most cooks usually rely on cans or cubes. Even in Italy, more and more working homemakers make risotto using bouillon cubes. Still, once you get in the habit of making your own stocks, you realize that they almost make themselves. The simple white stocks called for in most rice recipes require only that you throw a few vegetables into a pot with water and whatever bones or flesh you've chosen to define the broth, then leave it all to simmer slowly until the elements have given up their flavor. Spices and seasonings can be added later to suit the final dish.

These stocks will keep for several days in the refrigerator (vegetable stock will keep longer safely but might start tasting stale) or for weeks in the freezer. Freeze in appropriately sized containers, such as 2-cup portions for cooking a cup of rice at a time. Some boil down the stock, freeze it in ice cube trays, and add hot water to reconstitute as each cube is used.

Reduction

Boiling down, or reducing, a stock both concentrates its flavor and allows for easier storage. This can be done immediately after cooking the stock or the next day, after removing the surface fat. To reduce for flavor, simply boil steadily but not furiously until the stock is reduced to two-thirds of its original volume, or until the taste is full enough to suit. To reduce for storage, continue boiling until the stock is reduced to half its original volume. When cool, transfer to separate small containers and store in the refrigerator or freezer. To restore, dilute with hot water as you use it.

Vegetable Stock

2 stalks celery, trimmed and coarsely chopped
2 carrots, coarsely chopped
1 large onion, coarsely chopped
1 leek, trimmed, split, well washed, and cut into 3 or 4 lengths
1 white turnip, coarsely chopped
1 green bell pepper, cored, seeded, and coarsely chopped
1 red bell pepper, cored, seeded, and coarsely chopped
2 to 4 cloves garlic, smashed flat
1 small bunch parsley, stems and all
10 or 12 black peppercorns
1 tablespoon fresh thyme leaves or $\frac{1}{2}$ to 1 teaspoon dried
salt to taste

Put all ingredients except the salt in a large pot with 8 cups of cold water. Bring to a boil, taste, and salt lightly. Reduce heat and simmer, partially covered, 1 to 2 hours. Strain and discard the solids.

Variations and Additions
(all additions to be added with the vegetables at the start)

• Unpeeled potatoes, scrubbed and cut up, add flavor and body to vegetable stock and are sometimes used in stocks for risotto. However, their starchiness is unsuitable in broths for pilafs.

• A can of peeled tomatoes or a tablespoon of tomato paste added to a basic stock can enhance a wide variety of rice dishes.

• Save vegetable scraps, such as the stems from broccoli, parsley, and mushrooms, the stalk ends of asparagus, and the green ends of leeks or scallions, to use in vegetable stocks.

• For a delicious earthy flavor, add several chopped dried shiitake mushrooms, stems and all. (Dried mushrooms have a more intense flavor than fresh ones.) Use in rice dishes that can accommodate the robust flavor.

• Add a tablespoon of chopped fresh gingerroot, common in Asian dishes but good in many others as well.

• Add a few curry leaves (available from Indian grocery stores) if using in coconut rice or in a dish with currylike spices.

• If you are making the stock for a particular dish, add herbs to suit, such as a few sprigs of fresh rosemary or a teaspoon of dried rosemary needles for some risottos, or a few sprigs of fresh dill for many pilafs.

• Add the zest from an orange or lemon or a tablespoon of lemon juice.

• Add 2 or 3 whole cloves.

Chicken Stock

The most economical way to make chicken stock is to buy a whole chicken when you need only breasts, or breasts and legs, for cooking. Freeze the scrap parts (neck, back, and wing tips) for making stock.

Since I often go through stock faster than I accumulate scrap chicken parts, I sometimes use a whole cutup chicken for a broth, removing the breast and leg pieces and tearing off the meat after it has cooked for about half an hour. The bones can then be returned to the broth and the meat used in sandwiches or in a meal. At other times I make a broth with packaged inexpensive chicken parts.

2 pounds scrap chicken parts
1 stalk celery, trimmed and coarsely chopped
1 carrot, scrubbed or scraped and coarsely chopped
1 medium onion, coarsely chopped
1 leek, trimmed, split, well washed, and coarsely chopped
2 cloves garlic, smashed flat
1 small bunch parsley, stems and all
10 or 12 black peppercorns
salt to taste

Put all ingredients except the salt into a pot with 8 cups cold water. Bring to a boil, skimming off any scum that rises to the top. Taste and salt lightly. Reduce heat and simmer, partially covered, at least 2 hours, preferably 3 hours. Strain through a fine sieve, or through a colander lined with cheesecloth, and discard the solids. Let cool, then refrigerate overnight. The fat will rise to the top and can easily be removed.

Turkey Stock

After a holiday meal and the ritual day-after sandwiches, throw the turkey carcass and neck into a pot with vegetables and water, exactly as you would do with chicken parts. For seasoning add a teaspoon of dried thyme and a teaspoon of crumbled dry sage. When done, any meat remaining on the carcass should be discarded with the bones, because it will have given up its flavor.

Duck Stock

Use duck bones and scraps instead of chicken parts for a flavorful broth that's especially good in a rice and lentil combination, intensely so when browned.

Beef Stock

Again, follow the recipe for chicken stock but substitute 4 or 5 pounds of beef bones, with some meat still on, for the chicken. Shin bones are favored for making stock, and cracking the bones makes for stronger flavor. A cup of red wine makes a good addition to beef stock.

Beef and Chicken Stock

Follow the recipe for chicken stock but add 2 or 3 pounds of beef bones, with some meat still on, to the chicken parts. Use in some heartier risottos or in a rice side dish with meat. Reduced or browned, this stock adds rich flavor to a meat paella.

Lamb and Chicken Stock

This stock goes well with many Indian rice dishes and does great things for simple curried rice, either white or brown. (The 5-spice powder, an oriental standby, isn't used in India, but most of its components are at home there.)

1 to 2 pounds lamb bones with some meat attached
2 to 3 pounds chicken parts or scraps
1 large onion, coarsely chopped
1 large carrot, coarsely chopped
2 or 3 cloves garlic, smashed flat
1 stalk celery, coarsely chopped
1 small bunch parsley, stems and all
1 stick cinnamon
1 slice fresh gingerroot, about 1 inch in diameter
   $\times$ $\frac{1}{2}$ inch thick, quartered
12 black peppercorns
8 whole allspice berries
6 whole cardamom pods
2 whole cloves

1 teaspoon oriental 5-spice powder (optional)
salt to taste

Put all ingredients except salt in a pot with 8 cups cold water. Bring to a boil, skimming off any scum that rises to the top. Taste and salt lightly. Reduce heat to simmer gently, partially covered, for 3 hours. Strain through a fine sieve or a colander lined with cheesecloth and discard solids. Let cool, then refrigerate overnight. Before using, remove and discard any fat that has risen to the top.

Brown Stock

A stock can be made richer by browning the ingredients either on top of the stove or in the oven. This more intensely flavored broth can make all the difference for some rice dishes, such as paella.

For oven browning, put meat or poultry bones and scraps on a well-oiled pan and cook in a preheated 400°F oven for 30 minutes. Turn over the pieces, scrape up any stuck bits, and cook another 15 minutes or more until brown but not burned on both sides. Transfer to the stockpot with the pan scrapings. Add cold water to the stockpot and bring to a boil, skimming off the scum as in the recipe for white stock. Add parsley or other herbs and reduce the heat to boil very gently.

Add more oil to the browning pan if necessary, then distribute the chopped vegetables in an even layer. Return the pan to the oven and cook 15 minutes. Turn vegetables with a spatula and continue cooking until brown, checking to make sure the pieces do not burn. Add the vegetables to the stockpot and continue as in the recipe for white stock.

For faster browning, or in hot weather when you don't want to use the oven, brown the bones and scraps, then the vegetables, in a skillet on the stovetop. Transfer to the stockpot and scrape the pan as in oven browning.

Fish Stock

Fish stock should simmer for only half an hour, so it is easy to make just before you are going to use it.

*heads and bones from 1 or 2 red snappers or other mild
    white fish, rinsed, gills removed*
1 medium onion, coarsely chopped
2 cloves garlic, smashed flat
1 leek, white and light green parts, split and well washed
1 stalk celery, coarsely chopped
1 medium carrot, coarsely chopped
1 small bunch parsley, stems and all
1-inch piece fresh gingerroot
2 bay leaves
10 black peppercorns
1 cup dry white wine
juice 1 good lemon ($\frac{1}{4}$ cup)
1 teaspoon fresh thyme leaves or $\frac{1}{2}$ teaspoon dried
salt to taste

Put all ingredients in a large pot with 8 cups cold water. Bring to a boil, skimming off froth that rises to the top. Reduce heat and simmer, partially covered, for 30 minutes. Strain through a fine sieve or a colander lined with cheesecloth and discard solids. Refrigerate any leftover stock and use within 3 days, or freeze. Before using, simmer briefly with a little dry white wine.

Kevin Cahill's Lobster Stock

This is the stock that chef Kevin Cahill uses for the seafood risottos on pages 181–182. The lobster bodies are what is left after the tails and claws have been removed for other uses. Kevin suggests that you try to beg or buy them from a seafood restaurant or fish store that has bodies to spare. Or save the shells and bodies from a lobster cookout or a lobster salad and make lobster stock the next day. I've made a highly satisfactory stock for risotto using leftover shells and bodies from just two lobsters.

6 lobster bodies
3 tablespoons butter and/or olive oil
2 large carrots, diced

2 stalks celery, chopped small
2 Spanish onions, chopped small
3 tablespoons tomato paste
2 bay leaves
1 teaspoon dried thyme
1 teaspoon black peppercorns
salt to taste

Butterfly (spread open) the lobster bodies and roast in a 450°F oven until insides turn from green to red (about 20 to 30 minutes), but no longer than 30 minutes.

Heat butter or oil in a large kettle. Add carrots, celery, and onions, and sauté until golden. Stir in tomato paste. Sauté until no longer bright red. Add herbs, peppercorns, and salt and sauté 1 minute more. Add lobster bodies and water to cover. Boil gently 1½ hours. Strain. Return liquid to pot and boil down until somewhat reduced.

Shrimp Water

Too mild and simple to be called a stock, the water used to precook shellfish might still provide all the flavor needed for a seafood and rice dish. If shrimp or other shellfish is to be boiled briefly and then added to cooked rice, save the shrimp-boiling water for cooking the rice. For a little more flavor, return the shells to the water for 10 to 20 minutes after shelling the shrimp. If the shrimp is to be sautéed, boil just the shells for 10 minutes or more, along with fresh herbs and peeled smashed garlic cloves if it suits your dish, and use that water for the rice. If you can buy shrimp with heads on, use both heads and shells for making shrimp water.

Seaweed Stock

This is used in Japanese dishes such as miso soup and with brown rice in vegetarian cooking. The seaweeds, available at natural-food stores, come either crumpled or in smooth sheets and are known by both Japanese and English names. To make seaweed stock for rice cooking, simmer 1 sheet or a small handful of crumpled seaweed such as kombu (kelp) or nori (laver) in 4 cups of water for

30 to 60 minutes, depending on the strength desired. Strain and discard the solids.

Dashi

This all-purpose stock, the foundation for countless Japanese dishes, is sometimes poured over plain rice, often mixed with other flavorings such as soy sauce and rice wine.

One of the best things about dashi is that it can be made in about 5 minutes. The only ingredients, besides cold water, are kombu (kelp), a seaweed available at natural-food stores, and bonito flakes, a packaged product of shavings from dried bonito fish. Bonito flakes are sold in Japanese and some natural-food stores, as is dashi-no-moto, or instant dashi, a mixture of dried kombu and bonito flakes that makes a satisfactory substitute.

Here is a recipe for making 4 cups dashi from scratch.

> *1 sheet kombu about 3 inches square*
> *½ cup dried bonito flakes*

Drop kombu into 4 cups cold water. Bring to a boil and cook 2 or 3 minutes. Add dried bonito flakes and immediately turn off the heat. Wait a minute or two until the flakes sink to the bottom of the pan, then drain the stock through a cheesecloth-lined strainer. The solids can be discarded or used to flavor a vegetable stock.

If using instant dashi, or dashi-no-moto, drop it into boiling water, let it sink, and drain, as with the bonito flakes.

Toppings

When people eat rice every day — and many Asians have it two or three times a day — they tend to cook it plain and season it with sauces, condiments, and other toppings that are typically added at the table over individual servings.

Asian toppings for rice can be as simple as grated fresh ginger, thin-sliced scallions, or toasted sesame seeds. Alternatively, an entire Asian meal might be viewed as merely a judicious selection of toppings for the rice. According to Chinese food authority Kenneth Lo, a well-balanced rice meal should have at least two toppings: one meat and one vegetable, one dry and one with sauce.

Because entire Asian meals are beyond the scope of this book, the toppings in this section are limited to simple condiments and sauces. The eastern Asian toppings listed first are typically salty and emphatic and used in small amounts. (In addition, the Asian recipes in Chapter Five include some simple one-dish meals, such as Japan's donburi, that are essentially rice with meat and vegetable toppings.)

In Iran, home of pilau, and in other regions, from Greece to northern India, that follow one or another pilau (or pilaf or pullau) tradition, the rice is often cooked with other ingredients, usually including oil or butter along with herbs or spices. But even an elaborate pilaf might be embellished with a separately prepared topping. Pilaf toppings, which can verge on the rich and voluptuous, begin on page 42.

But not all rice toppings have to be homemade. Eastern Asian rice tables and Asian grocery stores here abound in bottled sauces and commercially prepared condiments. Browsing for these in New York's Chinatown or at the Japanese supermarket upriver from my home always turns up intriguing new pastes and sauces and powdered mixes (such as black sesame seeds with ground hot red pepper) for sprinkling over rice. But even our natural-food stores, our Korean-run neighborhood groceries, and, for most items, our standard American supermarkets have such basics as soy sauce, fish sauce, oyster sauce, rice wine vinegar, sesame seeds, gomasio (salted sesame seeds), dashi-no-moto (Japanese instant broth), Asian garlic chile paste, American Tabasco sauce, pickled ginger, pickled daikon (sometimes called turnip or radish), and ume-boshi (Japanese pickled plum). I keep them all on hand to use as is or in other preparations.

Although pilaf cooking calls on far fewer prepared condiments, the various chutneys sold in Indian groceries are handy extras. And the tiny bottles of aromatic orange flower water and rose water sold in Indian and Middle Eastern stores can give an atmospheric fragrance to the rice or to a fruit topping.

Korean and Japanese toppings are traditionally served over plain short-grain rice cooked as directed on page 17. All the others are used on long-grain rice.

Soy-Marinated Ginger or Daikon

Several Asian cuisines use this taste-intensive topping as a condiment with plain rice. To serve with rice for 4 to 8, use a 2- to 3-inch piece of ginger or daikon.

Peel the ginger or daikon, cut in half, then cut each piece along the grain into paper-thin slices. Cut slices into thin sticks. Pat dry with paper towel. Put the sticks in a small jar or dish and cover with soy sauce. Cover the container with a lid or foil and let stand several hours or overnight.

When pressed for time, you can get away with marinating for 1 or 2 hours. For faster saturation, make smaller pieces by shredding the ginger or daikon on the shredding side of a four-sided manual grater.

Sesame Chile Soy Sauce

This simple southern Chinese sauce can turn plain rice or rice noodles into a tasty snack or side dish. Use on cooked rice for 3 or 4, made from 1 cup raw rice, or on ½ pound rice noodles, soaked as directed on page 210.

> *2 tablespoons raw unsalted peanuts*
> *1 tablespoon plus 1 teaspoon corn, canola, peanut, or soy oil*
> *2 teaspoons Asian sesame oil*
> *2 teaspoons hot chile oil*
> *2 tablespoons sesame seeds*
> *2 tablespoons Chinese soy sauce*
> *2 tablespoons lime juice*

Crush peanuts with a rolling pin or in a food processor until broken into small pieces but not powder.

Heat the oils in a small skillet over medium-low heat. Add sesame seeds and fry until they sizzle and pop. (Stand back to dodge the sizzling and popping.) Add peanuts and fry very briefly until they darken or begin to darken; don't let the sesame seeds blacken. Remove from heat. Stand back and stir in the soy sauce and lime juice.

Egg Strips

Eggs turn up on top of rice all over Asia. The Japanese sometimes pour beaten raw eggs over hot cooked rice just as Italians sometimes add them to spaghetti. In Korea an egg fried sunny side up often crowns a mound of rice, with sticks and strips of cut vegetables surrounding it like rays from the sun. Often the egg itself is laid on in strips cut from a very thin omelet, as in the Japanese Chirashi-Zushi on page 204.

To make egg strips, cook 1 egg at a time, using 1 tablespoon of oil for each egg. Stir the egg (or beat very lightly) in a small bowl with 1 teaspoon water. Heat the oil in a medium-size nonstick frying pan (about 8 inches) over medium heat. Add the egg, tipping the pan to spread the egg in all directions. As soon as it is set (a matter of seconds), slip it onto a plate, then flip or turn with a spatula and return very briefly to the frying pan to cook the other side. Slip onto a plate or cutting board, roll it up, and cut into very thin slices. Arrange the strips over cooked rice.

For cholesterol watchers, 1 egg will do for 2 people, or for a bowl of cooked rice made from 1 cup raw rice.

Soy-Simmered Mushrooms

Here the simmered mushrooms absorb intense flavor for a delicious topping to use on Japanese Chirashi-Zushi (page 204) or on plain rice.

> 5 or 6 dried shiitake mushrooms, soaked in warm
> (not hot) water for 30 minutes, or 5 or 6 fresh
> shiitake mushrooms
> 4 tablespoons Japanese soy sauce
> 2½ tablespoons sugar
> 1½ tablespoons mirin or sake (Japanese rice wines)

Wipe mushrooms clean, remove and discard stems, and slice caps into thin strips. Mix soy sauce, sugar, and rice wine in a small frying pan. Add mushrooms and stir to coat. Simmer over low, then very low heat until liquid boils down and is almost dry, 15 to 20 minutes.

Soy-Marinated Cucumber

Use this to top 2 servings of short-grain Japanese-type rice, or serve with other condiments at a meal for 4.

> 3 tablespoons Japanese soy sauce
> 2 tablespoons rice vinegar
> 1 teaspoon sugar
> ½ kirby or ⅓ regular cucumber, peeled, seeded, and cut
>   into small, matchsticklike strips

Mix soy sauce, vinegar, and sugar in a wide-bottomed dish. Add cucumber to marinate while rice is soaking and cooking. When rice is ready, remove cucumber sticks with a slotted spoon and arrange over the rice.

Note: From my Korean neighbors I've learned that dropping a kirby cucumber into boiling water for a minute or two before peeling and cutting makes it crisper!

Roasted Seaweed and Sesame Seeds

This quick and easy topping for plain boiled rice or other rice-based dishes is a common finish, sometimes on top of other toppings, for short-grain rice in Japan or for brown rice in North American macrobiotic kitchens. Use over cooked rice to serve 2 to 4.

> 1 tablespoon sesame seeds (black if available)
> 1 sheet of nori (laver) or 1 strip 3 inches × 7 inches
>   of kombu (kelp), or some of each

Heat a medium-size dry skillet over medium heat. Add sesame seeds and cook until they begin to sizzle and pop. Add seaweed to skillet and toast briefly on each side until brittle but not burned. Remove from pan and crumble the seaweed. Scatter over individual portions of cooked rice.

Green Tea

Some say that the Japanese practice of pouring tea over cooked rice began as a way to soften dried-out leftover rice. Now it is also used on freshly cooked rice for everyday meals.

Use 1 cup of tea to top rice made from 1 cup of dry short-grain rice. Make the tea with 1 green tea bag or 1 teaspoon of green tea leaves per cup of boiling water. If using loose tea leaves, pour the tea through a small strainer. For a little bite, add up to 1 teaspooon of powdered wasabi (known as Japanese horseradish) before pouring over the rice.

Alone, this tea-flavored rice is rather austere. It is often topped with the seaweed and sesame seed topping described above and served with some condiments, such as soy sauce, soy-marinated or pickled ginger, or umeboshi plum (Japanese pickled plum available in jars at natural-food stores).

Korean Marinated Beef Strips

I recently had marinated beef strips at my neighborhood Korean restaurant in a dish called Bee Bim Bob. It consisted of a mound of rice, a sunny-side-up fried egg, and separate little piles of sautéed items: bean sprouts, shredded spinach, carrot matchsticks, chopped onion, chopped mushrooms, shredded Korean fish cake, and the beef strips. This was served with several condiments and sauces, such as marinated daikon, zucchini matchsticks in sesame oil and wine vinegar, and kimchee, the pickled cabbage preparation Koreans couldn't do without. Rather then try to re-create the dish, I used the beef and vegetables on rice for two to four, with prepared kimchee and other condiments.

1 tablespoon sesame seeds
2 tablespoons Asian sesame oil
2 tablespoons Japanese soy sauce
1 teaspoon hot chile oil
1 tablespoon mirin or sake (Japanese rice wines)
¼ teaspoon sugar
1 clove garlic, minced
1 tablespoon scallion (white only), sliced thin
a few twists freshly ground black pepper
½ pound beefsteak, cut into 1½- to 2-inch × ¼-inch strips

Toast the sesame seeds in a small unoiled frying pan until they begin to darken and pop. Mix with 1 tablespoon of the sesame oil and all the other ingredients except the beef. Add the beef and toss to coat. Marinate 20 to 30 minutes, then stir-fry briefly in the remaining tablespoon of sesame oil.

Finadene

Kristy Lee Carroll, who grew up on Guam, introduced me to this tasty and easy-to-make sauce that Guamanians of all backgrounds use as a topping for their version of red rice (page 75).

> *1 small onion, minced very small*
> *juice 1 lemon ($\frac{1}{4}$ cup)*
> *$\frac{1}{4}$ cup soy sauce*
> *1 small Indian chile or $\frac{1}{2}$ serrano or jalapeno pepper,*
>   *or to taste, minced very small*

Mix the onion with the lemon juice in a small bowl, pressing with a spoon to blend well. Mix in the soy sauce and chile. Pass at the table to spoon over rice.

Hot Pepper Sauce

With very slight variations, such as the choice of oil, this sauce might turn up anywhere from China to Italy to North Africa, where it is called harissa. Serve it, to be sampled sparingly along with soy sauce and other condiments, with the Senegalese cheb on page 116. Stir a small amount into fried rice. Or mix small amounts into other sauces such as tamarind, tomato, or sweet red pepper sauce. Some chile freaks put it on the table every night, like salt and black pepper.

> *1 cup whole dried hot red chile peppers*
> *2 cloves garlic, smashed flat*
> *$\frac{1}{2}$ to 1 teaspoon salt*
> *2 tablespoons olive, soy, peanut, vegetable, or sesame oil*

Put the peppers in a bowl and add boiling water to cover. Soak 1 hour. Drain. Puree (with seeds) in a food processor with the remaining ingredients.

Variations

• For a milder sauce, mix the dried hot peppers with milder dried chiles such as ancho or New Mexico type. Adjust the proportions to suit your tolerance for hot pepper.

• For flavor, add ½ teaspoon ground cumin, ½ teaspoon ground coriander, and ¼ teaspoon ground cinnamon to the processed mix.

• With or without the ground spices listed above, add 1 teaspoon ground caraway seeds as called for in some North African recipes.

• For a tart note, add 1 teaspoon to 1 tablespoon lemon juice, balsamic or other vinegar, or tamarind juice (page 50). (If using tamarind concentrate, mix ½ teaspoon tamarind with 1½ teaspoons water before stirring into the paste.)

Cumin Seeds in Oil

Indian cooks often enhance the flavor of cooked rice, lentils, or rice and lentils by adding sizzling oil and cumin seeds just before serving. I sometimes add some chile oil and some sesame oil for its smoky flavor. Use this amount for a dish made with 2 cups raw rice or 1 cup each rice and lentils.

> *3 tablespoons peanut, canola, or corn oil*
> *1 teaspoon Asian sesame oil*
> *½ to 1 teaspoon hot chile oil (optional)*
> *1 tablespoon cumin seeds*

Heat the oils in a small frying pan over medium-high heat. When hot, add the cumin seeds. As soon as they begin to darken, pour oil and seeds over the rice.

Persian Date and Raisin Topping

An easy way to dress up plain rice, this is also good as a topping for the Rice with Vermicelli on page 78 or as an alternative to the saffron butter on Persian chelo, page 62. My neighbors from Iran serve it on top of lamb or chicken stew over a bed of rice. This amount will top cooked rice made from 1½ to 2 cups raw rice.

     4 tablespoons unsalted butter
     ½ cup raisins
     10 pitted dates, cut in half
     ¼ teaspoon saffron threads, crumbled, or turmeric

Heat butter in a small frying pan over low heat. Add raisins, dates, saffron or turmeric, and 3 tablespoons water. Reduce heat to very low and cook 7 or 8 minutes. To serve, pour over cooked rice in a serving bowl or platter.

Persian Date and Raisin Topping with Nuts

Follow the directions for Persian Date and Raisin Topping, above, but add ¼ to ⅓ cup pine nuts or slivered almonds. Lightly brown the nuts in the butter before adding the other ingredients, or toast them in a 350°F toaster oven for 4 or 5 minutes, then stir them into the topping before serving.

Fruit Nut Topping with Lemon and Ginger

Here lemon and ginger provide a tart and zingy counterpoint to the sweetness of the fruit.

     4 tablespoons butter
     3 tablespoons pine nuts, cashew pieces, or unsalted pistachios
     ¼ teaspoon saffron threads, crumbled, or turmeric
     4 tablespoons raisins
     3 or 4 dried apricots, chopped
     1 tablespoon fresh gingerroot, cut into thin slivers
     zest ½ lemon, cut into thin slivers no more than ½ inch long
     1 teaspoon lemon juice
     ¼ teaspoon ground cinnamon

Melt butter over low heat in a medium-size saucepan. Add the nuts and cook until golden. Add remaining ingredients, reduce heat to very low, and cook 5 minutes. (Or toast the nuts separately in a 350°F toaster oven and stir in at the end.)

Crisp-Fried Onion Rings

From India to the eastern Mediterranean, fried onion rings commonly top plain rice, rice and lentils, or more elaborate pilafs. This recipe and the one following describe two versions.

vegetable oil to make at least 1 inch in a small frying pan
1 medium onion, sliced very thin

Heat the oil over medium heat until an onion ring sizzles when dropped in. Separate the onion slices into rings and drop into the oil. Fry until well browned but not burned. Remove with slotted spoon and spread on paper towel. (This might have to be done in batches, depending on the size of your pan.) Let sit 10 minutes or more to crisp.

Slow-Fried Onion Rings

3 tablespoons olive oil or butter, or a combination
2 medium onions (about 1 pound), sliced very thin

Heat oil or melt butter over low heat. Separate the onion slices into rings and drop them into the oil. Cook 30 to 45 minutes, stirring and scraping occasionally, until deep brown but not burned. While onions are browning, add small amounts of water if needed to prevent burning; water should boil off. (Sherry or dry white wine can be used instead of water.) Remove with slotted spoon.

Sweet and Sumptuous Onion Topping

Here two common toppings, sweet fruit and slow-cooked onions, are combined for a sauce that can set off plain long-grain rice, Indian rice with curry spices, or Persian chelo or chicken pilau. I pour it over cooked rice made with $1\frac{1}{2}$ to 2 cups raw rice.

3 tablespoons butter
½ cup golden raisins
8 or 10 dried apricots, cut into 6 pieces each
½ cup sherry
½ cup broth or water
¼ teaspoon saffron threads, crumbled
zest 1 orange, grated or minced
1 tablespoon honey
½ teaspoon turmeric
¼ teaspoon ground ginger or 1 teaspoon minced fresh gingerroot
½ teaspoon ground cinnamon
pinch salt
1 large onion, sliced very thin

Melt the butter in a small saucepan. Add remaining ingredients in the order listed, stirring to coat the onion. Reduce heat to very low, cover, and cook 45 minutes. Uncover and cook another 15 minutes or until thick but not dry.

Yogurt Topping with Toasted Cumin

Cooling yogurt sauces are used with rice, sometimes on top and sometimes on the side, in kitchens from Greece to India. Whipped yogurt is my favorite because it literally can be whipped up at the last minute. It's good in hot weather with rice that has been left to cool at room temperature for a half-hour or so before serving.

1 cup plain yogurt
½ teaspoon cumin seeds
salt and freshly ground black pepper to taste

Put the yogurt in a small bowl and beat with a fork for a minute or so to lighten. Toast the cumin seeds in a small unoiled frying pan until they darken and pop. Grind with a mortar and pestle or in a spice or coffee grinder and stir into the yogurt until evenly mixed. Stir in salt and pepper. Pass at table to spoon over or mix into plain rice or pilaf as desired.

Garlic Yogurt Topping

1 cup plain yogurt
1 clove garlic, peeled, smashed flat, and very finely minced
salt to taste
3 tablespoons chopped fresh dill or mint leaves

Pour the yogurt into a small bowl and beat with a fork for a minute or so to lighten. Stir in the garlic and beat again to mix. Mix in the salt and most of the chopped herb, reserving a bit to sprinkle on top. Pass at table to spoon over or mix into plain rice or pilaf as desired.

Garlic Yogurt Topping with Ground Spices

$\frac{1}{2}$ teaspoon cumin seeds
$\frac{1}{2}$ teaspoon whole allspice berries
all ingredients for Garlic Yogurt Topping, above

Toast the cumin seeds in a small unoiled frying pan until they darken and pop. Grind the toasted seeds and the allspice berries together in a spice or coffee grinder. Proceed with the Garlic Yogurt Topping, above, mixing the ground spices in after the garlic and before the herbs.

Yogurt-Cucumber Topping

This one is so cool that it can take a little heat in the form of ground chile pepper.

1 cup plain yogurt
1 small kirby or $\frac{1}{2}$ large regular cucumber
$\frac{1}{2}$ teaspoon cumin seeds
salt and freshly ground black pepper to taste
$\frac{1}{8}$ to $\frac{1}{4}$ teaspoon ground cayenne
3 tablespoons chopped cilantro (fresh coriander)

Put the yogurt in a small bowl and beat with a fork for a minute or so to lighten.

Peel the cucumber, cut it lengthwise, and scrape out the seeds. Chop the flesh as finely as possible (but not in a food processor, which will make it too watery) and stir into the yogurt.

Toast the cumin seeds in a small unoiled frying pan until they darken and pop. Grind with a mortar and pestle or in a spice or coffee grinder and stir into the yogurt.

Stir in the salt, pepper, cayenne, and most of the chopped cilantro, reserving a bit of the herb to sprinkle on top. Pass at table to spoon on or beside plain rice or pilaf.

Mexican Chiles in Lime Juice

This recipe derives from a relish recorded in Diana Kennedy's *Art of Mexican Cooking.* It can be very mild or very hot, depending on the type or combination of chiles used. Since poblanos are not available often in my neighborhood, I have used the long, thin, mild chiles that my local greengrocer calls "long hots" to distinguish them from Italian sweet peppers.

> *2 fresh poblano chiles or other large mild chiles, roasted*
> *and peeled as directed on page 49, then seeded,*
> *cored, and cut into strips*
> *1 or 2 serrano, jalapeno, or other fresh green chiles,*
> *seeded, cored, and cut into thin strips (optional)*
> *2 cloves garlic, smashed flat and mashed very fine*
> *½ small onion, sliced very thin, then cut in half to form*
> *thin half moons (¼ cup)*
> *juice 1 juicy lime (¼ cup)*
> *¼ teaspoon dried oregano, preferably Mexican,*
> *or 2 tablespoons chopped cilantro (fresh coriander)*

Mix all ingredients except the cilantro in a small bowl and toss to coat with juice. Let sit several hours or cover and refrigerate overnight. Serve over plain rice, sprinkled with the cilantro, if using, or use as the poblanos on Mexican Green Rice, page 70.

Sauces, Trimmings, and Special Effects

The recipes and notes that follow are for basic preparations, such as roasting peppers and processing bulk tamarind, that are called for in many of the rice recipes later in this book. Also included are some basic sauces derived from these preparations.

Tomatoes

Several recipes in this book call for tomatoes that have been peeled, seeded, and chopped. Unless local tomatoes are in season, canned tomatoes might be the best choice. The canned tomatoes I use, no matter what the ethnic origin of the dish, are the plum tomatoes imported from Italy, specifically from San Marzano, if available. These are already peeled. To seed, strain and reserve the juice, then cut the tomatoes in half lengthwise. Brush or rinse off the seeds, then chop the flesh in a bowl or food processor. Discard the seeds but save the juice or use it, according to the recipe.

If fresh vine-ripened tomatoes are available, use either plum tomatoes, good for chopping, or, when you want more juice, the big round ones of whatever variety is red, ripe, and juicy.

To peel fresh tomatoes, drop them into boiling water for 1 minute. Remove with slotted spoon and cut out and discard the stem end. The peel will then pull off easily.

To seed, cut tomatoes lengthwise into halves or quarters and scoop out the seeds. If you wish to keep the juice (which will thicken with long cooking) or the "jelly" that holds the seeds (the most nutrient-rich part of the tomato), do the seeding over a sieve that is propped over a bowl. Drop the solid, seeded tomato flesh into the bowl and push the pulp and juice through the sieve to strain out the seeds. (It is not necessary to get rid of every last seed, but a tomato sauce will be sweeter and more presentable with the seeds removed.) Chop flesh in the bowl or in a food processor.

Simple Tomato Sauce

Stir this into plain boiled rice or use as suggested in recipes for chicken or lamb stew cooked or served with rice.

Heat 4 tablespoons olive oil in a skillet and add 2 pounds peeled, seeded, and chopped fresh tomatoes (above) or 2 cups seeded, chopped canned tomatoes. Cook over low heat for 30 minutes. A chopped onion and/or some minced garlic can be sautéed in the oil before adding the tomatoes. Finish by adding salt, pepper, and herbs (chopped fresh parsley or basil leaves, fresh or dried oregano or thyme) to suit.

Roasted Peppers

"Roasted" peppers always means "charred and peeled." The process adds a depth of flavor and a smooth texture to large chiles, such as the very mild ancho, poblano, and New Mexico chiles, and to bell peppers of any color. But the bell peppers most often chosen for roasting are the red ones, which tend to be sweeter than the green ones and striking in appearance. Roasted red peppers in jars, sometimes called by their Spanish name, pimientos, are easy to find in supermarkets. These are fine for decorating the tops of casseroles or for some purees, but too limp and watery for other uses and without the flavor of good sweet red peppers that are fresh and ripe.

The best way to roast a pepper and maintain its fresh integrity is to char it with a flame. My husband uses a blowtorch for this chore. Outdoor charcoal or wood fires yield wonderful results. More commonly a broiler flame or stovetop gas burner is used.

To roast on the stovetop, hold the pepper with tongs over the flame, touching or almost touching the flame, to blacken or blister the skin. Keep moving and turning until all the skin is blackened or blistered, about 10 minutes, then cool for a few minutes and rub the skin off under running water.

If you are roasting more than one pepper, you'll save time by lining them up under the broiler portion of your oven, fairly close but not touching the flame or heat source. Watch them and turn them as they char, until they are blackened or blistered all around. Then cool and rub off the skin under running water.

Red Pepper Puree

The easiest way to puree a pepper is to core and seed it, chop it coarsely, and process in a food processor. However, smoother and tastier results are obtained by roasting or sautéing before processing.

If roasting, follow directions above to roast and peel, then remove the core, white veins, and seeds, and coarsely chop. Puree in a food processor.

If you are not roasting the pepper, it should be sautéed. For smoothest results, peel with a vegetable peeler. Then core, seed, and chop the pepper. Heat a tablespoon of olive oil per pepper in a skillet over medium heat. Add pepper and cook, stirring occasionally, until soft, reducing heat to medium-low if needed to prevent scorching. Then pick up with a slotted spoon and puree in a food processor.

If using pureed peppers directly on plain rice (or on pasta for that matter), give the sauce more flavor by sautéing chopped garlic and chopped onion (or leek or scallion whites) with the pepper — or sauté the other vegetables separately and add to the puree. To serve, stir in chopped scallion greens or chopped herbs such as basil leaves or broadleaf parsley.

Tamarind

The tart fruit of the tropical tamarind tree, native to the Indian subcontinent and a popular flavoring ingredient throughout the tropics, is often made into sauce or chutney, as in the recipe that follows, and sometimes mixed into plain rice or coconut rice, as on pages 85 and 86.

Although fresh tamarind pods are hard to find in this country, some form of tamarind is often available at Indian, Caribbean, African, or Southeast Asian groceries. Most often it is dried and packed in solid blocks of pulp, seeds, and fibers. I've also seen plastic pouches of ready-to-use tamarind pulp in refrigerated cases at stores with customers from the Caribbean. Indian stores carry a concentrated tamarind extract, a dense, jellylike paste that is easier to use than the blocks of dried pulp but less vibrant in flavor.

To get $\frac{1}{4}$ cup pulp from a block, break off a 1-ounce piece, cover with hot water, and soak for several hours or overnight. Then mash with the back of a spoon and pour tamarind and water through a sieve, pressing and mashing the pulp in the sieve and scraping the bottom of the sieve as pulp accumulates.

Depending on your strength and perseverance, you will end up, as my husband does, with a good quantity of thick sauce to use in cooking and only seeds and skin and stringy fiber in the sieve, or with the thinner tamarind juice I tend to settle for and more fibrous pulp to discard. When a recipe calls for strained tamarind pulp, use twice as much if you have only thin juice. If using concentrate, use only $\frac{1}{6}$ to $\frac{1}{4}$ as much and mix it with water before adding.

Tamarind Sauce

My husband often makes this "superketchup," derived from an Indian recipe by Madhur Jaffrey, and uses it on fish, shrimp, chickpeas, stuffed peppers, even french fries. I've used it with the Senegalese cheb on page 116 and stirred small amounts into other dishes such as the Spicy Rice and Vegetable Stew on page 94.

Since we like to have it on hand, we double the recipe and store leftover amounts in the refrigerator. It will keep, covered, for a good two weeks.

> *2 tablespoons peanut or corn oil*
> $\frac{1}{2}$ *teaspoon cumin seeds*
> $\frac{1}{2}$ *teaspoon black or yellow mustard seeds*
> *1 small onion, minced*
> *2 cloves garlic, minced*
> *minced fresh gingerroot to equal amount of garlic*
> *1 small hot green Indian chile or $\frac{1}{2}$ serrano or jalapeno*
> *   chile, or more to taste*
> $\frac{1}{2}$ *cup canned tomato sauce, or 2 tablespoons tomato paste*
> *   mixed with 4 tablespoons water*
> $\frac{1}{2}$ *teaspoon molasses*
> $\frac{1}{4}$ *cup strained tamarind pulp (for amounts of other*
> *   tamarind forms, see page 50)*

Heat oil in a heavy saucepan. Add cumin and mustard seeds. When the cumin seeds begin to sizzle and darken, add the onion and cook a few minutes until soft. Add garlic, ginger, and chile and cook, stirring, for about 2 minutes. Stir in the tomato sauce, molasses, and tamarind. Reduce heat to very low and cook 5 minutes, adding a little water if the sauce becomes too thick. Serve warm or at room temperature.

Coconut Milk and Shredded Coconut

There's no denying it: Fresh coconut milk adds a delicious velvety dimension to any number of rice dishes. But without the machetes that make short work of coconuts on tropical beaches, it's obtained through a labor-intensive process of whacking and shelling and peeling and shredding and straining.

Today, with canned unsweetened coconut milk from Thailand available in markets across the country, it's easy to make coconut rice dishes. I prefer, though, to mix canned coconut milk half-and-half with broth or water. Many excellent ethnic and regional cookbooks seem to disagree; but to my usually far from subtle taste, canned coconut milk at its fulsome strength imparts a cloying richness to most rice dishes.

There is, alas, another good reason for diluting coconut milk and for limiting indulgence in any form of coconut. Except for palm and palm oil, products of the coconut are the only foods of plant origin that are high in saturated fats. Coconuts contain no cholesterol; that substance is found exclusively in foods from animals. But according to U.S. Department of Agriculture tables (which are notoriously unreliable but remain the only guide we have to the nutritional content of most foods), a cup of coconut milk can burden your system with up to ten times as much saturated fat, and more than three times as many calories, as you would get from a cup of whole cow's milk! And saturated fat has a far greater effect than does dietary cholesterol itself in clogging our arteries with heart-threatening blood cholesterol. (Some Thai and American companies now put out "lite" canned coconut milk that claims far less fat and fewer calories than others; but since the cost is the same as the richer versions, that can be an expensive way of diluting the fat.)

To Make Fresh Coconut Milk

When choosing a coconut, shake it near your ear and buy it only if it sloshes vigorously. This indication that the inner cavity retains what is called the coconut water is a minimal test of freshness.

When you are ready to go to work on it, punch through 2 of the 3 "eyes" you will find at one end and drain the water out through them and into a cheesecloth-lined sieve held or propped over a 2-cup measuring cup. Add tap water to make 2 full cups. Set aside.

To split the coconut, whack it along the equator with a hammer, turning and whacking until you have circled the equator. You should then be able to pull it apart at the crack. Tap it with a hammer to break it up further, then remove the shell from all the pieces by working a sharp knife between the shell and the flesh. The white flesh will still have a thin brown skin around the outside. This can be pared away with a vegetable parer. Now chop up the flesh pieces with a knife, put them in a food processor, and process well until reduced to fine, fluffy shreds. Pour this into a large bowl.

Bring the 2 cups of coconut water to a boil, pour it over the shredded coconut, and let sit 15 to 20 minutes. Then, in batches if necessary, pour the coconut and soaking water into a sieve held over the 2-cup measure. (No cheesecloth is necessary at this stage.) Press down hard on the coconut and scrape the bottom of the sieve to get as much liquid as possible back into the cup. If you don't get a full 2 cups, make it up by pouring a little more hot water through the coconut in the sieve.

Use the milk for cooking rice, and keep the shredded meat to use in a rice pudding or other dish such as Wild Rice with Coconut and Raisins on page 81.

Clarified Butter

Clarified butter, called usli ghee in India, is pure butter fat that has been melted and separated to remove the milk solids. Its advantage over regular butter is that it can be heated to a somewhat higher temperature without burning. This can be helpful in an all-butter-based brown roux or in the tadig on page 64.

To make clarified butter, melt the butter, undisturbed, in a small skillet over low heat. Then remove from heat, skim off any foam, and carefully pour off the liquid butter into a small dish, leaving solids behind in the pan. Discard foam and solids. Or skim, pour the liquid through a fine strainer, and discard the solids left in the strainer.

If not using right away, refrigerate the clear butter in a covered container.

Achiote

Caribbean cooks often tinge their cooking oil with achiote, the brick-red seeds of the annato tree. The Caribe Indians used the color from annato seeds for body paint, but not, as far as we know, to color food. Whether achiote was first employed as a cheaper substitute for Spanish saffron, as is often maintained, or to imitate African cooks' orange-colored dende (palm) oil, as culinary scholar Jessica Harris suggests in her work on African–New World food connections, it can make plain rice either yellow or a golden orange, depending on the amount used. And though it is used primarily for color and has little if any discernible flavor of its own, achiote does seem to give an enriching roundness to the flavor of the oil.

Annato Oil

Caribbean cooks make large batches of annato oil, pour it through a sieve to strain out the seeds, and store it in jars to use as needed. Since I don't use it often, this is how I make a small amount to use right away, starting with whatever amount of oil my rice recipe requires.

> *2 to 4 tablespoons olive oil or other cooking oil*
> *1 to 2 teaspoons achiote (annato seeds)*

Heat the oil in a heavy saucepan over low heat. Add seeds and cook briefly, until the seeds darken and the oil turns a deep reddish orange. Remove from the heat. Remove the seeds from the oil with a perforated spoon and discard the seeds. Return oil to burner and proceed with your recipe.

Annato Water

In the Philippines and on the island of Guam, annato seeds are used to tint the rice cooking water rather than the oil, an alternative that lends itself to nonfat cooking (though Pacific island cooks still sauté their "red rice" in oil).

To tint 2 cups of water (enough to cook 1 cup of raw rice), soak 1 or 2 tablespoons achiote for 30 minutes in $\frac{1}{2}$ cup warm water. Then pour the soaking water through a strainer into a small saucepan with another $1\frac{1}{2}$ cups water. Press the seeds to extract as much of the color as possible. (Or wrap the achiote in cheesecloth before soaking, then squeeze to extract the colored juice.)

Bijol

Bijol (pronounced bee-*hole*) is a deep, vibrant orange powder, available in Cuban bodegas, containing ground dried corn, ground cumin, and the annato seeds described above, also ground. A drawback for some is that it also contains MSG.

Bijol gives cooked rice a rich golden color and a faint but enhancing depth of flavor; and it's far easier to use than the pebblelike achiote. Just stir $\frac{1}{2}$ teaspoon bijol into each cup of sautéed rice before adding the cooking liquid. If rice is not to be sautéed, stir bijol into the liquid before adding the rice.

THREE

Pilaf and Its Extended Family

✂

PALOV. Pelau. Pelo. Pilaf. Pilao. Pilau. Pilav. Pilaw. Plav. Plavi. Pollo. Polo. Pullao. Pullow. Purloo. Purlow. Blof. And so on. There must be as many ways to say and spell this infinitely variable and widely traveled rice construction as there are to cook it.

Culinary historian Karen Hess, who explored its evolution in her book *The Carolina Rice Kitchen,* calls it *pilau,* the term still used in Carolina as well as the original one coined by the Persians who initiated this way of cooking rice in the early centuries A.D. Persian native Nesta Ramazani calls it *pollo,* the modern Persian usage, in her Persian cookbook published here in 1974. To my rice cooking tutors from Iran, of Sunni Muslim background, it is *pullau.* In India, where the concept was introduced by Moghul (Muslim) conquerors, the common English spelling is *pullao.* Most cookbooks published in this country call it *pilaf,* a variant attributed to the Turks. I favor *pilaf* in these pages simply because it's most familiar in America; but I'll also use other variants depending on the source I'm citing or the cuisine I'm discussing.

Definitions of the dish can be more confusing than the spellings. Countless cookbooks and culinary guides in several languages, including French and English, define pilaf or pilau as "boiled rice with meat," "fish or meat cooked with rice and seasonings," or, more specifically, "rice made with meat broth and bacon fat." Yet some of those same books then proceed to illustrate the dish with completely vegetarian recipes. And early rice cooks in European Catholic countries routinely substituted almond milk for meat broth on days of mandated abstinence from meat.

In parts of Central Asia and the Middle East, lamb is part of the definition of pilov (or plov) and the cooking fat is not bacon but the rendered tail fat from a special breed of fat-tailed sheep. As far west as Greece there are whole communities of cooks who would not make pilaf without cooking it in sheep's-tail fat. Yet in India, another country with a dazzling repertoire of lamb pullao, it's cooked in rendered butter or oil, not tail fat, and the lamb versions coexist with an equally impressive tradition of vegetarian pullao. Yamuna Devi's Indian vegetarian cookbook, *Lord Krishna's Cuisine,* includes dozens of sumptuous and fragrant examples that contain no trace or flavor of fish, fowl, or flesh.

Karen Hess seems to have hit on an essential element when she observes that every pilau contains some fat, whether oil, butter, bacon, or some other regional preference. Besides enriching the flavor, the fat coats the grains of rice, thus helping to ensure the outcome devoutly sought by pilaf cooks everywhere: When the rice is cooked, "each grain must stand alone," without the clumping or clinging that is standard in eastern Asia, where cooked rice has to hold together when picked up with chopsticks.

To achieve the Western ideal of separate grains, almost all pilaf cooks use long-grain rice, which tends to cook up fluffier than short-grain varieties. Many include this requirement in their definitions of the dish. Yet several traditional and serious pilafs are made with short- or medium-grain rice. Authoritative Greek and Turkish cookbooks, for example, have recipes for both long-grain and short- or medium-grain pilafs. The plavi recipes in Julianne Margvelashvili's *Cuisine of Soviet Georgia* call for short- or medium-grain rice only. And in Uzbekistan, I was told by a transplanted Uzbek native who seemed pained that I would suspect otherwise, "We don't use long-grain rice."

With so many contradictory specifications, it's not surprising that some cooking authorities throw up their hands and define pilaf or pilau simply as "rice cooked with other things." But what of the traditional Central Asian pilaf that combines the rice and the "other things" *after* separate cooking? And what of the eastern Asian rice dishes "cooked with other things" that bear no historical or other association with pilaf?

Instead of trying to pin down all pilaf with one definition or set of rules, it might help to look at the different categories of rice constructions commonly covered by the term. My aim in these summary descriptions is merely to convey some sense of the concept, not to impose any judgment as to what is or is not a true pilaf.

• In the original Persian version, rinsed and presoaked rice is boiled in several times its volume of water. Then it is drained, spread over some fat in a closed pot on low heat, and left to steam until light and dry. When serving it plain, Persians call this rice preparation *chelo* (or *chilau*); when other ingredients such as cooked meat, herbs, or dried beans are steamed with the rice or mixed in later, it's *pilau* (or *pollo,* or *pullau*).

• In *kateh* (or *cha,* or *kaethe*), an everyday Persian rice treatment that Persians themselves don't grace with any form of the term *pilau* but many latter-day pilaf cooks do, the soaked rice is put into a pot with twice its volume of water, a lump or spoonful of fat, and whatever other ingredients are wanted; then it's covered and cooked over low heat until the liquid is absorbed. This is the method favored in our own rice cooking state of South Carolina, though today's Carolina cooks often skip the soaking stage and might or might not dispense with the rinse. A common variation uses broth instead of water.

• A practice shunned by Persian and Carolina rice cooks but common in Turkish, Greek, Egyptian, and some Indian pilaf cooking is to sauté the rice before adding the liquid, again in a roughly two-to-one ratio. Meats, if any, might be sautéed first, removed, and returned to cook with the rice. Many of the pilaf side dishes in this book start with a sauté, which makes it easy to achieve the requisite separateness of grain.

• In Central Asian recipes such as Tali Benjamin's Ohs-Blof on page 125, meats and vegetables (often carrots and onions) are sautéed and partially cooked in liquid; then the rice is added, often with more liquid. This is the procedure followed in a recipe from Baghdad dating to 1226 and cited by Hess and others; it's also standard in Uzbekistan (once part of Persia), where the art of pilaf goes way back.

In *Please to the Table,* a delightful cookbook and culinary travel guide from the then Soviet Union, Anya von Bremzen and John Welchman show us how seriously pilaf is taken among the Uzbek men. Every year they display their skills at fiercely competitive lamb pilaf cook-offs; and they put their sons through rigorous apprenticeships to maintain, in the authors' words, their "venerable dynasties of pilaf wizards." The rules and standards for these culinary performances are exacting, but quite different from those of neighboring Azerbaijan and Iran.

About pilau's origins, though, everyone seems to agree that this concept of combining rice with meats, seasonings, or other ingredients began with the Persians and captivated all they encountered. When the Persian Empire fell to the Arabs in the early seventh century, the conquerors yielded in the kitchen to the Persians' more refined and sophisticated practices. Most enthusiastically, the Arabs adopted the Persians' ways with rice and passed them on as they moved west through the Middle East, across northern Africa, and into Mediterranean Europe. Around Valencia, in Spain, rice planted by Arab conquerors became a staple food, and the invaders' pilaf evolved into Valencia's own sautéed rice specialty, paella. In northern Africa rice was already an ancient grain; Africans were cultivating a native species (*Oryza glaberrima*) for about two thousand years before the Arabs' arrival and were no doubt cooking from wild grains long before that. But eventually Africans also adopted the varieties of Asian *Oryza sativa* introduced by Arab traders and invaders. And with the new rice, as culinary historians find likely, they assimilated Arab ways of cooking it as well.

Indians have also been cooking rice since well before the Persians knew it, probably cultivating it for at least five thousand years. Today rice is the staple food for two-thirds of India's people, those in central and southern India where most of the country's rice is grown. But it was the Moghul Empire, established in the early 1500s and seated in the north, where wheat is the prevailing grain, that brought pullao to India. There it took root and flowered in distinctly Indian versions, made with northern India's exceptional basmati rice, that are still associated with "royal" kitchens and occasions. Among the most esteemed and seriously festive of pullao forms is biryani, an elaborate, layered, baked pullao typically replete with lamb or chicken, often cooked with yogurt (a Moghul introduction), and enhanced by the complex and inspired spicing that marks Indian cooking.

While Moghul India was developing its sumptuous pullao repertoire, the New World colonies of Spain and Portugal were establishing their own lustier rice cooking ways. There was no true rice (as opposed to North America's "wild rice") in the Americas before Columbus, but by 1570 Spanish Mexico was importing Asian rice through the Philippines. And though Mexican cooks continued to revere and rely on their native maize, they readily embraced the new grain as well and took up the Old World's sautéed pilaf with a vengeance, creating their own now classic style of cooking rice by actually scorching the raw grains and pulverizing the additions in ways that the original pilau cooks would no doubt deem abusive.

Elsewhere in the Americas, slaves brought from African rice country were generating new local specialties based on the dishes of their homelands. Culinary historian Jessica Harris, an authority on African contributions to New World kitchens, has pointed to the African roots of various rice dishes now closely associated with particular spots and regions of the Caribbean, Brazil, and the North American South. Karen Hess agrees that all the New World's rice and bean specialties, from South Carolina's hoppin' John to Cuba's Moros y

Cristianos and other Caribbean islands' signature dishes, originated with slaves from Africa who knew similar dishes back home — and they, in turn, Hess believes, had been influenced by the bean pilau that traveled with the Arabs.

In the New Orleans melting pot, Spanish, French, and African ways came together in that city's signature rice specialties: jambalaya, gumbo, Monday's washday red beans and rice, and other less famous daily fare. My brother-in-law Tony LaRocca, who grew up in New Orleans in a Sicilian-American family, remembers spaghetti dinners as a twice-a-week treat: with meat on Sundays and without meat on Fridays. The other days were rice days, and they followed one upon the other with gratifying predictability. "You always knew," Tony recalls, "that Tuesday was the day for snap beans with the rice, and on Wednesday it would be cabbage."

But this country's true riceland was coastal South Carolina, where for more than two centuries the world's most esteemed rice, known as Carolina gold, was cultivated by slaves from rice-growing West Africa, and where black and white, rich and poor, in sophisticated urban Charleston and in primitive rural cabins, still eat rice every day if not at every meal, though commercial rice has not been cultivated in the state for more than sixty years. (The Carolina brand rice sold today is grown in Arkansas or Texas or Louisiana and has no association with Carolina gold except for appropriating the prestigious name.)

How Carolina's rice culture came about in a nation of generally indifferent rice cooking is the subject of Hess's enlightening study, *The Carolina Rice Kitchen*. Like other historians, Hess credits the African slaves with the knowledge of rice growing and rice cooking that made it happen. She also notes that almost half of South Carolina's white settlers were French Huguenots fleeing religious persecution at home, and she explains how they could have picked up pilau cooking in Provence from their fellow religious outcasts: Sephardic Jews who had brought the pilau to Provence from Persia, either directly or as victims of the Spanish expulsion.

So pilau/pilaf/plavi/pullao/pollo/perloo has all but spanned the world. The variety of dishes that answer to some version of the name only testifies to that rice cooking concept's long history, wide travels, and myriad attractions.

It must be said that not all the dishes that follow are considered forms of pilaf. But other traditional dishes, such as Mexico's sautéed rice specialties, can reasonably be viewed as natural members of the extended family with ultimate roots in pilaf tradition; and the original dishes without a specific pilaf lineage are constructed in one or another pilaf mode. As for gumbo, really a sort of stew that is customarily served over rice, I've adopted that dish into the extended family and appended it to this section simply because it's an important part of New Orleans's rice cuisine, in repertoire with true members of the pilau family that come from the same ethnic cooks, and too delicious to leave out for reasons of culinary genealogy.

Persian Versions

Persia, once an empire that extended well beyond the boundaries of present-day Iran, is generally credited as the birthplace of pilau. But whereas we might apply that name to all Persian rice dishes, Persians themselves have an entire system of inspired and clearly differentiated rice preparations, each with its own name.

Nesta Ramazani, the Iranian-born and -raised author of *Persian Cooking,* calls rice "the mainstay of the Persian cuisine" and observes that any Persian hostess is likely to put several different rice dishes on the table, together with several kinds of meat or meat dishes to go with them. Her word order is worth noting: Where Americans might serve rice to go with the meat, with Persians it's the other way around.

In the introduction to her cookbook, Ramazani quotes from three centuries of travel notes by Westerners who were dazzled by the sumptuous profusion of rice dishes offered by their Persian hosts. According to one 1824 account, "First came the chilau, white as snow"; then one pilau after another, the first containing lamb, the second chicken, the next peas and saffron, the last sugar and spices; then a similar parade of ragouts of meat or fowl cooked up with nuts and fruits and seasoning and poured over chilau. "Then came the roasts" — and the list goes on.

Thanks to my Hoboken neighbor Soheila Sobsey and her mother, Mrs. Zivar Mostafavi, I have learned not only to distinguish among chilau, pilau, and kateh (an everyday version that would not have been served at the nineteenth-century banquet) but also to prepare them. As mentioned in the introduction to this chapter, when the pure white rice is soaked, boiled, steamed, and served as is, it is called chelo (the modern term for chilau). When meat stews or other ingredients are layered or mixed with the rice, it is pollo in Iran today; or pullau, in my neighbors' Muslim usage; or pilau, the original Persian term, which unlike chilau survives in French and English usage. Kateh (or kaethe, or cha) is cooked by the total absorption method, either on the stovetop or in the oven; it's less fluffy and less fussed over but can contain the same ingredients as a chelo or a pilau. Then there is the tadig, the bottom crust that Persian rice cooks deliberately induce by long, slow cooking of a chelo, pilau, or kateh, but also the name Soheila sometimes uses for the entire dish, just as a queen or king might be referred to as "the crown." ("You should try her tadig with beans and herbs — out of this world," her husband Michael will say.)

The recipes that follow are for chelo, simple pilau with herbs, different varieties of tadig, and basic kateh. Other pilau recipes can be found later in this chapter in the sections on Rice and Beans, Rice with Poultry, and Meaty Rice Dishes.

Chelo with Tadig

Serves 6 to 8 as a side dish

Here in its classic purity is Persian chelo, as demonstrated to me by Mrs. Zivar Mostafavi from Iran. Mrs. Mostafavi served her chelo with a meat stew in tomato sauce, which I have adapted in the recipe on page 138. For a lemon chicken stew to serve with chelo, see page 126.

> *2 cups Indian basmati rice, preferably dehradun*
> *3 tablespoons salt*
> *4 tablespoons butter*
> *1 teaspoon saffron threads, crumbled*
> *3 tablespoons extra-virgin olive oil*

Pick over the rice to remove any impurities. Working in the sink, pour rice into a large bowl and add cold water to cover by 2 inches. Let stand 1 or 2 minutes, then drain through a large sieve. Repeat several times (8 or 9 rinses is not too many) until the water runs clean and clear of starch. Add more water to cover and the 3 tablespoons salt. (The salt is added to keep the rice from breaking.) Let soak 2 hours.

When the soaking period is over, gently pour the rice and soaking water into 3 quarts boiling water. (Some drain and rinse the soaked rice before boiling, a good idea if your soaking water is not clear of starch.) After the water returns to a boil (2 to 5 minutes), cook another 2 to 5 minutes, or until you can break a grain of rice but it is still slightly al dente inside. (Rice should be at this stage about 6 or 7 minutes after being poured into the boiling water.) Drain through a sieve and rinse with cold water.

In a small saucepan, combine butter and saffron with 3 tablespoons water and heat just to melt the butter.

Spoon the oil into a large heavy pot over low-to-medium heat. When warm, lay down a solid layer of rice and drizzle with a little of the saffron butter. Then pour in the rest of the rice to form a mound and pour the remaining saffron butter over the top. Do not mix in.

Wrap the pot lid in a cloth dish towel as directed on page 16. Cover the pot and cook 15 minutes, then turn the flame as low as it will go without flickering out. (The single-ring burners on my otherwise unimpressive gas stove do this beautifully. If working on an electric stove, or a gas stove with too high a flame, you might have to use a heat-diffusing pad or raise the pot from the burner on a wok ring or other device to keep the crust from burning.) Let steam another 45 minutes.

Before serving, set the pot for 1 or 2 minutes in about 2 inches of cold water in a low pan or sink; this should loosen the bottom crust, or tadig. To serve, spoon rice into a mound on a serving platter. You can then either lift out the crust in one piece with a spatula and serve it on a separate plate or break up the crust and sprinkle pieces over or around the mound. The mounded rice will be light, in separate intact grains, and attractively stippled with saffron butter.

Variations

If you prefer, drizzle the platter of mounded rice with more saffron butter before serving. Or cook the rice plain and save all the saffron butter to pour on just before serving. Another alternative is to mix a cup of the cooked rice with the saffron butter just before serving, then arrange that on top of the white rice. I prefer the stippled effect.

Tadig Variations

Having perfected the bottom rice crust cultivated in different ways by rice cooks around the world, the Persians have gone on to create intriguing variations, some enhancing the rice crust and some making the crust of other foods instead. Here are the most common, all of them delicious.

Potato Tadig. While the rice is soaking, peel 2 medium baking potatoes and cut them into ¼-inch-thick slices. (Cut a few slices crosswise off each end, then slice the large middle part lengthwise.) Drop the slices into a pan of water until ready to use, then blot on paper towel.

As in the recipe for chelo, spoon the oil into a large heavy pot over low-to-medium heat. When warm, lay down the potato slices in one layer to cover as much of the pot bottom as possible. Cut up leftover slices as needed to fill in any large gaps. Cover potatoes with a thin layer of rice and dribble with a little of the saffron butter. Then pour in the rest of the rice, shape into a mound, and proceed as in the recipe for chelo.

To serve, surround the mounded rice with the potato slices. They should be deliciously crisp and golden.

Bread Tadig. The best bread for tadig is a Middle Eastern flatbread such as lavash, if available, or, if not, pita or damascus bread. If using pita or damascus, you will have to pull or cut the layers apart to make a slice half the usual thickness (easily done with thin pocket pita). Some cooks here substitute flour tortillas, though my sources sniff at this.

As with the rice tadig in the chelo recipe, spoon the oil into a large heavy pot over low-to-medium heat. When warm, lay down the bread, tearing extra pieces to fill in around the edges if needed to cover the pot bottom. Use 2 or 3 layers of lavash, a half-thickness of pita or damascus bread, or 2 flour tortillas. Cover the bread with a thin layer of rice and drizzle with a little of the saffron butter. Then pour in the rest of the rice, shape into a mound, and proceed as in the recipe for chelo.

Egg Tadig. I've tried it both ways, and my family agrees that this crust must be made with butter, not oil. Because butter burns at a lower temperature than oil, it is safer to use clarified butter (page 53).

Melt 3 tablespoons unsalted butter in a large heavy pot over low to medium heat. Mix 1 or 2 beaten eggs with 1 cup of the cooked rice. (Two eggs are favored by some but to my mind make the crust less like a tadig and more like a frittata.) When the pot is warm, spread the egged rice over the butter on the bottom of the pan. Drizzle with a little of the saffron-butter-water mixture. Pour in the remaining rice to form a mound, and proceed as in the recipe for chelo.

Egg and Yogurt Tadig. Follow the directions for egg tadig, above, but add ½ cup yogurt. Mix the yogurt with 1 beaten egg yolk, then mix in 1 cup cooked rice and proceed, laying down the tadig over butter as in the directions for egg tadig.

Herbed Pilau with Tadig

Serves 6 to 8 as a side dish

Once another ingredient is added to the rice, a Persian chelo becomes a pilau. For this simplest but tasty pullau, follow the directions for Persian chelo (page 62) but add the following ingredients:

> *1 cup chopped fresh dill*
> *½ cup chopped cilantro (fresh coriander)*
> *½ cup chopped fresh broadleaf parsley*
> *3 or 4 scallions, green part only, trimmed and sliced very thin*

Wash, soak, boil, and drain the rice as directed in the recipe for Persian Chelo with Tadig (page 62). Toss the drained rice with the chopped herbs, then proceed with the recipe for chelo, using the tadig of your choice. Garnish with sliced scallion greens.

Variations

• Instead of the herb mixture above, use only chopped dill, but increase the amount to 2 cups. Scallions optional.
• Instead of mixing the herbs with the rice, lay down a layer of plain rice over the tadig, then a layer of herbs, then the mounded rice.
• When tossing or layering in the herbs, save a bit to toss over the mounded rice and saffron butter for serving.

Streamlined Chelo or Pilau

For a first attempt, for special occasions, or for best results at all times, the directions given in the previous chelo and pilau recipes should be followed precisely. However, I have taken the following shortcuts with respectable results:

Presoak the rice for only ½ hour, as the Indians do, or just wash it in a strainer under running water to remove the starch and skip the soaking. Add salt with the rice to the boiling water, and skim off any starch that rises to the top of the water during the boiling process. Boiling will take a few minutes longer with unsoaked rice. This shortcut knocks 1½ to 2 hours off the entire process.

For the steaming stage, cook over low-to-medium heat 15 minutes as directed, then reduce heat to low (instead of "as low as possible") for 20 to 25 minutes, followed by a 5- to 10-minute rest off heat. This saves about 15 minutes and is recommended in some cookbooks, but, depending on your burner and equipment, might risk burning the tadig.

Kateh

Serves 3 to 4 as a side dish

Persians prepare kateh, their everyday rice dish, very much as Americans cook rice by the total absorption method, except that kateh is cooked longer at a lower temperature to produce a bottom crust. The rice does not come out as celestially fluffy as it does for chelo and pilau, and the crust is not as impressively intact, but kateh lends itself to just as many interesting and delicious variations. My Iranian source Soheila Sobsey, who spells the dish *kaethe* or *cha,* soaks the best Indian basmati rice for kateh as for chelo and (as she spells it) pullau, but I make kateh with American basmati or other long-grain American rice and skip the soak.

To make plain kateh, drop 1 cup rice, 3 tablespoons butter, and salt and freshly ground black pepper to taste into a saucepan containing 2 cups of water. Add a pinch or two of saffron if desired. Bring to a boil, reduce heat to as low as possible, and cook 1 hour. Spoon onto a serving platter. Scrape up the bottom crust with a spatula — it will probably come up in bits and pieces — and sprinkle over or around the rice, discarding any burned pieces.

Baked Kateh

Serves 6 to 8 as a side dish (plain) or a main dish (with a stew filling)

When kateh is baked, it comes out with a crust not only on the bottom but all around the sides as well. It is then inverted and presented as a golden crusted cake.

Kateh can be made with plain rice or rice mixed with herbs, baked as is for a side dish or filled with any of the stews (such as the chicken on page 126 or the lamb on page 138) that are used to layer or accompany a Persian pilau or chelo. Here is a recipe for plain baked kateh made to fit a 1½-quart baking dish, with appended directions for making a filled kateh.

> *2 cups long-grain white rice*
> *1 whole egg and 1 egg yolk, beaten*
> *½ cup plain yogurt*
> *5 tablespoons melted butter, plus more for buttering the baking dish*
> *1 cup chopped fresh dill (optional)*

Put the rice in a saucepan with 4 cups water. Bring to a boil, cover, reduce heat to low, and cook 20 minutes.

Preheat the oven to 350°F.

Mix the beaten eggs, yogurt, and 2 tablespoons butter in a medium-size bowl. Add 1 cup of the cooked rice and mix well.

Liberally butter the inside surface of a 1½-quart casserole or baking dish. Put the egg-yogurt-rice mixture on the bottom and shape with a rubber spatula to come partway up the sides of the dish. Add a thin layer of plain rice, then the dill, then the remaining rice. Drizzle half the remaining butter around the edge between the rice and the sides of the dish. Drizzle remaining butter over the top of the rice.

Bake uncovered 45 minutes. Then run a spoon handle around the edge between the rice and the sides of the dish. Put the dish in 2 inches of cold water for 2 minutes. Cover with an inverted platter and flip so that the platter is on the bottom and the kateh is on the platter. Lift off the baking dish, using a spatula to unmold if necessary.

Variations

• To make a filled kateh, you will need a large dish. Press the egg-yogurt-rice mixture into the baking dish as directed, then put in the filling, pushing the egg-yogurt-rice mixture up the sides to completely surround the stew. Top the stew with the remaining cooked rice. Drizzle with butter as directed and proceed with the recipe.

• Another alternative is to bake the kateh without a filling in a ring mold, then serve with a stew heaped into the center of the ring.

Sopa Seca: The Mexican First Course

When the Spanish introduced rice to Mexico in the late 1500s, it was not the short-grain type that grows in Spain and has shaped the development of Spain's paella cooking, but the long-grain Asian rice, more typical of pilaf, brought to the New World through Spain's trading outpost in the Philippines. Although Mexican rice dishes are not classed as pilaf, they clearly descend from the pilaf cooking that the Arabs introduced earlier to Spain; and in procedure they're just a step beyond the Turkish-style pilaf that begins by sautéing the rice: Mexican cooks simply continue the sautéing until the rice is literally scorched, then they add a paste of mashed onion and other vegetables and fry that until dry. The combination of long-grain rice and vigorous sautéing results in a dish that rivals any for the separate integrity of each grain.

Traditionally, Mexican cooks fried their rice in lots of lard. Today many have switched to oil, but they still use generous amounts, at least $\frac{1}{4}$ cup for 1 cup of rice, typically tipping the pan and pouring off any oil that remains after the rice has browned. I find it easier, and the outcome no poorer, just to start with a little less oil so none is left to pour off. At a certain point in the frying process, the rice might tend to stick in spots and you might feel like giving up, but keep stirring and this phase will pass as the oil is absorbed. (The extensive frying can, however, make the pot so hot that the liquid boils and splashes furiously when added. Stand back as you pour it in.)

In Mexico, as in Spain and Italy, rice is served as a first course before the entrée. It's then called *sopa seca* (dry soup), maybe because wet soup also comes before the main course. (A formal full-service meal would start with both, first the wet soup and then the dry one.) In North America, where simultaneous service is the everyday norm, Mexican-style rice makes a memorable side dish for meat, poultry, or fish; a stylish companion for a vegetarian bean dish; or a good light supper by itself.

Arroz Blanco
Mexican White Rice

Serves 3 or 4 as a first course or side dish

The basic Mexican rice on which the others are based.

> *1 cup long-grain white rice*
> *½ medium onion, chopped*
> *1 clove garlic, chopped*
> *3 tablespoons olive or peanut oil*
> *2 cups hot chicken or vegetable broth*
> *salt and freshly ground black pepper to taste*

Put the rice in a bowl and add hot water to cover. Let soak 10 to 15 minutes. Drain through a large sieve, then hold under cold running water and rinse until the water runs clear of starch. Shake sieve and rake with your fingers to drain off residual water.

Process onion and garlic in a food processor until they form a paste but have not turned watery.

Heat oil over medium-high heat in a large heavy saucepan or Dutch oven. Add rice and cook, stirring, until golden, about 10 minutes. Stir in the processed onion and garlic. Pour in the hot broth. Add salt and pepper. Reduce heat to bubble gently for 5 or 10 minutes, until the surface liquid has disappeared and steam holes appear on top. Cover, reduce heat to very low, and cook another 10 to 15 minutes, for a total of 20 minutes' cooking time. Remove from heat and let sit, covered, another 10 minutes.

Arroz Gualdo
Mexican Golden Rice

To give Mexican Arroz Blanco an appetizing deep yellow tinge, first tint the cooking oil with achiote seeds as directed on page 54, then proceed with the recipe above.

Arroz Verde
Mexican Green Rice

Serves 3 or 4 as a first course or side dish

Arroz verde is not just a Spanish term for rice with parsley; in Mexico it signals the presence of poblanos, the large and very mild chile peppers. Still, I much prefer this rice without the peppers mixed in, and I am emboldened to say so by Mexican food authority Diana Kennedy's expression of the same sentiment. Her solution is to serve the chiles in strips on top of the rice, an idea I've borrowed for this different recipe.

The green herbs in arroz verde might be added in any amount from a few sprigs to a good fistful; this recipe reflects my taste for a deep green version.

1 cup long-grain white rice
1 or 2 fresh mild chiles such as poblano (preferred), New
*   Mexico, or anaheim, roasted and peeled as directed*
*   on page 49*
⅔ cup chopped parsley leaves and small branches
⅓ cup chopped cilantro (fresh coriander) leaves and small branches
1 large clove garlic, chopped
1 small onion, chopped
3 tablespoons olive or peanut oil
2 cups hot chicken or vegetable broth
salt and freshly ground black pepper to taste

Put the rice in a bowl and add hot water to cover. Let soak 10 to 15 minutes. Drain through a large sieve, then hold under cold running water and rinse until the water runs clear of starch. Shake the sieve and rake with your fingers to drain off residual water.

Core and seed the chiles and cut them into long thin strips. Set aside.

Put parsley, cilantro, garlic, and onion together in a food processor and process to a paste.

Heat oil over medium-high heat in a large heavy saucepan or Dutch oven. Add rice and cook, stirring, until golden, about 10 minutes. Stir in the mixture from the food processor. Pour in the hot broth. Add salt and pepper. Reduce heat to bubble gently for 10 minutes, or until the surface liquid has disappeared and little steam holes appear on top. Arrange pepper strips in a lattice pattern on top of the rice. Cover the pot, reduce heat to very low, and cook another 10 minutes. Remove from heat and let sit, covered, another 10 minutes.

Stuffed Chiles for Arroz Verde

Serves 4 as a first course or side dish, 2 or 3 as a light supper with salad

My husband recently cooked up these stuffed chiles for a more substantial version of arroz verde. For this variation, follow the previous recipe, but instead of the pepper strips, top the rice with the following preparation:

> *4 or 6 small fresh mild green chiles such as poblano,*
> *   New Mexico, or anaheim*
> *1 dried mulatto chile*
> *4 tablespoons olive or peanut oil*
> *4 tablespoons onion, chopped small*
> *1 large clove garlic, minced*
> *$\frac{1}{4}$ cup fresh or canned crushed tomatoes (page 48)*
> *$\frac{1}{2}$ teaspoon dried oregano*
> *$\frac{1}{4}$ teaspoon dried epazote (if available)*
> *$\frac{1}{8}$ teaspoon ground cinnamon*
> *$\frac{1}{2}$ pound Monterey Jack cheese, shredded*

Roast and skin the poblano chiles as in the directions on page 49. Make a lengthwise slit in each chile and remove the seeds.

While the rice is soaking, toast the mulatto chile for a minute on each side in an unoiled skillet over medium heat. Then cut open and remove and discard stem, seeds, and veins. Break into pieces and grind to a powder in a spice or coffee grinder.

Heat the oil in a small frying pan over medium heat. Add onion and garlic and cook until soft. Add tomatoes and spices and cook 10 minutes, reducing heat and/or adding water if needed to prevent sticking. Put a little of this sauce into each chile, then top with the cheese.

After the rice has simmered uncovered for about 10 minutes, or when the surface liquid has disappeared, lay the peppers on top of the rice. Cover, reduce heat to very low, and cook another 10 minutes. Remove from heat and let steam, covered, another 10 minutes.

Arroz a la Mexicana

Serves 3 or 4 as a first course or side dish

This classic Mexican rice dish has been widely and poorly imitated in mushy canned and packaged "Spanish rice" and in those North American "Mexican" restaurants that seem to specialize in leftover baby food. Nothing could be further from the real thing, a masterpiece of separate, stand-alone grains.

To demonstrate some of many small variations in procedure, this recipe follows those used by Reina Beceira Mejia, a recent visitor from Puebla, Mexico, who learned the dish from her mother. They are a little different from the ones in the three preceding Mexican rice recipes.

1 cup long-grain white rice
½ medium onion, chopped
1 large clove garlic, chopped
1 medium fresh ripe tomato or 2 fresh ripe plum tomatoes
    or canned Italian plum tomatoes, peeled and seeded
    as directed on page 48
4 tablespoons olive or peanut oil
2 cups reduced chicken broth
salt and freshly ground black pepper to taste
½ cup shelled fresh peas or thawed frozen peas or diced
    carrots (optional)

Rinse the rice in a sieve under cold running water until the water runs clear. Put rice in a bowl and add hot water to cover. Soak 5 minutes. Drain through a large sieve. Return to the bowl and add cold water to cover. Soak 5 minutes. Drain again. Shake the sieve to drain off residual water.

Puree onion, garlic, and tomato in a food processor.

Heat oil over medium-high heat in a large heavy saucepan or Dutch oven. Add rice and cook, stirring constantly to prevent sticking, until golden, about 10 minutes. Tip pot and pour off unabsorbed oil, if any. Stir in the mixture from the food processor and continue to cook and stir a minute or two until no longer soupy. Pour in the broth. Add salt, pepper, and optional peas or carrots. (Frozen peas should not be added until the final 10-minute resting period.) Cover the pot but leave the lid slightly ajar. Then reduce heat to very low. (Reina slips a comal, a porous stone slab used in Mexican slow cooking, under the pot.) Cook 20 minutes or until all the liquid is absorbed. Then remove from heat and let sit 10 minutes before removing the lid.

Side Dishes

Yellow Rice with Turmeric

Serves 3 or 4

Turmeric, a spice-shelf staple in the ancient Orient and throughout the modern world, gives rice an attractive yellow tinge and adds a pleasant dusky dimension to the flavor.

> *2 tablespoons cooking oil*
> *1 small onion, chopped fine*
> *2 cloves garlic, minced*
> *minced fresh gingerroot to equal amount of garlic*
> *1 cup long-grain white rice*
> *1 teaspoon turmeric*

1¾ cups hot chicken or vegetable broth or water
salt and freshly ground black pepper to taste

Heat the oil in a heavy saucepan over medium heat. Add onion and sauté 5 minutes, until soft. Add garlic and ginger and sauté about 2 minutes, until garlic begins to turn golden. Add rice and cook, stirring, 2 or 3 minutes, until translucent. Stir in the turmeric. Add broth or water, then salt and pepper. Bring to a boil. Cover the pot, reduce heat, and simmer 20 minutes. Remove from heat and let sit, still covered, another 10 minutes.

Variations

For the simplest of side dishes to call itself a curried rice, add ½ teaspoon ground cumin and ½ teaspoon ground coriander with the turmeric. For more cumin flavor, change the proportions, using 1 teaspoon cumin and ½ teaspoon turmeric. Or give coriander the leading role for a sweeter effect.

Arroz Amarillo con Achiote
Caribbean Yellow Rice with Annato Oil

Serves 3 or 4

Achiote, the red seed of the tropical annato tree, is described on page 53, along with directions for making the annato oil that Caribbean cooks use to color rice and the annato water used for the same purpose in the Pacific. Here is a standard Caribbean recipe for annato-tinted rice.

2 tablespoons annato oil (page 54)
4 tablespoons onion, chopped fine
1 cup long- or short-grain white rice
1¾ cups hot chicken broth or water
salt and freshly ground black pepper to taste

Heat the oil in a heavy saucepan over medium heat. Add onion and sauté about 5 minutes, until soft. Add rice and cook, stirring, 2 or 3 minutes, until translucent. Add broth or water, then salt and pepper. Bring to a boil. Cover pot, reduce heat, and simmer 20 minutes. Remove from heat and let sit, covered, another 10 minutes.

Variations

• For Cuban Arroz Amarillo, follow the same recipe, but instead of coloring the oil with achiote, sauté the onion in regular cooking oil and then stir in the rice and $\frac{1}{2}$ teaspoon bijol, a powdered form of annato described on page 55, just before adding the broth.

• For Guamanian Red Rice (actually no redder than Caribbean Yellow Rice unless more achiote is used), sauté the onion and rice in untinted peanut oil, then instead of using chicken broth add annato water produced according to the directions on page 54. If desired, stir in $\frac{1}{2}$ cup of fresh or thawed frozen peas with the water. My daughter's friend Cristy Lee Carroll, who grew up on Guam, tops this rice with Guam's Finadene sauce (page 41).

Golden Rice with Saffron

Serves 3 or 4

The royalty of yellow rices, saffron rice has such an enticing fragrance, delicately pungent flavor, and sumptuous aura that it is usually referred to as "golden." Saffron is also costly, because it consists of stigmas laboriously handpicked from a particular Mediterranean crocus, and thousands of flowers are needed to get 1 tablespoon of saffron. Fortunately, a small amount can be transporting. This recipe represents saffron rice at its simplest; still, the royal ingredient calls for a little extra care and rates a special aromatic rice, whether Indian basmati, American popcorn rice, or jasmine rice from Thailand.

> *1 cup aromatic long-grain white rice*
> *1$\frac{3}{4}$ cups chicken broth*
> *$\frac{1}{4}$ teaspoon saffron threads, crumbled*
> *2 tablespoons unsalted butter or olive oil*
> *1 small onion, chopped fine*
> *salt and freshly ground black pepper to taste*

If using Indian basmati, wash, soak, and drain the rice as directed on pages 13–14.

Heat the chicken broth in a small saucepan. Crumble the saffron threads between your fingers and drop them into the broth.

Melt the butter or heat the olive oil in another, heavy saucepan over medium heat. Add the onion and sauté 5 to 10 minutes, until soft but not browned. Stir in the rice. Add broth with saffron, then salt and pepper. Reduce heat to bubble gently about 10 minutes, or until surface liquid has been absorbed and small steam holes appear on the surface of the rice. Wrap the pot lid in a cotton or linen dish towel, as explained on page 16, and cover the pot with the wrapped lid. Reduce heat to very low and cook another 10 minutes. Remove from heat and let sit, still covered, another 10 minutes.

Fragrant Golden Pilaf

Serves 3 or 4

Almost every ingredient in this eclectic pilaf adds to the inviting fragrance. Delicious made with jasmine rice from Thailand, it's also a good way to use American brown basmati. It's a good accompaniment for chicken or duck.

> *¼ cup golden raisins*
> *¼ cup sherry*
> *1 tablespoon walnut oil*
> *½ onion, minced (⅓ to ½ cup minced)*
> *1 tablespoon minced fresh gingerroot*
> *1 cup jasmine or other white or brown long-grain rice*
> *1¾ cups hot chicken or duck broth*
> *grated zest 1 orange*
> *pinch saffron threads, crumbled*
> *salt and freshly ground pepper (white if you have it), to taste*
> *3 curry leaves, if available (do not substitute curry powder)*
> *2 tablespoons pine nuts*

Put the raisins into a cup with the sherry to plump.

Heat the oil in a heavy saucepan over medium heat. Add onion and sauté a few minutes until soft. Add ginger and sauté another minute. Stir in the rice, then the sherry and raisins. Add broth and then the orange zest, saffron, salt, and pepper. Reduce heat to bubble gently 10 minutes, or until surface liquid largely disappears and small steam holes appear on top of the rice. (Brown rice will take longer.) If using curry leaves, push them into the rice. Wrap the pot lid in a dish towel as directed on page 16, then cover the pot, reduce heat to very low, and cook another 10 minutes (25 minutes if using brown rice). Remove from heat and let rest another 10 minutes before serving.

While the rice is resting, toast the pine nuts in a 350°F oven or toaster oven for 5 minutes, or until golden but not dark brown. Stir into the rice.

Carolina Red Rice

Serves 3 or 4

Classic Carolina red rice was a plain dish that stood on the quality of its ingredients: the rice itself, grown in lowland Carolina and prized throughout the world; fresh vine-ripened local tomatoes; and the fat that my Carolina rice adviser Kathryn Lotson, who has been cooking rice for sixty years, refers to as "white bacon" or "a streak of fat, a streak of lean." Today it's often made with canned tomatoes, converted rice, and a range of other ingredients, including tomato paste or even ketchup, put in to make it redder.

This recipe falls somewhere between the old and the "improved" versions.

> *1 cup long-grain white rice*
> *2 ounces slab bacon or salt pork, diced*
> *1 pound fresh ripe local tomatoes, peeled, seeded, and*
> *   chopped as directed on page 48 (1 cup chopped),*
> *   or 1 cup canned imported Italian plum tomatoes,*
> *   seeded and chopped, with juice*
> *1 cup hot chicken or vegetable broth or water*
> *1 small onion, chopped small*
> *½ green bell pepper, chopped small*
> *¼ teaspoon sugar (optional)*
> *½ teaspoon hot red pepper flakes (optional)*
> *1 teaspoon fresh thyme leaves (optional)*
> *salt and freshly ground black pepper to taste*

Rinse the rice under cold running water until the water runs clear or almost clear. Drain in a strainer and shake to get rid of the water. Leave in the strainer to drain.

Cook bacon in a heavy-bottomed saucepan until fat is melted and meat lightly browned. Remove any remaining solid fat pieces with a slotted spoon. Stir in tomatoes and cook, stirring, until thick. Add broth and all remaining ingredients except the rice. Bring to a rapid boil and add the rice. Don't stir the rice, Mrs. Lofsen advises, but shake the pot to make it settle evenly. Then turn down the heat, cover the pot, and simmer 20 minutes. Remove from heat and let sit, covered, 10 minutes.

Rice with Vermicelli

Serves 4 or 5

Rice cooked with toasted or sautéed noodles is a traditional dish in pilaf country from the eastern Mediterranean region to the Caspian Sea. Marie Alberian of Weehawken, New Jersey, makes an Armenian version using vermicelli. She serves it plain at holiday feasts alongside several other traditional dishes, including lamb or poultry. I like to add a yogurt topping or the Persian Date and Raisin Topping with Nuts on page 43 and serve with chicken, duck, or just vegetables such as squash or sweet potatoes.

> *4 tablespoons walnut oil or butter or 2 tablespoons each*
> *½ cup vermicelli, broken into pieces about 1½ inches long*
> *1 cup long-grain white rice*
> *2¼ cups hot chicken or duck broth or water*
> *salt to taste*

Heat the oil or butter over medium-low heat in a large heavy saucepan. Add vermicelli and cook, stirring, until golden. Add rice and cook, stirring, 2 or 3 minutes. Add broth or water and salt. Adjust heat to boil gently 10 minutes, or until surface liquid has been absorbed. Cover pot, turn heat to very low, and cook another 10 minutes. Remove from heat and let sit covered another 10 minutes.

Pilaf with Carrot, Dill, and Orange Zest

Serves 3 or 4

This pilaf with its fresh, naturally sweetish flavors is a favorite among my steady tasters. I serve it with any fish or fowl. For a meatless dinner for 2, stir in a cup of cooked chickpeas with the broth or serve the rice beside a black bean stew.

> *2 tablespoons butter or extra-virgin olive oil*
> *2 medium carrots, shredded (about 1 cup)*
> *1 cup long-grain white rice*
> *grated zest 1 orange*
> *1 bunch fresh dill leaves, washed and chopped ($\frac{1}{2}$ cup chopped)*
> *1$\frac{3}{4}$ cups hot chicken or vegetable broth*

Melt butter or heat oil over medium heat in a heavy saucepan. Add carrots and cook, stirring occasionally, 5 minutes. Add rice and cook, stirring, 2 or 3 minutes. Stir in orange zest, then dill, then broth. When boiling well, cover, reduce heat to very low, and cook 20 minutes. Turn off heat and let sit 10 minutes.

Pilaf with Carrots and Coconut

Serves 5 or 6

Tart and sweetish flavors give this pilaf a pleasing dimension.

> *4 tablespoons raw unsalted cashew pieces (available at*
> *   natural-food stores)*
> *2 lemons*
> *4 tablespoons unsalted butter*
> *2 tablespoons minced shallots*
> *2 medium carrots, shredded*
> *$\frac{1}{2}$ cup unsweetened shredded coconut*
> *$\frac{1}{3}$ cup golden raisins*
> *1$\frac{1}{2}$ cups long-grain white rice*

1 teaspoon turmeric
2½ cups hot chicken or vegetable broth
salt and freshly ground black pepper to taste

Spread cashews on a baking sheet and cook in a preheated 350°F oven until a light golden brown, 4 or 5 minutes.

Grate the zest of the 2 lemons and reserve both zest and lemons.

Melt butter in a heavy saucepan over medium heat. Add shallots and carrots and cook, stirring, 5 minutes. Stir in coconut, cashews, raisins, and lemon zest, then the rice and turmeric. Add broth, salt, and pepper. When boiling well, wrap the pot lid in a dish towel as directed on page 16. Cover the pot with the wrapped lid, reduce heat, and simmer 20 minutes. Remove from heat and let rest, still covered, 10 minutes before serving.

Cut the lemons into quarters and pass at table for squeezing over the rice.

A Touch of Coconut

Serves 3 or 4

The coconut flavor in this simple curried rice comes through as both rich and subtle, smooth and full.

2 tablespoons peanut oil
½ teaspoon cumin seeds
1 cup long-grain white rice
1 teaspoon turmeric
½ teaspoon ground ginger
¼ cup shredded dried coconut
½ cup canned coconut milk ("lite" is fine)
1½ cups hot chicken broth

Heat oil in a heavy saucepan over medium heat. Add cumin seeds. When they begin to darken, sizzle, and pop, add rice and stir to coat. Stir in turmeric, ginger, and shredded coconut, then the coconut milk. Cook briefly until most of the coconut liquid is absorbed. Add broth. When boiling well, cover, reduce heat, and simmer 20 minutes. Remove from heat and let sit 10 minutes.

Wild Rice with Coconut and Raisins

Serves 5 or 6

This is one of several recipes provided by Maria Alvarez, a beautiful New Jersey pharmacist and talented Cuban cook. In Cuba, where Maria grew up, the dish is made with long-grain white rice, but Maria's family likes her North American wild rice version as a side dish with a roast or ham. It's also good with duck or turkey.

Maria cooks all rice, including wild rice, in an equal volume of water, though most wild rice recipes call for $2\frac{1}{2}$ to 4 cups liquid per cup of wild rice. After trying different proportions, I take a compromise position.

> *2 tablespoons butter*
> *$1\frac{1}{2}$ cups wild rice, washed and drained*
> *$\frac{1}{2}$ cup grated or shredded coconut*
> *$\frac{1}{2}$ cup raisins*
> *salt to taste*

Bring 3 cups water to a boil. Add butter and rice. Return to boil, reduce heat, and simmer uncovered for 10 minutes. Stir in coconut, raisins, and salt. Cover, reduce heat to very low, and cook another 35 minutes, or until all the water is absorbed. Remove from heat and let sit, covered, another 10 minutes.

Brown Rice with Lemon, Dill, and Feta

Serves 3 or 4

The zippy flavors borrowed from Greek pilafs give life to the brown rice in this sprightly match for beans or fish or for a Mediterranean vegetable dish such as baked eggplant or ratatouille.

> *2 tablespoons olive oil*
> *$\frac{1}{2}$ medium onion, chopped small*
> *1 clove garlic, minced*

> *1 cup long-grain brown rice*
> *2 cups hot vegetable broth or water*
> *grated zest 1 lemon*
> *⅛ teaspoon ground cinnamon*
> *salt and freshly ground black pepper to taste*
> *1 small bunch fresh dill, chopped (½ to ¾ cup chopped)*
> *⅓ to ½ cup crumbled feta cheese*
> *1 lemon, cut lengthwise into crescents*

Heat oil in a heavy saucepan over medium heat. Add onion and cook, stirring occasionally, until soft. Add garlic and cook, stirring occasionally, until soft. Add rice and cook, stirring, until it begins to turn golden brown, about 5 minutes. Reduce heat and pour in the hot broth or water. Add lemon zest, cinnamon, salt, pepper, and dill. Adjust heat to bubble gently 10 to 15 minutes until surface water has been absorbed. Cover, reduce heat to very low, and cook another 25 to 30 minutes, for a total of 40 minutes' cooking time. Remove from heat and let sit covered another 10 minutes. Just before serving, stir in the feta. Pass lemon wedges at table.

Brown Rice with Lemon and Ginger

Serves 3 or 4

If you share my taste for tart flavors, you will find this simple side dish refreshing with fish or fowl or in a vegetarian meal.

> *2 tablespoons walnut oil or other cooking oil*
> *1 small onion, chopped small (about ⅓ cup chopped)*
> *1 large clove garlic, minced*
> *minced fresh gingerroot to equal amount of garlic*
> *1 cup long-grain brown rice*
> *1 tablespoon fresh lemon juice*
> *zest 1 lemon, grated or minced*
> *salt and freshly ground black pepper to taste*

Heat oil in a heavy saucepan over medium heat. Add onion and cook 2 or 3 minutes until soft. Add garlic and ginger and cook 2 or 3 minutes until soft. Add rice and stir to coat. Add 2 cups steaming-hot water, then the lemon juice, lemon zest, salt, and pepper. When boiling, cover, reduce heat, and simmer 40 minutes. Remove from heat and let sit, still covered, another 10 minutes.

Brown Rice with Apples, Raisins, and Walnuts

Serves 3 or 4

This sweetish side dish also makes a nice stuffing for vegetables or poultry or a delicious weekend breakfast, topped if you like with a little honey or maple syrup.

> *2 tablespoons walnut or canola oil*
> *1 small or $\frac{1}{2}$ medium onion, chopped ($\frac{1}{2}$ cup chopped)*
> *1 cup brown rice (long- or short-grain)*
> *1 teaspoon oriental 5-spice powder or the following 3 spices:*
> > *1 teaspoon ground coriander*
> > *$\frac{1}{2}$ teaspoon ground cinnamon*
> > *$\frac{1}{8}$ teaspoon ground cloves*
> *1 Granny Smith apple, or other firm, tart apple, peeled,*
> > *cored, and diced*
> *4 tablespoons raisins*
> *4 tablespoons walnuts, chopped*

Heat the oil in a heavy saucepan over medium heat. Add the onion and cook, stirring occasionally, until soft, about 5 minutes. Add the rice and cook, stirring frequently, until translucent, 2 or 3 minutes. Add 2 cups steaming-hot water, the ground spices, and the apple and raisins. Bring to a boil, then lower heat to boil gently until surface water has disappeared and small steam holes appear on top of the rice. Cover, reduce heat to very low, and cook another 30 minutes. Remove from heat and let rest, still covered, another 10 minutes.

While the rice is resting, roast the walnuts for 5 minutes on an unoiled sheet in a toaster oven or oven preheated to 350°F. Fold walnuts into rice before serving.

Turkish Pilaf with Herbs

Serves 3 or 4

Ayla Algar, an authority on Turkish cooking, hints in her book *Classic Turkish Cooking* that the Turks, as much as the Persians, were responsible for the early flowering of pilaf. In any case, the variety of Turkish pilaf styles and dishes is impressive. In some the rice is boiled in the old Persian way, but the quick sauté that begins this recipe is typical of what the world has come to know as Turkish pilaf. I serve this with chicken or lamb and a separate dish of the Garlic Yogurt Topping on page 46.

> *1 cup Indian basmati rice*
> *2 tablespoons butter*
> *3 tablespoons pine nuts*
> *1 medium onion, chopped small*
> *1¾ cups hot chicken stock*
> *¼ teaspoon saffron threads, crumbled*
> *3 tablespoons golden raisins*
> *3 tablespoons chopped fresh dill*
> *3 tablespoons broadleaf parsley*
> *½ teaspoon ground allspice*
> *¼ teaspoon ground cinnamon*
> *⅛ teaspoon freshly grated nutmeg*
> *pinch ground cloves*
> *salt and freshly ground black pepper to taste*
> *3 tablespoons chopped fresh mint leaves, plus several*
> *   small whole leaves*
> *1 teaspoon rose flower water (optional)*

Clean and wash the rice in several changes of water as directed on page 13. Cover by 1 inch with cold water and leave to soak for 30 minutes. Drain through a strainer, and shake the strainer to drain off the water.

Heat butter in a heavy saucepan over medium heat. Add nuts and cook, stirring, 5 minutes or less, until lightly browned. Remove with a slotted spoon and set aside. Add onion to the saucepan and cook, stirring occasionally, until it turns golden. Add rice and cook, stirring, 5 minutes, until translucent and almost chalky white. Add stock. Stir in all the remaining ingredients except the nuts, the whole mint leaves, and the optional rose flower water. Bring to a boil, then reduce heat to bubble gently until the surface water has disappeared, about 10 minutes. Wrap the pot lid with a dish towel as directed on page 16 and cover the pot with the wrapped lid. Reduce heat to very low and cook 10 minutes. Remove from heat to rest, covered, another 10 minutes. Toss in the nuts, sprinkling some bits over the rice. Scatter the whole mint leaves on top and sprinkle with the rose flower water.

Tamarind Rice

Serves 3 or 4

The fruit of the tropical tamarind tree lends a pleasantly tart flavor to this Indian-style rice dish, essentially a pilaf translation of the Tamarind Sauce on page 51. Try it with fish or lentils.

> *1-ounce piece bulk tamarind or 1 level teaspoon*
> *concentrated tamarind extract (see page 50)*
> *4 tablespoons canned tomato sauce*
> *¼ teaspoon molasses*
> *2 tablespoons peanut or corn oil*
> *½ teaspoon cumin seeds*
> *½ teaspoon black or yellow mustard seeds*
> *½ medium onion, minced*
> *1 clove garlic, minced*
> *minced fresh gingerroot to equal amount of garlic*
> *1 tablespoon minced fresh chile*
> *1 cup long-grain white rice*
> *pinch ground cinnamon*
> *salt to taste*

If using bulk tamarind, break off a 1-ounce piece, soak it for several hours or overnight, then mash and strain it as directed on page 50. If using tamarind concentrate, mix it with the tomato sauce. Stir the molasses into the tomato sauce.

Heat oil in a heavy saucepan. Add cumin and mustard seeds. When cumin seeds begin to sizzle and darken, add onion and cook, stirring, a few minutes until soft. Add garlic, ginger, and chile, and cook, stirring, another 2 minutes. Add rice and cook, stirring, until translucent, 2 or 3 minutes. Stir in molasses and tomato sauce with the tamarind concentrate, if using. If using bulk tamarind, and if the material you strained through the sieve has a juicelike consistency, add $\frac{1}{2}$ cup to the rice mixture and cook until liquid thickens. If it has more the consistency of ketchup, add $\frac{1}{4}$ cup and stir. Add $1\frac{3}{4}$ cups water, then the cinnamon and salt. When boiling well, cover the pot, reduce heat, and simmer 20 minutes. Remove from heat and let sit uncovered another 10 minutes.

Coconut Tamarind Rice

Use all the ingredients for Tamarind Rice, above, plus $1\frac{3}{4}$ cups fresh or a 14-ounce can coconut milk. Proceed as for Tamarind Rice but add the coconut milk instead of water. To reduce the amount of saturated fat, or for a lighter coconut flavor (as I prefer), use 1 cup coconut milk and $\frac{3}{4}$ cup water.

Indian-Style Lemon Ginger Rice I: With Whole Spices

Serves 3 or 4

The three recipes in the progression that follows demonstrate how a rice side dish can be made as simple or as elaborate as you like. The first is tasty, with a pleasant tang; the second is a little more complex; and the last is dressed up with a spicy, festive topping. Although white rice is traditional and cooks up lighter and fluffier, these recipes also work for brown rice.

In India, whole spices are sometimes cooked with rice and left in when the rice is served, though they are not eaten. Here, if you choose to follow that custom, it is best to alert your guests to their tooth-jolting presence.

1 cup Indian or American basmati or other long-grain rice
1 tablespoon butter or oil

slivered zest ½ lemon
2 teaspoons slivered fresh gingerroot
1 stick cinnamon
2 whole cloves
5 whole cardamom pods
salt to taste
1 tablespoon freshly squeezed lemon juice

If using Indian basmati, wash the rice several times to remove starch, then soak in 2 cups cool water for 30 minutes before cooking, as directed on pages 13–14. (This preparation is optional if using American rice.)

Pour the rice and its soaking water (or pour unsoaked rice and 2 cups water) into a saucepan and add the butter or oil, lemon zest, ginger, cinnamon, cloves, and cardamom. Bring to a boil, then reduce heat to boil gently until surface water disappears and small steam holes appear on top, about 10 minutes. Add salt. Wrap the pot lid in a dish towel as directed on page 16. Cover the pan with the wrapped lid, reduce heat to very low, and cook 10 minutes. Remove from heat and let rest, still covered, another 10 minutes. Remove cinnamon stick and other whole spices if you wish. Toss in the lemon juice and serve.

Indian-Style Lemon Ginger Rice II: With Whole and Sizzling Spices

Serves 3 or 4

A sizzling sauté at the opening gives the fragrant rice some punch.

1 cup Indian or American basmati or other long-grain rice
2 tablespoons canola or corn oil
1 teaspoon cumin seeds
1 teaspoon mustard seeds
1 small or ½ medium onion, minced
2 teaspoons turmeric
slivered zest ½ lemon
2 teaspoons slivered fresh gingerroot

1 stick cinnamon
2 whole cloves
5 whole cardamom pods
salt to taste
1 tablespoon freshly squeezed lemon juice

If using Indian basmati, wash and soak the rice as directed above. (This preparation is optional if using American rice.)

Heat the oil in a medium-size saucepan over medium heat. Add the cumin and mustard seeds and cook until they sizzle or pop and the cumin seeds darken. Add onion and cook, stirring occasionally, about 5 minutes until soft. Add drained rice, reserving the soaking water, and cook, stirring frequently, until translucent, 2 or 3 minutes. Stir in the turmeric. Add soaking water (or, if rice has not been soaked, add 2 cups steaming-hot water). Add lemon zest, ginger, cinnamon, cloves, and cardamom. When water returns to a boil, adjust heat to boil gently until the surface water disappears and small steam holes appear on top. Add salt and finish cooking as in the recipe above.

Indian-Style Lemon Ginger Rice III: With Whole Spices and Sizzling Festive Topping

Serves 3 or 4

In India, as in Iran and its neighbors, an already tasty rice dish is often made sumptuous with a buttery or oil-fried topping. This one uses the same fried seeds and onions that are cooked with the rice in version II, above, but gives them a more prominent presence and a festive accompaniment of fried nuts.

all the ingredients for Indian-Style Lemon Ginger Rice I, plus:
3 tablespoons ghee (see clarified butter, page 53) or butter
1 small onion or $\frac{1}{2}$ medium onion, sliced very thin
2 tablespoons unsalted, shelled pistachio nuts
2 tablespoons unsalted, raw cashew pieces
1 teaspoon mustard seeds

1 teaspoon cumin seeds
2 teaspoons turmeric

Follow the recipe for Indian-Style Lemon Ginger Rice I, but do not stir in the lemon juice at the end. (Instead, it will go in with the topping.)

When the rice is cooking, heat the ghee in a small frying pan over medium heat. Break the onion slices into rings and fry, in batches so as not to crowd, until brown but not burned. Remove to paper towel. Reduce heat to low and fry the pistachios and cashews until the cashews are lightly browned but not burned. Remove to paper towel. Add mustard and cumin seeds and cook until cumin seeds have darkened. Reduce heat to very low and stir in the turmeric and lemon juice.

To serve, transfer the rice to a serving bowl or platter. Fluff with 2 forks and jab some holes in the mound of rice for the topping to trickle into. Pour contents of frying pan over the rice, tossing gently. Top with onion rings and nuts.

Vegetable Pilaf

Waves Edge Vegetable Pilaf

Serves 8 as a side dish

When my daughter had the vegetable rice side dish at Waves Edge restaurant in Waves, North Carolina, she asked Waves Edge proprietor Harry White if he would send me the recipe. It turns out that the Waves Edge kitchen mixes wild rice with a basmati-wheat-tomato orzo blend sold only to restaurants, so this is only my approximation. The orzo, a rice-shaped pasta, provides some interesting textural variety but is not essential. For a nuttier, whole-grain alternative, use one of the Lundberg company's brown rice mixes instead of the basmati and orzo.

This recipe makes a large quantity of pilaf, but leftovers are good cold with an oil and vinegar dressing.

1 cup American basmati rice
¾ cup wild rice
¼ cup wheat berries
½ cup orzo (optional)
4 or 5 tablespoons butter or olive oil
1 medium-small onion, chopped small
1 large carrot, diced
1 green bell pepper, diced
2 fresh plum tomatoes, peeled, seeded, and chopped
½ roasted red pepper, diced
¼ cup chopped parsley
1 tablespoon fresh thyme leaves
salt and freshly ground black pepper to taste

Add basmati rice to 1¾ cups boiling salted water. Return to a boil, then cover, reduce heat to low, and cook 20 minutes.

Add wild rice and wheat berries to a separate pot with 2 cups boiling salted water. Return to a boil, then cover, reduce heat to low, and cook 40 to 45 minutes.

If using orzo, drop into 2 cups boiling water with ½ teaspoon butter or oil to prevent clinging. Return to a boil, stir, and boil gently 6 to 8 minutes or until done. Drain through a strainer and rinse under warm running water, then turn into a large bowl and mix in another ½ teaspoon butter or oil.

While rice is cooking, heat 4 tablespoons butter or oil in a skillet and sauté onion, carrot, and green pepper 7 or 8 minutes until soft but not brown. Add tomatoes for the last 2 minutes. Remove from heat and stir in the diced red pepper.

Add rice and vegetables to the bowl with the orzo and mix with a serving spoon and fork. Mix in parsley, thyme, salt, and pepper.

Potato Rice with Seeds and Garlic

Serves 4 as a side dish, 2 or 3 as a meal with lentils

There are several Persian and Indian versions of potato rice; both must have evolved after potatoes from the New World made their way around the Old.

This recipe derives from my Iranian neighbor's family standby, but my sauté and spicing give it an Indian spin.

3 fresh plum tomatoes
3 tablespoons mustard or peanut oil
½ teaspoon mustard seeds
½ teaspoon cumin seeds
1 small onion, chopped small (about ½ cup chopped)
1 large clove garlic, minced
1 small to medium boiling potato, peeled and diced (⅔ to 1 cup diced)
1 cup long-grain white rice
2 cups hot chicken or vegetable broth or water
¾ teaspoon turmeric
¼ teaspoon ground cayenne, or to taste
salt and freshly ground black pepper to taste

Skin, seed, and chop tomatoes as directed on page 48. Heat the oil in a heavy saucepan over medium heat. Add mustard and cumin seeds and cook 2 to 3 minutes until the cumin seeds begin to darken. Add onion and cook 5 minutes, then add garlic and cook 2 to 3 minutes until soft. Add potato and cook another 5 minutes or more until onion turns golden brown. Add rice and cook, stirring, 2 to 3 minutes. Stir in the tomatoes. Add broth. Stir in the turmeric, cayenne, salt, and pepper. Adjust heat to bubble gently for 10 minutes, until surface liquid has disappeared. Cover, reduce heat to very low, and cook 10 minutes. Remove from heat and let sit, still covered, another 10 minutes. Toss gently to stir in any tomatoes or other ingredients that have risen to the top. (The tomatoes will be in pieces, not dissolved into a sauce.)

Curried Cauliflower Rice with Yellow Dal

Serves 6 to 8 as a side dish, 4 as a main dish

Cauliflower, rice, and curry flavors seem to have a natural affinity. The ingredients in this recipe and the one that follows can be mixed, matched, and varied almost infinitely. I've served this version as a main dish with a spinach-mushroom-yogurt salad.

½ *cup yellow split peas (dal in India), rinsed*
1 *teaspoon turmeric*
salt to taste
1½ *cups long-grain white rice*
3 *to 4 tablespoons sesame or peanut oil*
1 *teaspoon mustard seeds*
1 *teaspoon cumin seeds*
1 *small to medium cauliflower, cut into small florets*
    (4 or 5 cups florets)
2 *or 3 large cloves garlic, minced*
minced fresh gingerroot to equal amount of garlic
1 *medium-large onion, chopped*
¼ *to* ½ *teaspoon ground cayenne, to taste*
½ *cup chopped fresh dill leaves*

Put split peas in a small saucepan with 1½ cups water. Bring to a boil. Skim froth from the top with a slotted spoon or skimmer. (Don't worry if you don't get it all.) Cover pot, remove from heat, and let stand 1 hour.

Bring 1½ cups water to a boil in another, medium-size saucepan. Stir in ½ teaspoon turmeric and salt to taste, then add the rice. When water has returned to a low boil, cover pot, remove from heat, and let stand 1 hour.

Preheat oven to 350°F.

Heat 2 tablespoons oil in a heavy Dutch oven over medium heat. Add mustard and cumin seeds. When they begin to darken and pop (a matter of seconds), add half the cauliflower and cook, turning occasionally, until golden brown in spots. (Cauliflower will not brown evenly. Better to miss some spots than to burn some.) Remove to paper towel. Add another tablespoon of oil if needed and repeat with the remaining cauliflower.

Add another tablespoon of oil if necessary. Stir in the garlic, ginger, and onion. Cook until turning golden, about 5 minutes. Add rice. Cook, stirring, until well coated. Return the cauliflower to the pot and stir in the remaining ½ teaspoon of turmeric and the cayenne, then the split peas with any water remaining with them in the saucepan. Stir in all but 1 tablespoon of the dill. Pour 2 cups boiling water evenly over the mixture. Cover pot and bake 20 minutes. If top layer of rice has not cooked, stir it under and return to oven for another 10 minutes if needed. Sprinkle with reserved dill to serve.

Curried Cauliflower Rice with Coconut

Serves 6 to 8 as an ample side dish, 4 as a main dish

Here is a richer but not necessarily better version of my infinitely variable curried cauliflower rice. Serve as a side dish with fish or as a main dish with a fresh fruit salad.

> $\frac{1}{3}$ cup golden raisins
> 4 tablespoons corn or peanut oil
> 1 tablespoon minced fresh gingerroot
> 1 medium to large onion, chopped small
> 1 small to medium cauliflower, cut into small florets
>   (4 or 5 cups florets)
> $\frac{1}{3}$ cup shredded coconut
> 1$\frac{1}{2}$ cups long-grain white rice
> 1 teaspoon ground coriander
> $\frac{1}{2}$ teaspoon ground cumin
> $\frac{1}{2}$ teaspoon turmeric
> $\frac{1}{2}$ teaspoon ground cardamom (optional)
> $\frac{1}{2}$ teaspoon allspice or mace (optional)
> $\frac{1}{4}$ teaspoon ground cinnamon
> salt to taste
> 1$\frac{1}{2}$ cups coconut milk
> 1 tablespoon freshly squeezed lemon juice
> 1 lemon, cut in wedges

Put the raisins in a small saucepan with 1$\frac{1}{2}$ cups water and keep hot (but not boiling) over a low flame.

Heat oil in a large nonstick skillet over medium heat. Add ginger and cook 1 minute. Add onion and cook, stirring occasionally, about 5 minutes until soft. Add cauliflower and cook, turning occasionally, until all or most pieces are turning golden brown in spots. Add the coconut and rice, then the ground spices and salt. Pour the coconut milk evenly over the mixture and bring to a boil. Add the lemon juice and the raisins with their soaking water. Cover, reduce heat to medium-low, and cook 20 to 30 minutes, moving the skillet an inch or two now and then if needed to ensure even cooking. Serve lemon wedges at table.

Spicy Rice and Vegetable Stew

Serves 4 or 5 as a main dish

This substantial melting-pot stew came about in an off-campus apartment oc-cupied by an ever-changing stream of graduate students from East and West. While the students came and went, the stew evolved. In that spirit, consider this recipe an outline for improvisation. For example, potatoes, sweet potatoes, or other root vegetables might be added with the broth. The stew will be a little soupier than a standard pilaf.

> *3 tablespoons peanut oil*
> *1 teaspoon black mustard seeds*
> *1 teaspoon cumin seeds*
> *1 teaspoon fenugreek seeds*
> *1 medium onion, chopped*
> *2 large cloves garlic, minced*
> *1 tablespoon minced fresh gingerroot*
> *2 jalapeno chile peppers, minced*
> *1 small eggplant (about $\frac{1}{2}$ pound), cut into $\frac{3}{4}$-inch cubes*
> *1 teaspoon turmeric*
> *1 teaspoon ground coriander*
> *$\frac{1}{4}$ teaspoon ground cinnamon*
> *1 half-pound piece calabaza squash or 1 very small*
>   *butternut squash (about $\frac{1}{2}$ pound), cut into 1-inch cubes*
> *2 cups canned plum tomatoes, with juice*
> *salt to taste*
> *2 cups chicken or vegetable broth or water*
> *2 cups cooked or canned chickpeas*
> *$1\frac{1}{2}$ cups long-grain rice*
> *4 tablespoons chopped cilantro (fresh coriander)*
> *2 tablespoons freshly squeezed lemon juice*

Heat oil in a large heavy pot. Add seeds. When they begin to pop, add onion, garlic, and ginger. Add chile, with seeds if you like it hot, without seeds for a milder effect. Cook, stirring occasionally, 5 minutes. Add eggplant and cook, stirring, another 5 minutes. Stir in ground spices. Add squash, tomatoes, and salt. In the pot, break up the tomatoes with your stirring spoon. Add broth and bring to a boil. Cover, reduce heat, and simmer gently 20 minutes, stirring once or twice to prevent sticking on the bottom. Add chickpeas with their liquid. Stir in the rice and boil gently 10 minutes. Then cover, reduce heat to very low, and cook 20 minutes. Stir in the cilantro and lemon juice.

Rice and Beans

Japan's favorite sweet treat is made with short-grain "sticky" rice and red adzuki beans. Italians wax nostalgic about risi e bisi (rice and peas). A classic Persian pilau layers rice with lima or fava beans. In much of southern India, whatever else is on the table, there is always rice and dal, the word for dried beans and peas and lentils. The same is true in the Caribbean, where the poor eat rice and beans and the better off eat rice and beans and other things. The population in and around Havana, Cuba, devours black beans and rice as an almost patriotic affirmation of identity; on the eastern end of the same island they swear by congris (red beans) and rice.

So many cultures have their own rice and bean combinations that the two foods must have been made for each other. They've been enjoyed together for millennia, and together they provide vegetarians with protein that mainstream nutritionists now recognize as equal to what others get from meat. And they're better for you, being high in complex carbohydrates and virtually fat free. When meat or fat is added, it can be done in small amounts, for flavor, as doctors are advising.

I don't claim all rice and bean combinations for the pilaf family. I mention the Japanese treat (not included here) simply as an example of how various and widespread is this happy pairing. But the dishes in this section either are cooked in a pilaf manner or are so similar in origin and ingredients to those that are that they belong together. As for the versions in which the rice and beans are cooked separately and combined at table, there is precedent for viewing them as deconstructed pilau; other examples of this structure can be found in Africa, whence the New World rice and bean dishes derive, and for that matter in Persia.

Herbed Fava Bean Pilau with Tadig

*Serves 6 to 8 as an American-style side dish, 4 to 6 with a little meat or chicken on
the side*

Fresh fava beans are so good in this Persian pilau that I make it only when they
are in season, but cooked dried or frozen lima beans also work.

Some Persian cooks layer this dish for a more formal presentation. My neighbor from Iran, Soheila Sobsey, who cooked it for me, mixes the beans and dill
with the boiled rice before steaming. Here is yet a third alternative.

You will need all the ingredients for Persian chelo (page 62), plus the tadig of
your choice (the crusts described on pages 64–65), and the following:

> *1 pound fresh fava beans in pods or 1 10-ounce or 12-ounce
> package frozen lima beans or 1½ cups cooked dried lima
> or fava beans
> 1½ cups chopped fresh dill or ¼ cup dried*

Wash, soak, boil, and drain the rice, and prepare the saffron butter as directed
in the recipe for Persian Chelo with Tadig on page 62.

If using fresh fava beans, remove from pods. Steam or simmer the beans until
just tender (10 to 15 minutes, depending on size and age). Cool under running
water until cool enough to handle and remove skins. Thaw the frozen lima
beans, if using. If limas are large, steam 5 minutes to partially cook.

Heat the oil as in the recipe for chelo, lay down the tadig of your choice, and
cover with a thin layer of rice. Spread the beans over the layer of rice. Mix the
dill with the remaining rice and put on top of the beans, shaping the rice with
your hands to form a mound. Proceed as in the recipe for chelo.

Soheila's Kateh with Beans and Dill

In addition to her splendid pilau, above, Soheila uses fava beans and dill in her
everyday kateh. To cook this easier Persian rice dish, drop 1 cup of rice with the
dill and partly cooked beans into a saucepan containing 2 cups of water. Soheila
also adds ¼ teaspoon of a mix of sugar, saffron, salt, and pepper. Bring to a boil,
cover, reduce heat to as low as possible, and cook 1 hour. Spoon onto a serving

platter. Scrape up the crust with a spatula and sprinkle over or around the rice. (If no crust is desired, cook only half an hour. But this is not the Persian way.)

Variation

Instead of dill and beans, Soheila sometimes cooks her kateh with chopped fresh spinach leaves (about ½ pound for a cup of raw rice) and thin-sliced scallions.

Maria's Cuban Moros y Cristianos

Serves 6 to 8 as a side dish

This classic Cuban dish of black beans and white rice is named for the dark-skinned Moors who invaded Spain in the early 700s and the light-skinned Spanish Christians who lived for centuries under Moslem rule. Maria Alvarez, who grew up in Cuba, makes this pristine Moros y Cristianos without meat or spices and serves it as a side dish with roast pork or ham. (I've added a little more liquid to her proportions.) When making Moros y Cristianos for a main dish, Cubans often cook a ham hock or a meaty leftover ham bone with the beans.

> ⅔ *cup dried black beans (2 cups cooked) or 1 16-ounce can*
> *black turtle beans*
> *4 tablespoons olive oil*
> *1 medium onion, sliced thin, with slices cut in half*
> *1 green bell pepper, cut into thin strips*
> *2 cloves garlic, mashed*
> *1 tablespoon chopped cilantro (fresh coriander)*
> *2 cups long-grain white rice*
> *1 teaspoon salt*

If using dried beans, rinse them and put them in a heavy pot with 2 cups of water. Bring to a boil, boil 1 or 2 minutes, then cover and remove from heat for 1 hour. Return to a boil, reduce heat to a very low boil, and cook 1 to 2 hours until done but not mushy.

Ladle the cooked beans into a large heavy saucepan. Some liquid will come along with the beans. Measure the bean liquid that remains behind and, if needed, add enough water to equal 2 cups. Add to the beans and keep warm over low heat. If using canned beans, put beans and liquid in the pot with 2 cups hot water.

Heat oil in a skillet and sauté the onion and green pepper until soft but not brown. Add garlic and cilantro and cook, stirring, for 1 or 2 minutes. Then add contents of the skillet to the beans.

Rinse the rice under running water. Drain and add to the bean pot with the salt. Bring to a boil, then cover and reduce heat to simmer 20 minutes.

Vegetarian Black Beans and Rice

Serves 4 to 6 as a main dish

When I serve black beans and rice as a meatless main course, I add a little more spice and flavor than is traditional or needed when the dish is served with meat. Here the beans are enriched by a sofrito, a fried tomato-based sauce that takes different forms in different Spanish-speaking countries.

Also, whereas Maria's Cuban Moros y Cristianos are mixed together, I cook the beans and rice separately and enjoy the contrast of the rich dark beans over stark white rice. Another option is to use brown rice — the spicy bean mixture can stand up to the coarser grains.

> *1 pound dried black beans (about 2¼ cups)*
> *2 cups long-grain white rice*
>
> ### The sofrito:
>
> *4 tablespoons olive oil*
> *1 large or 2 medium onions, chopped fine*
> *1 large green bell pepper, chopped fine*
> *1 or 2 jalapeno or serrano chile peppers, minced*
> *2 or 3 large cloves garlic, minced*
> *minced fresh gingerroot to equal amount of garlic*
> *4 ounces tomato paste (½ small can)*
> *1 teaspoon dried thyme*
> *1 teaspoon ground cumin*
> *½ teaspoon ground coriander*

salt and freshly ground black pepper to taste
1 16- or 20-ounce can Italian plum tomatoes, juice reserved
⅓ cup feta cheese, crumbled, or 1 tablespoon vinegar or
        2 tablespoons rum
3 or 4 tablespoons chopped cilantro (fresh coriander)
pimiento strips for garnish (optional but dashing)

Rinse the beans and put them in a large heavy pot with 6 cups water. Bring to a boil. Boil 1 or 2 minutes, cover, and remove from heat for 1 hour. Then return to a boil, reduce heat to a very low boil, and cook 1 to 2 hours until done but not mushy. Check after the first hour and add more water if needed.

Rinse rice under running water and leave in sieve to drain.

While beans are cooking, make the sofrito: Heat oil in a skillet and sauté onions, pepper, chile, and garlic over medium heat about 10 minutes, until they are soft and the onions clear. Stir in the ginger, tomato paste, and spices, and cook in the oil until tomato paste is darkened, about 10 minutes.

When beans are nearly done, bring 3 cups water to a boil in another heavy saucepan. Add rice. When water returns to a boil, cover pot and reduce heat to very low. Cook 20 minutes (40 minutes if using brown rice), then remove from heat to rest for 10 minutes.

Add sofrito to the cooked beans with the salt, pepper, and canned tomatoes, reserving the juice from the can. In the pot, break up the tomatoes with your stirring spoon. If the beans are dry, add reserved tomato juice, but not enough to make them soupy. Cook over low heat, stirring as needed, until rice is ready. Then stir in the cheese or vinegar or rum.

Serve on a platter or on individual plates with a bed of rice topped by a generous cover of beans, then a sprinkling of cilantro and a pimiento cross.

Cumin Rice with Black Beans

Serves 4 as a side dish

No one would call this side dish beans and rice; the fluffy, cumin-flavored rice clearly comes first here and the black beans second. The beans should be drained of their cooking juice and scattered discretely through the dish. Good with pork, duck, or baked squash.

1 tablespoon peanut oil
1 large clove garlic, minced
1 tablespoon minced fresh gingerroot
1 cup long-grain white rice
1 teaspoon cumin seeds, ground in a spice mill or coffee grinder
salt to taste and generous amount of freshly ground black pepper
½ cup plain cooked or canned black beans, drained or
*   removed from liquid with a slotted spoon*

Heat the oil in a heavy saucepan. Add garlic and ginger and cook, stirring, until soft. Add rice and cook, stirring to coat the grains. Stir in the ground cumin, then add 1¾ cups boiling or steaming-hot water. Sprinkle with salt and pepper. Cover, reduce heat, and simmer 20 minutes. Remove from heat and let sit 10 minutes. Turn into a large bowl and gently stir in the beans.

Hoppin' John

Serves 6 as a hefty side dish, 3 as a main dish

Culinary historians agree that it was Africans brought as slaves to work the Carolina rice fields who gave the South its body-and-soul-sustaining comfort food and New Year's Day good-luck dish, hoppin' John. The earliest recipes, like today's, call for either black-eyed peas or pigeon peas (known also by such variant forms and names as field peas, cow peas, and the crowder peas beloved of Elvis Presley), both carried here from the slaves' homeland in rice-growing West Africa. Jessica Harris, an authority on African–New World food connections, tells us that West Africans still enjoy those same peas mixed with rice.

Of the three ingredients essential to hoppin' John — rice, peas, and pork fat — this recipe uses half the traditional amount of pork fat and then discards some of that. The flavor remains. And though Southerners accompany hoppin' John with greens cooked in pork fat, I have it with a spinach salad.

¼ pound slab bacon or salt pork
1 medium onion, chopped
1 cup dried black-eyed peas, washed and picked over
½ teaspoon hot red pepper flakes, with no or few seeds

1 teaspoon fresh thyme leaves (optional)
1 cup long-grain white rice
salt to taste

Try to buy or cut off a quarter-pound piece of bacon or salt pork that is about half meat and half fat. Separate the meatier portions from the fatty ones by slicing, then dice both meaty and fatty parts.

Heat a heavy saucepan or Dutch oven over medium heat. Add the fatty pieces of the bacon or salt pork and cook 3 to 5 minutes until they have yielded enough fat to cook the onion and rice. Remove the fatty cubes with a slotted spoon and discard.

Add the meaty pieces to the pot and cook to brown lightly. Add onion and cook 5 minutes until soft. Add peas, pepper flakes, thyme, and 5 cups cold water. Bring to a boil, cover, and reduce heat to simmer gently until peas are tender but not mushy, about 45 minutes. (But see Note below on timing.)

Turn up the heat and add the rice and salt. When boiling, cover and reduce heat to very low. Cook 20 minutes, then remove from heat and let sit, still covered, another 10 minutes.

Note: This recipe calls for far less cooking time than others I've read. Some would have you soak the peas overnight, then cook them for an hour or more before adding the rice. The brands of black-eyed peas I've used would be mush long before that time is up. (I don't presoak the peas at all.) It seems to me that many of today's dried beans cook faster than was once the case. I can only assume that brands vary and advise you to get to know your own.

LaRoccas' New Orleans Red Beans and Rice

Serves 5 or 6 as a main dish

Anyone who grew up in New Orleans remembers Monday as red-beans-and-rice day, when the beans simmered untended on the stove while the mothers bent over their scrub boards with the family wash. Jazz great Louis Armstrong, a New Orleans native, remembered the dish so fondly that throughout his life he closed his letters with "Red beans and ricely yours."

My brother-in-law Tony LaRocca, also a New Orleans native and a jazz pianist there before he became a physicist, still likes his beans cooked to a creamy consistency, the way his mother made them, as opposed to the soupy style some others favored; this recipe honors that longstanding family preference. Tony also remembers that his mother always washed her rice, to get the starch off, before she cooked it. That ritual is no longer observed by her descendants, who have converted to Uncle Ben's.

> *1 pound dried red kidney beans*
> *2 bay leaves*
> *4 tablespoons olive oil*
> *1 slice ham, cubed*
> *1 large onion, chopped fine*
> *1 green bell pepper, chopped fine*
> *2 stalks celery, chopped fine*
> *2 to 4 cloves garlic, minced*
> *1 large or 2 small carrots, sliced thin*
> *1 teaspoon dried thyme*
> *¼ teaspoon ground cayenne, or more to taste*
> *salt and freshly ground black pepper to taste*
> *2½ cups long-grain white rice*
> *bottled Tabasco or other hot sauce*

Rinse and sort the beans, and soak them for several hours or overnight in enough water to come 1 inch above the level of the beans. (Or put beans in a pot with 6 cups water. Bring to a boil, remove from heat, cover, and let sit 1 hour.)

About 2 hours before mealtime, bring beans and water to a boil. Add bay leaves. Cover pot and reduce heat to a simmer.

Heat the oil in a skillet. Brown ham in the olive oil, then remove and set aside. Cook the onion in oil until light brown. Add green pepper, celery, and garlic and cook until soft. After beans have cooked 1 hour, add the cooked vegetables to the bean pot with chopped ham, sliced carrots, and spices. Return cover and cook until beans are soft, checking now and then, and adding water if needed.

When beans are nearly done, bring 3½ cups salted water to a boil. Add rice, return to a boil, then cover, reduce heat to very low, and cook 20 minutes. Remove from heat and let sit, covered, another 5 to 10 minutes, then spoon onto plates and top with bean mixture. Put out the hot sauce to add at table as desired.

Puerto Rican White Rice and Kidney Beans

Serves 8 to 10 on the side, 4 to 6 as a meal

A white rice dish in Spanish-speaking countries is simply rice cooked plain as a side dish in whatever manner locally prevails. In Puerto Rico, rice and beans might be served side by side or together as a meal, or as separate side dishes to accompany a main dish of meat or chicken. Another major use for the kidney bean preparation used in this dual recipe is with Arroz con Pollo (page 121), which is always served with peas or beans either on top or on the side.

This recipe calls for medium-grain rice, traditional in Puerto Rican cooking. The Japanese type grown in California is good. The recipe departs from tradition, as do today's health-conscious Puerto Rican cooks, in using oil instead of lard for the cooking fat.

The aji dulce chile used in the recaito (a made-from-scratch flavoring paste essential to Puerto Rican cooking) is a tiny, wrinkled, flying-saucer-shaped sweet chile that looks and smells like the incendiary habanero or scotch bonnet chile but lacks the heat. Sometimes simply called *aji* in Puerto Rico (though that word just means chile in other parts of Latin America), it is available in mainland grocery stores with Puerto Rican customers. If unavailable, just do without — don't substitute hot chiles.

The beans:

1 pound dried red kidney beans
½ pound calabaza (Caribbean squash or pumpkin)
    or butternut squash, peeled and cut into 2-inch pieces

The recaito:

1 medium onion, peeled
2 Italian green peppers or 1 green bell pepper, cored and seeded
2 large cloves garlic, smashed flat
3 aji dulce chiles, if available (see headnote above)
6 to 8 sprigs cilantro (fresh coriander)

2 tablespoons olive or corn oil
¼ cup diced ham or salt pork (traditional but optional)

4 ounces (½ can) tomato sauce (not needed if beans are
to be served with Arroz con Pollo)
salt and freshly ground black pepper to taste

The rice:

3 tablespoons cooking oil
2 cups medium-grain rice
2 teaspoons salt

Rinse the beans and pick out any pebbles, dirt, or other stray bits of matter. Then put the beans in a large pot with 6 cups of water to soak overnight — or bring to a boil, boil for 1 minute, remove from heat, cover, and soak for 1 hour. After the soak, bring to a boil, add the calabaza, reduce heat, and simmer 1 to 2 hours, or until the beans are tender but not mushy.

While the beans are cooking, prepare the recaito. Coarsely chop all the ingredients listed and process in a food processor until very finely minced but not watery.

Heat the oil over medium heat. Add the ham or salt pork, if using, and cook 5 minutes. Remove any solid fat pieces but leave the meat in the pot. Add the recaito and cook 5 minutes, stirring occasionally. Add tomato sauce, if using, and cook, stirring, to reduce and darken. Stir into the beans and cook together until the beans are done. With a wooden spoon, smash the calabaza pieces against the sides of the pot and stir them into the bean juice to thicken the juice. Add salt and pepper to taste.

When the beans are partially cooked, prepare the rice. Put 3 cups cold water in a large heavy kettle over medium-high heat. Add the oil. Put rice in a large strainer and rinse under cold running water until the water runs clear. Shake and rake the rice to drain. When the water is boiling, add the salt and the rice. Return to a boil, then adjust heat to boil moderately, uncovered, until surface water disappears (Puerto Rican cooks say "until the rice is dry"). Reduce heat to very low. With a wooden spoon, turn rice once from bottom to top, then cover the pot and cook 10 minutes. Turn once more, replace cover, and cook another 10 minutes, or longer if a pegao, or crust, is desired (see recipe for Arroz con Gandulez, which follows). When serving, scrape up any rice that has stuck to the bottom and serve on a separate plate.

Geri's Puerto Rican Arroz con Gandulez

Serves 4 to 6 as a main dish

According to my Hoboken neighbor Geri Wasserman Hernandez, who learned Puerto Rican cooking from her husband Orlando's mother and aunts on the island, you can't visit a Puerto Rican home at Christmastime without being served arroz con gandulez (rice with pigeon peas), cooked in a large cast-iron or aluminum caldero, or kettle, and accompanied by pastelles, little bundles of pork and seasoning tied up in edible wrappings. You can go to a different home every night for a week and the menu is the same; only the details vary from house to house.

Whereas traditional cooks would add some chopped ham or cook their rice in salt pork or lard, Geri uses only cooking oil; but she uses more of it than is her health-conscious custom — because, she says, Orlando is adamant: In true arroz con gandulez, or in any Puerto Rican rice dish, every grain of rice must be coated with fat.

There's another reason for not skimping on the oil: Puerto Rican rice cooks are among the many in the world who cultivate a bottom crust by cooking the rice for an extended period over very low heat. The fat on the bottom helps form the desired golden brown pegao (from *pegado,* literally "stuck to").

The recaito and the adobo in this recipe are typical homemade seasoning pastes that almost define Puerto Rican cooking.

The recaito:

1 small onion, coarsely chopped
1 small or ½ large green bell pepper, coarsely chopped
6 aji dulce chiles, seeded and cored, if available
    (see headnote to preceding recipe)
6 to 8 sprigs cilantro (fresh coriander)
    (1 tablespoon leaves), chopped

6 tablespoons annato oil (page 54)

The adobo:

1 tablespoon dried oregano
½ teaspoon freshly ground black pepper

2 cups cooked pigeon peas (from ⅔ cup dried)
     or 1 16-ounce can, drained
2 cups medium-grain white rice
4 ounces canned tomato sauce
12 pitted green olives, cut in half
2 teaspoons capers
salt to taste

To prepare the recaito, coarsely chop the onion and pepper. Reserving a bit of each to chop with a knife, put remaining pieces into a food processor with the aji and cilantro. Process to a paste. (This paste is the recaito.) Fine-chop the reserved onion and pepper and mix into the recaito.

Heat the oil in a large heavy pot over medium-high heat. Add the recaito and cook, stirring, 5 minutes. Add the adobo ingredients and stir to mix. Stir in the pigeon peas, then the rice. Cook, stirring, to coat the rice with oil. Add the tomato sauce, olives, capers, and salt, then 3 cups hot water. Bring to a boil, adjust heat to boil moderately, and cook uncovered, frequently turning the rice up from the bottom, until the surface liquid has disappeared. (Orlando's mother says to cook it uncovered until you can stand a spoon up in it.) Then shape the mixture into a mound. Cover the pot, reduce heat to as low as possible, and cook 1 hour. Remove from heat and let sit, still covered, 10 minutes or longer. (Puerto Rican cooks might make the dish an hour or a few hours ahead of time, then reheat gently before serving.)

To serve, spoon onto a serving dish or platter. Then scrape up the pegao, in pieces, and serve in a separate dish.

Os's Mom's Masoor Dal and Rice

Serves 4 to 6 as a side dish, 3 as a main dish

When Osmond Ahmad left Bangladesh for the University of Chicago in the mid-1970s, he brought an everyday family recipe that is still a staple in his Chicago kitchen and wherever in the world his college friends have set up theirs.

Like other living recipes, this one has evolved some in its travels. I have toned down the hot pepper quantities from Mrs. Ahmad's 4 fresh chiles and full tea-spoon of ground cayenne. In Bangladesh, Os tells me, the rice is boiled in several quarts of water, and the starchy water is saved to do the wash.

Masoor dal is a small, salmon-colored lentil available in Indian groceries and some natural-food stores. (*Dal* is an Indian word for legumes — beans, peas, or lentils.)

> *1 cup masoor dal (see headnote above)*
> *5 tablespoons peanut oil*
> *1 medium onion, chopped small*
> *1 tablespoon minced garlic*
> *1 tablespoon minced fresh gingerroot*
> *2 fresh green chiles, chopped small*
> *1 teaspoon ground coriander*
> *½ teaspoon turmeric*
> *1 teaspoon ground cumin*
> *¼ to ½ teaspoon ground cayenne*
> *1 medium tomato, chopped*
> *salt to taste*
> *1¼ cups long-grain white rice*
> *2 or 3 tablespoons chopped cilantro (fresh coriander)*

Rinse and drain the dal. Heat 4 tablespoons oil in a heavy pot over medium heat. Add half the onion and fry until brown. Reduce heat to low. Add the dal, garlic, ginger, chiles, and spices. Fry, stirring, about 2 minutes, taking care not to burn the spices. Add 2½ cups water, bring to a boil, then lower heat so the water is just simmering. Add tomato, salt, and remaining onion. Cook uncovered for about an hour until thick and pastelike at the bottom. (The mixture will be thinner toward the top.)

Bring 3 quarts of water to a boil. Add salt, then swirl in the rice. Stir to prevent sticking. Adjust heat to boil steadily about 15 minutes (10 or less for basmati), or until tender but not mushy. (Timing varies with the type, age and condition of the rice.) Drain through a sieve.

Serve individual portions of rice topped with ladles of dal and sprinkled with chopped cilantro.

Aegean Lentil Pilaf

Serves 6 with other dishes, 3 or 4 as a main dish

It was impossible to choose between this delicious lentil pilaf and the one that follows. Try them both.

$\frac{3}{4}$ *cup lentils*
4 tablespoons olive oil
1 tablespoon cumin seeds
1 medium-large onion, chopped small
1 large clove garlic
3 medium carrots, peeled and shredded
2 teaspoons ground coriander
1 teaspoon allspice berries, crushed in a coffee or
    spice grinder, or $\frac{1}{2}$ teaspoon ground allspice
$\frac{1}{2}$ teaspoon ground cinnamon
1 cup long-grain white rice
$2\frac{1}{4}$ cups warm chicken broth
salt and freshly ground black pepper to taste
$\frac{1}{3}$ cup feta cheese
2 teaspoons freshly squeezed lemon juice
4 tablespoons Italian parsley, chopped
4 tablespoons cilantro (fresh coriander), chopped
4 tablespoons fresh mint, chopped

Rinse lentils and put them in a saucepan with $1\frac{1}{2}$ cups of water. Bring to a boil. Cover, reduce heat to very low, and cook 20 minutes. Remove from heat but keep covered until ready to add to the rice.

Heat oil over medium heat in a heavy saucepan or Dutch oven. Add cumin seeds. In a few seconds, when the seeds begin to darken, add the onion and cook 5 minutes. Add garlic and cook 3 minutes. Add carrots and cook another 3 or 4 minutes. Add spices and cook, stirring, 1 minute. Add rice and cook, stirring, 2 or 3 minutes, until grains turn translucent. Stir in the lentils with their liquid. Add broth, salt, and pepper. Adjust heat to boil gently and cook uncovered 10 minutes, until surface liquid disappears and small steam holes appear on top.

Cover, reduce heat to very low, and cook another 15 minutes. Remove from heat and wait another 5 minutes before removing the lid. Crumble and stir in the feta cheese, lemon juice, and herbs.

Fragrant Lentils and Rice with Fried Onions

Serves 3 as a main dish, 6 as a side dish

Middle Eastern, Persian, and Indian cooks have long traditions of topping lentil pilafs with fried onions. For other onion toppings, see the section on toppings in Chapter Two.

> *1 cup lentils*
> *2 cups chicken or vegetable stock*
> *1 stick cinnamon*
> *2 whole cloves*
> *zest 1 orange, grated or cut into slivers no more than $\frac{1}{2}$ inch long*
> *$\frac{1}{4}$ teaspoon ground coriander*
> *$\frac{1}{4}$ teaspoon turmeric*
> *$\frac{1}{2}$ teaspoon allspice berries or ground allspice*
> *$\frac{1}{2}$ teaspoon cardamom pods or $\frac{1}{4}$ teaspoon ground cardamom*
> *$\frac{1}{2}$ teaspoon cumin seeds or ground cumin*
> *salt and freshly ground black pepper to taste*
> *1 cup basmati or other long-grain white rice*
> *vegetable oil to make at least 1 inch in a small frying pan*
> *1 medium onion, sliced very thin*

Rinse the lentils and put them in a saucepan with the stock, cinnamon, cloves, orange zest, and ground spices, including salt and pepper. Bring to a boil, then reduce heat to a slow simmer.

If using whole spices, remove seeds from cardamom pods and toast the cardamom seeds and cumin seeds in a small unoiled frying pan until the cumin seeds begin to darken and jump. Put the seeds in a coffee or spice grinder with the allspice berries and grind to a powder. Add to the lentils. The lentils should simmer covered for 30 minutes, or until they are tender but intact and all the water is absorbed.

If using Indian basmati, wash in several changes of water as directed on page 13, then soak for 20 minutes in water to cover by 1 inch. Drain through a sieve.

Pour the rice into 2 quarts salted boiling water and cook 10 minutes. Drain through a sieve and shake the sieve to drain off the water.

Heat 1 inch of oil in a frying pan. Break the onion slices into rings and add to the oil in batches. Fry until brown but not burned. Remove with slotted spoon and let rest on paper towel to dry and crisp.

Remove and discard cloves and cinnamon stick. Mix the rice with the lentils. Wrap the pot lid with a dish towel and cover the pot with the lid. Remove from heat and let stand, covered, 10 minutes. Top with fried onions to serve.

Brown Rice, Lentil, and Spinach Curry

Serves 3 or 4 as a main dish

Warm pita bread, baked or steamed squash, and a small serving dish of whipped plain yogurt sprinkled with ground paprika and cayenne and chopped cilantro make this a complete meal.

> $\frac{3}{4}$ *cup lentils*
> *5 tablespoons canola or olive oil*
> *1 small onion, chopped small*
> *1 stalk celery, chopped small*
> *3 cloves garlic, minced*
> *1 medium carrot, shredded*
> *1 small green chile, minced*
> *2 teaspoons ground cumin*
> $\frac{1}{2}$ *teaspoon ground coriander*
> $\frac{1}{4}$ *teaspoon turmeric*
> $\frac{1}{4}$ *teaspoon ground cinnamon*
> $\frac{1}{4}$ *teaspoon ground cardamom*
> $\frac{1}{8}$ *teaspoon ground cloves*
> *1 cup long-grain brown rice*
> *salt and freshly ground black pepper to taste*

2¼ cups vegetable broth or water
½ pound fresh spinach leaves, cut into 1-inch-wide strips
1 teaspoon cumin seeds
1 tablespoon freshly squeezed lemon juice

Wash lentils and put them in a saucepan with 1½ cups of water. Bring to a boil. Cover, reduce heat to very low, and cook 20 minutes. Remove from heat until ready to add to the rice.

Heat 4 tablespoons of the oil in a large heavy saucepan or Dutch oven. Add onion and celery and cook 5 minutes. Add garlic and cook 3 minutes. Add carrot and chile. Cook, stirring, 1 or 2 minutes. Add ground spices and cook, stirring, about 1 minute. Add rice. Cook, stirring, about 5 minutes, until grains turn translucent, then opaque, but not scorched. Stir in the lentils and any unabsorbed water in the lentil pot. Add salt, pepper, and broth or water. Cook at a low boil for 15 minutes. Then add spinach, pushing it down into the rice mixture. Cover, reduce heat to very low, and cook 30 minutes.

Heat the remaining tablespoon of oil in a small skillet or saucepan. Add cumin seeds and cook until they begin to darken and pop. Pour over the lentil-rice mixture, add the lemon juice, and serve.

"Wild" Rice with "Wild" Mushrooms and Black-Eyed Peas

Serves 3 as a meatless main dish, 6 as a side dish with turkey, duck, or pork

As mentioned on page 10, wild rice is not really rice and most of the wild rice we buy today is not really wild. The same is true of many types of mushrooms, still called "wild" but increasingly cultivated here and abroad. Wild or not, they make an earthy combination, especially when reinforced with leeks and black-eyed peas.

¾ cup wild rice
¾ cup dried black-eyed peas
4 tablespoons walnut oil
6 ounces mixed fresh mushrooms such as cepes, shiitake,
*   and portobello, chopped*

1 medium leek (about ½ pound), white part and first
  2 inches of green, chopped (1 cup chopped)
¾ cup long-grain brown rice
¼ cup dry white wine or dry sherry (optional)
1½ cups chicken, turkey, duck, or vegetable broth, warm
1 tablespoon crumbled dried sage or 3 tablespoons
  chopped fresh sage leaf or 1 teaspoon ground sage
1 tablespoon fresh thyme leaves or 1 teaspoon dried
⅓ cup chopped broadleaf parsley
salt and freshly ground black pepper to taste

Add the wild rice to 1½ cups boiling salted water. When the water returns to a boil, cover, reduce heat to low, and cook 15 minutes. Then reduce heat to very low, and cook another 20 to 30 minutes until water is absorbed and rice is cooked but still slightly chewy.

While wild rice is cooking, add the black-eyed peas to 2½ cups boiling water. Return to a boil, cover, reduce heat to very low, and cook until done, about 35 to 45 minutes.

Meanwhile heat 2 tablespoons oil in a third heavy saucepan. Add mushrooms and stir-fry over moderately high heat until soft. Remove with slotted spoon and set aside. Add another tablespoon of oil, then the leek. Stir-fry until softened but not limp. Remove with slotted spoon and add to mushrooms. Reduce heat to medium. Add remaining 1 tablespoon oil, then the brown rice. Cook, stirring, 2 or 3 minutes. Return mushrooms and leek to the pot, then add wine and cook until it is mostly absorbed or evaporated. Add broth, herbs, salt, and pepper. When boiling, cover, reduce heat to very low, and cook 40 minutes or until liquid is absorbed and rice cooked. Let sit off heat, still covered, another 10 minutes.

Turn brown rice into a large serving bowl and stir in the wild rice and black-eyed peas.

Fish and Seafood in Rice

Coconut Rice with Shrimp

Serves 4 as part of a seafood dinner, 2 as a main dish

This variation on a tropical curry is delicious with fresh coconut milk. If using canned, mix with water flavored by boiling the shrimp shells for 15 minutes.

1 teaspoon cumin seeds
½ teaspoon coriander seeds
½ teaspoon allspice berries
6 whole cardamom pods
½ teaspoon ground mace
¼ teaspoon ground cinnamon
1½ teaspoons turmeric
2 tablespoons peanut oil
½ pound medium shrimp, shelled and deveined
1 lime, cut in half crosswise
1 large clove garlic, minced
minced fresh gingerroot to equal amount of garlic
½ to 1 fresh green chile, such as jalapeno or serrano,
*   seeded and minced*
1 cup long-grain white rice
2 cups fresh coconut milk or 1 cup canned coconut milk
*   and 1 cup shrimp water (see headnote above), warm*
1 cup fresh green peas or thawed frozen peas
salt and freshly ground black pepper to taste

Toast the cumin seeds in a small ungreased skillet over medium heat until they just begin to darken and pop. Put them in a spice or coffee grinder with the coriander seeds, allspice berries, and cardamom pods. Grind to a powder, then mix with the mace, cinnamon, and ½ teaspoon of the turmeric. Set aside.

Heat the oil over medium heat in a large heavy saucepan or Dutch oven. Add the shrimp and cook 45 seconds on each side. Remove with a slotted spoon to a small bowl. Sprinkle with the remaining 1 teaspoon turmeric and the juice from half the lime. Mix and set aside.

Add garlic and ginger to the saucepan and cook, stirring, 1 minute. Add chile and cook until soft. Add rice and stir to coat with oil. Stir in the ground spices. Add coconut milk (with shrimp water, if using canned coconut milk) and adjust heat to bubble gently about 10 minutes, until surface liquid is mostly gone and small steam holes appear on top of the rice.

Stir in the peas. Add salt and pepper. Cover, reduce heat to low, and cook another 10 minutes. Lift lid and gently but rapidly push the shrimp into the rice. Replace cover, remove from heat, and let sit covered another 10 minutes. Toss with 2 forks and sprinkle with the juice of the remaining lime half.

Salmon Pilaf

Serves 6 as a first course, 3 or 4 as a main dish

This modern-day hybrid, executed in the manner of a Turkish pilaf, starts out like a risotto and ends with a typical Mexican finish.

> 3 tablespoons olive oil
> ½ pound salmon steak or fillet, cut into 1-inch × 1½-inch pieces
>   (about 20 pieces)
> 4 scallions, white part only, trimmed and chopped fine
> ½ jalapeno or serrano chile, seeded and minced
>   (1 tablespoon minced), or more to taste
> 1½ cups long-grain white rice
> ½ cup dry vermouth, dry sherry, or other dry white wine
> 3 cups mild fish, vegetable, or chicken stock, hot
> salt and freshly ground black pepper to taste
> 1 tablespoon freshly squeezed lime juice
> 4 tablespoons chopped cilantro (fresh coriander)

Heat the oil in a large heavy saucepan over medium heat. Add salmon. Cook 1 minute on each side. Remove and set aside. Add scallions and chile. Cook, stirring, until soft but not brown. Add rice and cook, stirring, 2 or 3 minutes. Add wine and cook, stirring, until liquid is absorbed. Add stock, salt, and pepper and adjust heat to bubble gently 10 minutes or until surface liquid disappears. Return salmon pieces. Cover, reduce heat to very low, and cook 10 minutes. Remove from heat and rest 10 minutes. Sprinkle with lime juice and 3 tablespoons of the cilantro. Toss to distribute the salmon, lime juice, and cilantro, then scatter remaining cilantro over the top.

Christmas Eve Baccalà

Serves 4 as a main dish

This is my version of one Sicilian-American family's holiday salt cod, called *baccalà* in Italy and *bacalao* in Spain and Spanish-speaking America. The rice is a recent addition, making a meal of what was formerly one of several fish courses.

Around the winter holidays some markets sell salt cod floating in water, already soaked and ready to cook. Usually, though, you have to soak the dried fish before cooking. This can take from a few hours to a few days, depending on its form and condition and your taste for salt cod. If using packaged fillets, remove from the package, cover with water, and put to soak in the refrigerator overnight or for 24 hours. Change the water every 8 hours or so. Then drain and, if it's still too salty for your taste, rinse it a few times in warm water.

> *5 tablespoons pine nuts*
> *3¼ cups mild fish stock, clam juice and water, or vegetable broth*
> *½ teaspoon hot red pepper flakes*
> *½ teaspoon saffron threads, crumbled*
> *4 tablespoons olive oil*
> *2 large cloves garlic, sliced thin*
> *1½ cups long-grain rice*
> *½ pound salt cod, soaked, drained, and cut into 1-inch squares*
> *½ cup dry vermouth or other dry white wine*
> *½ cup raisins*
> *12 large black olives, pitted and quartered*
> *8 to 12 capers, rinsed and cut in half*
> *½ cup chopped parsley*
> *1 roasted red pepper (page 49), diced*

Spread pine nuts on an ungreased baking sheet in a preheated 350°F oven or toaster oven and toast 5 minutes or until golden (not brown). Remove and set aside.

Heat stock in a small saucepan and stir in the pepper flakes and saffron. Keep warm.

Heat oil in a large nonstick skillet over medium-low heat. Add garlic and cook 1 or 2 minutes until soft. Add rice and stir to coat with oil. Add cod and cook, stirring, 5 minutes. Add wine and cook, stirring, until mostly absorbed or evaporated. Stir in pine nuts, raisins, olives, capers, parsley, and roasted pepper. Bring stock to a boil and pour it evenly over the rice. When boiling well, cover tightly, reduce heat, and simmer for 20 minutes, moving the skillet an inch or so occasionally if needed for even cooking (in which case the cooking time might be a few minutes longer). Remove from heat and let sit, covered, another 10 minutes.

Senegalese Thiebou Dienne

Serves 6 for a one-dish meal

Spelled *thiebou dienne* or *cheboudiene,* pronounced *cheb-oo-djin* or just cheb, this Senegalese national dish is best known as a fish dish but is sometimes made with chicken, beef, or lamb, often with dried fish added. And though a proper cheb contains 4 or 5 vegetables, they are not always the same 4 or 5. But always there is rice, cooked in the tomato-flavored water after the fish (or meat) and vegetables are removed.

According to Mamadou Jalo, who introduced me to Gnagna Diene's cheb at Manhattan's Lucky Star Deli, on any given day in Senegal 90 percent of the people are having cheb for lunch. They have it with a very hot red pepper sauce, essential to the cheb experience but used in very small amounts. You can use a bottled garlic chile paste or make the hot red pepper sauce on page 41. The Lucky Star serves cheb with hot sauce and bottled Maggi seasoning; Ms. Diene suggests plain soy sauce as a substitute. Another common accompaniment is tamarind sauce; I use the Indian tamarind sauce on page 51.

For the fish, use thick steaks of any firm fresh fish that will not fall apart when cut up and cooked. Swordfish or tuna steaks are good. For more flavor, cook the cheb in a quick broth made with a fish head and bones instead of in water.

Simmer the broth while you stuff the fish and sauté the fish and onions, then strain and add it to the tomato paste as directed.

> *1 bunch cilantro (fresh coriander) (about ½ cup)*
> *1 bunch broadleaf parsley (½ to 1 cup)*
> *3 or 4 medium to large scallions, trimmed and coarsely chopped*
> *3 cloves garlic, smashed flat*
> *½ teaspoon hot red pepper flakes*
> *5 tablespoons peanut oil*
> *2 pounds fish (see headnote above), cut into large chunks*
> *1 large onion, coarsely chopped*
> *1 6-ounce can tomato paste*
> *1 pound yucca (cassava), peeled of bark and skin and*
>   *cut into roughly 1½-inch × 2-inch pieces, or*
>   *1 pound frozen yucca cut into 1½-inch × 2-inch*
>   *pieces, if available*
> *1 pound calabaza or butternut squash, seeded, peeled,*
>   *and cut into 2-inch pieces*
> *1 pound African yam or white potato or sweet potato,*
>   *peeled and cut into 2-inch pieces*
> *1 pound eggplant, cut into 2-inch pieces*
> *3 or 4 large carrots, cut into thirds*
> *1 small or ½ large cabbage, cored and cut into 6 wide arcs or wedges*
> *2½ cups long-grain white rice*

Put the cilantro, parsley, scallions, garlic, pepper flakes, and 1 tablespoon of the oil in a food processor and process to a paste.

Cut 1 or more deep slits in each piece of fish to make small pockets for stuffing. Stuff with the processed paste and rub more paste on the fish pieces. Reserve any leftover paste.

Heat the remaining oil in a large heavy pot over medium heat. Add fish and cook a minute or so on each side. Remove with slotted spoon and set aside. Add onion to the pot and cook 10 minutes, stirring occasionally. Stir in leftover herb paste, then the tomato paste. Add 5 cups of water, stirring to mix with the paste, and bring to a low boil. Add yucca and cook, covered, 10 minutes. Add calabaza or squash and yam or potato and cook, covered, 5 minutes. Add eggplant and carrots and cook, covered, 10 minutes. Add cabbage and cook 15 minutes or until all vegetables are done. With a slotted spoon, remove vegetables from the cooking pot and transfer to a heated bowl. Tip any liquid from the vegetables back into the pot. Cover bowl and set aside. Return fish to cooking pot and cook 10 minutes or until done. Remove with slotted spoon and add to vegetables in covered bowl.

If cooking liquid has boiled down substantially, add water to total $3\frac{1}{2}$ cups. Bring to a boil and add the rice. When the liquid returns to a boil, cover the pot, reduce heat to very low, and cook 20 minutes. To serve, put the rice in a large wide bowl or on a platter and top with the other ingredients.

Rice with Poultry

Louisiana Dirty Rice

Serves 6 as a side dish, 3 as a main dish

Today's quick-and-dirty version of a bayou favorite calls for pantry-staple ingredients, Uncle Ben's rice, and a time-saving food processor. To serve as a one-dish meal, throw in a cup of thawed frozen peas with the broth.

> *1 small onion, coarsely chopped*
> *2 cloves garlic, smashed flat and cut crosswise*
> *1 small or $\frac{1}{2}$ large green bell pepper, seeded, cored, and*
>   *coarsely chopped*
> *1 large stalk celery, trimmed and coarsely chopped*
> *$\frac{1}{2}$ pound chicken liver*
> *1 14-ounce can chicken broth plus enough water to*
>   *make 2 cups or 1 chicken bouillon cube dissolved in*
>   *2 cups hot water*
> *4 ounces slab bacon or salt pork, chopped, or 2 tablespoons corn oil*
> *1 cup Uncle Ben's or other long-grain white rice*
> *$\frac{1}{2}$ teaspoon Tabasco sauce, or to taste*
> *salt and freshly ground black pepper to taste*

Process the onion, garlic, pepper, and celery in a food processor until finely minced. Remove to a bowl and set aside. Process the chicken liver until no longer in pieces. Heat chicken broth on a back burner and keep just below a boil.

Heat the bacon or pork or the oil in a large heavy saucepan. If using bacon or pork, cook until grease separates from solids and remove solids with a slotted spoon. Reserve meaty pieces and discard chunks of fat. Add chopped vegetables to the pan and cook over medium heat until golden, about 10 minutes. Add rice and stir to coat with oil. Add chicken liver and cook, stirring, until it turns to a crumbled solid consistency, 2 or 3 minutes. Add the broth, then the Tabasco sauce, reserved bacon bits, salt, and pepper. Bring to a boil. Cover, reduce heat to very low, and cook 20 minutes. Remove from heat and let rest, still covered, another 10 minutes.

Hoppin' John Taylor's Carolina Pilau

Serves 4 to 8

In its three centuries of serious rice cooking, coastal South Carolina has given birth or new life to a whole repertoire of pilau dishes. But the one that natives and strangers alike identify as Carolina pilau — or pielow, or perloo, or however any given native says it and any given stranger hears it — is this straightforward combination of chicken, rice, and tomatoes. Since I could not improve on the classic recipe in John Martin Taylor's *Hoppin' John's Lowcountry Cooking*, I reproduce it here with his generous permission. (We differ, though, on portion estimates—he would serve this at a meal for 8; in my house, 4 to 6 would finish it off.)

> *1 3½- to 4-pound chicken*
> *2 quarts water*
> *¼ pound (1 stick) unsalted butter*
> *1 large onion, chopped (about 1½ cups)*
> *2 cups chopped celery*
> *2 or 3 large tomatoes (about 1 pound), peeled and chopped*
> *1 tablespoon fresh thyme leaves or 1 teaspoon dried*
> *½ teaspoon hot red pepper flakes*
> *salt and freshly ground black pepper to taste*
> *2 cups long-grain white rice*

Cover the chicken with the water and boil in a large pot, uncovered, for 30 minutes. Remove the chicken from the broth and reserve the broth. Skin the chicken and remove the bones, pulling the meat from the bones. Cut the meat into uniformly sized pieces. Set aside.

Melt the butter in a Dutch oven on top of the stove, then add the onions and the celery and cook over medium heat until the onions start to brown, about 10 minutes. Add the tomatoes and their juice and the seasonings, adding a little more salt than you might think is necessary. Add the chicken meat, the rice, and 1 quart of the reserved broth. Cover, bring to a simmer, and cook slowly, without lifting the lid, for 30 minutes. Serve with a green salad and corn bread.

Jollof Rice

Serves 4 to 6

This tasty West African dish, named for the Wolof people, is one of those regional specialties cooked differently from nation to nation and from kitchen to kitchen. Sometimes other meats and other vegetables are added, but chicken seems to be the best-traveled version.

The marinade:

1 fresh chile pepper, seeded and coarsely chopped
2 cloves garlic, smashed flat and cut crosswise
juice 1 lemon ($\frac{1}{4}$ cup)
salt and freshly ground black pepper to taste

1 chicken, cut into 8 to 10 pieces
2 to 3 tablespoons peanut or corn oil
$\frac{1}{2}$ pound ham, diced, or $\frac{1}{2}$ pound shrimp, shelled and deveined
2 medium onions, coarsely chopped
1 green bell pepper, seeded, cored, and coarsely chopped
2 cloves garlic, chopped
1 28-ounce can tomatoes, juice reserved
$1\frac{1}{2}$ teaspoons dried thyme
1 teaspoon ground ginger

½ teaspoon hot red pepper flakes, or more to taste
3 tablespoons tomato paste
½ medium cabbage, cored and cut into 4 or 5 wide arcs or wedges
2 cups long-grain white rice
salt and freshly ground black pepper to taste

In a food processor, make a paste of the marinade ingredients. Remove skin and removable fat from chicken and cut slits into the flesh. Put the chicken in a flat-bottomed dish and add the marinade. Turn to coat chicken and let sit at room temperature for 1 hour.

Heat 2 tablespoons of the oil in a large heavy kettle or Dutch oven over medium-high heat. Add ham and sauté to brown lightly, or add shrimp and cook 1 minute on each side. Remove and set aside. Add chicken with marinade and cook, stirring and scraping the bottom of the pan, until liquid in marinade evaporates and chicken browns. Remove chicken with slotted spoon and set aside. Add another tablespoon of oil to the pan, if needed (or pour off excess chicken fat if indicated). Add the chopped onion and pepper. Cook, stirring and scraping the bottom of the pan occasionally, until the onion is golden, about 10 minutes. Add garlic and cook 2 or 3 minutes until golden. Add tomatoes from can, breaking them up in the pan with your stirring spoon. Add juice from tomato can with enough water to make 3 cups. Stir in the seasonings and tomato paste. Bring to a boil. Cut the chicken into 2-inch cubes, discarding bones. Return to the skillet. Return ham if using. Reduce heat to a low boil and cook 5 minutes. Add cabbage and cook another 5 minutes. Pour rice evenly over the mixture and add salt and pepper. Return to the boil, cover, reduce heat to very low, and cook 20 minutes. If using shrimp, remove cover, put the shrimp over the rice, and return cover. Remove from heat and let sit 10 minutes.

Arroz con Pollo I
Puerto Rican Chicken and Rice

Serves 5 or 6 as is, 8 with the kidney beans on page 103

Every Spanish-speaking Caribbean island has its own arroz con pollo; Puerto Rico's has the status of a national dish. But even among serious cooks, the old rules for constructing it are changing. The freshly made seasoning pastes adobo and recaito, as well as the flavor-intensive olives, capers, and pimientos, still define the dish. But without the lard and the salt pork that health-conscious modern cooks have put behind them, the proud insistence on cooking the rice in plain water is yielding to the richer flavors of chicken broth or beer. This recipe retains a little of the old, ubiquitous chopped ham as an option, but since ham is also in the kidney beans that usually accompany the dish in Puerto Rico, you might prefer to omit it from the chicken if serving both.

1 whole chicken, cut up as directed

The adobo:

2 teaspoons olive oil
2 large cloves garlic, minced
1 tablespoon oregano
1 teaspoon vinegar or freshly squeezed lime juice
2 teaspoons salt
$\frac{1}{2}$ teaspoon freshly ground black pepper

The stock:

1 clove garlic, smashed flat
1 small onion, coarsely chopped
1 stalk celery, cut up
4 or 5 sprigs cilantro (fresh coriander)

The recaito:

1 small onion
2 Italian green peppers or 1 green bell pepper,
*   cored and seeded*
6 aji dulce chiles, if available, cored and seeded
several sprigs cilantro (fresh coriander), to taste

3 tablespoons annato oil (page 54) or olive oil
$\frac{1}{4}$ cup ham or salt pork, diced (optional)
1 8-ounce can tomato sauce
$1\frac{1}{2}$ cups beer (optional)
2 cups medium-grain white rice

18 pimiento-stuffed olives, cut in half
1 tablespoon capers, cut in half if large
1 roasted red pepper (page 49) or 1 small jar roasted red
    pepper (pimiento), cut into strips
1 cup fresh or frozen peas (if not serving kidney beans)

Cut the chicken, or have it cut, into 2 thighs, 2 drumsticks, 2 wings, 2 wing tips, a back piece, and 4 breast pieces. Reserve the neck, back, and wing tips for stock.

Mix all the ingredients for the adobo and rub over the remaining pieces. Refrigerate several hours or overnight, or let sit at room temperature 1 hour to absorb the flavors.

Meanwhile, make the stock. Put the neck, back, and wing tips (and giblets if you like) in 4 cups of water with the garlic, onion, celery, and cilantro. Cook uncovered 2 to 3 hours, then strain out the solids and return the stock to the pot.

Coarsely chop the recaito ingredients, then process them together in a food processor until very finely minced but not watery.

Heat the oil over medium heat in a large, wide, heavy-bottomed saucepan, Dutch oven, or skillet. Add diced ham or salt pork, if using, and cook 3 to 5 minutes. Remove any solid fat pieces but leave the meat in the pot. Add chicken thighs and drumsticks and cook 5 minutes. Add remaining chicken pieces and cook another 10 minutes to brown all pieces on both sides. Remove and set aside. Add the recaito and cook 5 minutes. Add tomato sauce, then 3 cups hot stock (or 1½ cups stock and 1½ cups beer) and the rice. Bring to a boil. Return chicken to pan. Stir in the olives and capers, and some salt, if needed. Reduce heat and boil gently, uncovered, until all the surface water disappears (Puerto Rican cooks say to cook uncovered until the rice is dry). With a wooden stirring spoon, turn up the rice from the bottom of the pot.

Reduce heat to very low, cover the pot, and cook for 1 hour, uncovering briefly every 15 minutes to turn up the rice from the bottom of the pan.

Turn the rice and chicken onto a serving platter and garnish with the pimiento strips and the peas, if using. For a heartier and more interesting meal, skip the peas and accompany the arroz con pollo with the kidney beans on page 103. Serve the beans in a separate serving bowl to be dished out on top or on the side, according to individual preference. Scrape up the pegao (the bottom crust) with a spatula (it will come off in pieces) and pass in a separate serving dish, or scatter the pieces around the edges of the platter. It should be crisp and colored anywhere from gold to brown, but not burned.

Arroz con Pollo II
Cuban Chicken and Rice

Serves 4 to 6

This is my reconstruction of a dish described to me in detail by Maria Alvarez, who contributed several Cuban recipes to this book. Maria points out that this is not *the* Cuban arroz con pollo but is a special one she favors for entertaining.

The mayonnaise in this recipe might have evolved from the Spanish use of homemade aioli (garlic mayonnaise), but most Cubans buy it by the jar — and so do I, especially now that raw egg contamination makes homemade mayonnaise risky.

If you can't find the Cuban coloring agent bijol (page 55), cook the chicken in annato oil (page 54) or add a teaspoon of turmeric to the cooking water.

> 3 tablespoons olive oil
> 1 chicken, cut into 8 to 10 pieces, excluding neck and wing tips
> salt and freshly ground black pepper to taste
> 1 medium onion, chopped small
> 3 large cloves garlic, minced
> 2 teaspoons bijol (see headnote above)
> 2 cups long-grain white rice
> 1 cup beer, at room temperature
> $\frac{1}{2}$ cup mayonnaise
> 18 to 20 large green Spanish olives, sliced or chopped
> 1 roasted red pepper (page 49) or the equivalent from a
>   jar of roasted peppers or pimiento, cut into thin strips
> 1 tablespoon capers, chopped if large
> 1 cup fresh or frozen green peas, cooked, or 1 cup canned peas
> 2 hard-boiled eggs, sliced (optional)

Heat oil over medium heat in a large nonstick skillet. Sprinkle chicken with salt and pepper, then add to skillet and cook, turning to brown on all sides, about 15 minutes. Remove chicken and set aside. Add onion and garlic to the pan and cook until soft and turning golden, 5 to 10 minutes. Return chicken to pan. Add 2 cups steaming-hot water, the bijol, and more salt and pepper if desired.

Bring to a boil and reduce heat to simmer about 20 minutes, or until chicken is done. Remove chicken and set aside.

Bring the water to a boil and add the rice. Cover pan, reduce heat to low, and cook until water disappears, about 10 or 15 minutes. (It might be necessary to move the skillet an inch or two now and then to ensure even cooking of the rice.) Add the beer, replace cover, and cook another 10 to 15 minutes, until rice is done and no liquid remains in the bottom of the pan.

While rice is cooking, tear the chicken meat from the bones and shred the meat, discarding the skin and bones.

To serve, lay down a third of the rice in a flat baking dish, preferably clear glass (Pyrex). Cover with a third of the mayonnaise, then all the chicken; half the remaining rice; half the remaining mayonnaise; half the olives, pimiento strips, and capers; the remaining rice; the remaining mayonnaise; the remaining olives, pimiento, and capers; and the cooked peas. If using sliced eggs, arrange on top before adding the peas. Serve warm.

Tali Benjamin's Ohs-Blof
Rice with Chicken and Carrots

Serves 4 to 6

Tali Benjamin, now a New Jersey resident, learned this dish in Israel from her grandmother, who brought the recipe from the Caucasus region, south of Russia. I have since come across almost the identical recipe, called *plov* and attributed to Bukhara, in Copeland Marks's *Sephardic Cooking*.

Tali says to cook this in a nonstick skillet, because the onions on the bottom tend to stick and blacken. Another caution: If you don't have a deep enough skillet you might have to reduce the amounts to $1\frac{1}{2}$ pounds carrots and $1\frac{1}{2}$ cups each rice and water just to fit everything into the pan.

> *2 cups long-grain white rice*
> *4 or more tablespoons butter or olive oil*
> *2 medium-large onions, 1 chopped small and 1 cut in*
>   *half and then into thin slices*
> *1 chicken, cut into serving pieces*
> *2 pounds carrots, cut into matchsticks (julienne)*
> *salt and freshly ground black pepper to taste*

Add the rice to 2 cups boiling water. Cover, remove from heat, and let steam 1 hour.

Heat 2 tablespoons butter or oil in a large nonstick skillet. Add the chopped onion and then the chicken. Brown the chicken on both sides and remove from pan.

Heat remaining butter or oil, then add the sliced onion; cook until soft and turning golden. Mix about one-fourth of the carrot sticks into the onion in the pan and spread the mixture across the pan. Put the chicken on top of this layer, then spread the remaining carrots over the chicken and into the spaces between chicken pieces. Sprinkle the carrots with black pepper. Add the rice, then salt it well, as your taste and diet allow. Bring 2 cups of water to a boil in a separate saucepan and pour it over the rice. Cover and cook over medium heat for 10 minutes, then lift the lid very briefly to poke a few holes in the rice with the handle of a wooden spoon. (If you find that the water is not simmering near the edges of the pan or the center is cooking too fast, move the pan an inch or so now and then during the cooking time to ensure even cooking.) Turn heat to low and cook, covered, 20 or 30 minutes until the chicken and rice are done. (You can check the bottom and the water level by poking the wooden spoon handle down into the holes, a venerable and useful practice.)

To serve, Tali says the rice should go on the bottom, then the carrots, topped by the chicken. (The onions will be caramelized and much reduced.) I accomplish this by holding the serving platter upside down over the uncovered skillet with one hand while holding the skillet handle with the other hand (an oven mitt comes in handy here), then flipping them together and setting them down with the platter on the bottom. Any onions that are stuck but salvageable can be scraped off with a spatula.

Variation

Add 4 tablespoons golden raisins with the carrot layer.

Zesty Chicken in Tomato Sauce

Serves 4 or 5

I devised this dish to go with the Persian Chelo with Tadig on page 62. The lemon zest and juice are a sort of substitute for dried Persian lime. Some serve the chicken on top of the chelo; some layer it in with the steaming rice as in the recipe for Chicken Pilau that follows; I prefer to serve the beautiful saffron-buttered rice on its own platter and let guests have their chicken over or beside their rice, as they choose.

> *4 tablespoons extra-virgin olive oil*
> *10 fresh ripe plum tomatoes, if in season, peeled, seeded,*
>   *and chopped, or 1 28-ounce can Italian plum toma-*
>   *toes, drained, seeded, and chopped (page 48)*
> *1 3½- to 4-pound chicken, cut into 8 or 10 pieces,*
>   *sprinkled with salt and freshly ground black*
>   *pepper to taste*
> *1 medium onion, minced*
> *4 tablespoons parsley*
> *2 cloves garlic, minced*
> *grated zest 1 large lemon*
> *2 tablespoons freshly squeezed lemon juice*
> *¼ teaspoon ground cinnamon*
> *pinch ground cloves*
> *¼ teaspoon ground cardamom or ginger*
> *18 black olives such as gaeta or kalamata, pitted and cut in half*
> *salt and freshly ground black pepper*
> *thin strips lemon zest for garnish*
> *1 lemon cut into 4 or 5 wedges (1 for each diner)*

Heat 1 tablespoon oil in a medium-size skillet or large saucepan. Add tomatoes and simmer, stirring occasionally, while browning the chicken and vegetables.

Heat remaining oil in a large heavy skillet. Add chicken pieces and cook until golden brown on both sides, 10 to 15 minutes. Remove to paper towel. Add onion to pan and cook about 10 minutes until soft and turning golden. Add parsley, garlic, and grated lemon zest. Cook up to 5 minutes, without browning the garlic. Add tomatoes, lemon juice, and ground spices. Return chicken to pan and add a little water if tomatoes are too thick to coat chicken. Stir in the olives. Cover and simmer 15 minutes. Uncover, turn chicken pieces, and spoon sauce over the chicken. Add salt and pepper if desired and/or a little water if needed to keep sauce from sticking. Cook another 15 minutes or until chicken is done. (Longer cooking over very low heat also produces excellent results.) Serve over chelo or on a separate platter, garnished with strips of lemon zest. Serve lemon wedges on the side for individual adjustments.

Chicken Pilau with Tadig and Dried Fruit

Serves 4 or 5

This is a sweeter alternative to the preceding Zesty Chicken, and the chicken is layered into the rice rather than served beside. Make it with any of the tadigs (bottom crusts) described on pages 64–65: flatbread, bread, potato, rice alone, or rice with egg or yogurt.

> $1\frac{1}{2}$ *cups basmati rice*
> *6 tablespoons walnut or olive oil*
> *1 chicken, cut into 10 pieces (2 thighs, 2 drumsticks,*
>   *4 breast pieces, and 2 wing pieces, with wing tips*
>   *removed)*
> *salt and freshly ground black pepper*
> *1 large onion, chopped*
> *2 large carrots, cut into julienne*
> $1\frac{1}{2}$ *cups chicken broth*
> $\frac{1}{2}$ *teaspoon ground coriander*
> $\frac{1}{2}$ *teaspoon ground cinnamon*
> $\frac{1}{2}$ *teaspoon ground ginger*
> *2 cups cooked chickpeas or 1 16-ounce can, drained*
> $\frac{1}{2}$ *cup chopped fresh broadleaf parsley*
> *grated zest 2 oranges*
> *4 tablespoons butter*
> $\frac{1}{2}$ *teaspoon saffron threads, crumbled*
> *10 dried apricots, cut into 6 pieces each*
> *10 pitted dates, cut in half*
> $\frac{1}{2}$ *cup golden raisins*
> *flatbread, potato, egg, or egg and yogurt, for the tadig*

Put the rice in a large bowl with water to cover by about 1 inch. Swirl it around with your fingers, then carefully drain off the water through a large sieve. Repeat several times until the water runs clear. Then put the rice back in the bowl with more water to cover by 1 inch. Add 2 tablespoons salt. Set aside to soak while chicken is cooking.

Heat 3 tablespoons of oil in a large skillet over medium heat. Sprinkle the chicken pieces with salt and pepper. In batches, if necessary, add chicken pieces to skillet. Brown on all sides, and remove to paper towel. Add onion to pan and cook, stirring occasionally, about 5 minutes or until golden. Stir in carrots and cook 1 to 2 minutes. Return chicken to pan. Add 1 cup broth, the coriander, and half the cinnamon and ginger. Bring to a boil, cover pan, and adjust heat to simmer 30 minutes.

After 30 minutes, stir in the chickpeas and parsley and half the orange zest. Cook uncovered 10 minutes or until chicken is tender and broth is reduced. (If stew is too soupy, the rice will be soggy.) Remove from heat.

Melt the butter over low heat in a small frying pan or saucepan. Add the remaining $\frac{1}{2}$ cup broth, the remaining cinnamon, ginger, and orange zest, and the saffron, apricots, dates, and raisins. Reduce heat to very low and cook 10 minutes. Remove from heat.

Bring 3 to 4 quarts of water to a boil. Add the rice with its soaking water and cook until tender but not mushy, about 7 minutes after adding to the boiling water. Drain through a sieve and shake to remove any residual water.

Heat remaining oil in a large heavy saucepan or Dutch oven over medium-low heat. Lay down the tadig of your choice (such as bread, potato, or rice). Check the clock. Add a thin layer of rice, then half the chicken-chickpea stew. Add half the remaining rice and all the remaining stew. With a slotted spoon, scoop up half the dried fruit and distribute it over the stew. Top with the remaining rice. Form into a mound and poke four or five steam holes with the handle of a wooden spoon. Wrap the pot lid with a dish towel as directed on page 16 and cover the pot. Fifteen minutes after laying down the tadig, reduce heat to very low and cook 45 minutes. Remove from heat.

To loosen the tadig, set the pan in 2 inches of cold water in a sink or large pan for 2 minutes. Remove lid and spoon the pilau onto a serving platter. Pry up the tadig with a spatula and cut into wedges like a pie. Serve on a separate plate or scattered around the pilau.

Reheat the remaining dried fruit and broth mixture over very low heat, then pour over the pilau to serve.

Murgh Biryani
(Indian Baked Chicken and Rice)

Serves 4 to 6

Indian cooks have developed countless versions of this tangy and intriguingly spiced baked pilaf, a legacy of Moghul rule and a favorite for grand occasions. The preparation can be an all-day process, but the complex flavor and opulent presentation are well worth the time expended. Serve with a whipped yogurt dish, such as the Yogurt Topping with Toasted Cumin on page 45 or the Yogurt-Cucumber Topping on page 46, and a green vegetable such as spinach or broccoli.

The marinade:

1 teaspoon cumin seeds
1 teaspoon coriander seeds
1 teaspoon cardamom seeds removed from pods
6 whole cloves
½ teaspoon black peppercorns
½ teaspoon ground mace
½ teaspoon ground cinnamon
¼ teaspoon ground cayenne
2 teaspoons salt
3 cloves garlic, smashed flat and minced
1-inch piece fresh gingerroot, minced
2 large or 4 medium onions, chopped
2 tablespoons freshly squeezed lemon juice
1 cup plain yogurt

1 chicken, cut into 8 or 10 pieces
2 cups Indian basmati rice
2 tablespoons salt
4 tablespoons cooking oil
3 tablespoons milk
½ teaspoon saffron threads, crumbled

Suggested garnishes:

1 large or 2 medium onions, sliced and crisp-fried
   as on page 44
2 tablespoons unsalted cashew pieces, almond slices,
   shelled pistachio nuts, or any combination,
   lightly browned over low heat in 4 tablespoons
   melted butter
3 tablespoons raisins, plumped in warm water or
   in melted butter with the nuts
2 tablespoons fresh mint leaves, whole or (if large)
   cut into strips
2 teaspoons rose flower water

Early in the day, prepare the marinade: First roast the cumin, coriander, and cardamom seeds in a small unoiled frying pan until the cumin seeds begin to darken. Put the seeds in a coffee or spice grinder with the cloves and peppercorns. Grind to a powder. Then put the contents of the grinder into a food processor with the mace, cinnamon, cayenne, salt, garlic, ginger, and half the onion. Puree to a paste. Put the lemon juice and yogurt in a small bowl and whip with a fork to lighten, then mix the contents of the food processor into the yogurt. Spread a layer of the yogurt mixture on the bottom of a large pan.

Skin the chicken pieces and remove and discard excess fat. Jab a small knife into the chicken flesh in several places. Lay the chicken over the yogurt mixture in the pan and cover with the remaining yogurt mixture. Marinate 1 hour at room temperature or refrigerate for 2 or more hours, turning once or twice.

Wash the rice several times until the water runs clear, as directed on page 13, then soak it for half an hour in 4 cups cold water and 1 tablespoon salt. Drain through a strainer.

Meanwhile, heat the oil in a large nonstick skillet. Add the remaining onions and cook, stirring occasionally, about 10 minutes or until very soft and turning golden. Remove with slotted spoon and reserve on paper towels. Add the chicken and all the marinade to the skillet and cook until the chicken is just done and the yogurt much reduced and very thick but not dry. As the chicken pieces cook, remove them and cut into large ($1\frac{1}{2}$- to 2-inch) chunks, discarding the bones and returning any undercooked pieces to the pan. (Midway in this process preheat the oven to 325°F and bring 3 or 4 quarts of water to a boil in a large pot with the remaining tablespoon of salt.)

When the yogurt has cooked down and thickened, remove from heat, stir all the chicken pieces back in, then transfer the contents of the skillet to a large casserole. Top chicken with the onions and cover the casserole.

Warm the milk in a small saucepan. Add the saffron and keep warm but do not boil.

Add the drained rice to the pot of boiling water and return to a boil. Boil 2 to 5 minutes (for a total of 6 or 7 minutes after adding to the water) or until just tender, then drain through a strainer and shake well to dry. Turn the strainer of rice over the chicken and onions in the casserole. Top with streaks of the saffron milk. For beautifully dry, white, saffron-streaked rice, leave this layering undisturbed. But for rice that partakes of the delicious spiced yogurt-onion gravy, gently turn contents of casserole with a wooden spoon so that the rice will absorb the flavors during baking. Either way, wrap the casserole lid with a cloth dish towel as directed on page 16. Cover casserole and bake 30 minutes. Turn onto a serving platter and sprinkle with garnishes.

Variations

• For a juicier biryani with a meatier flavor, make a broth of the scrap parts of the chicken (neck, back, and wing tips) and use it for cooking the rice *or* for saucing it at table, as outlined below.

• To make the broth, start a day or several hours before making the biryani. Bring the chicken parts to a boil in a large pot with 4 cups water. Skim the surface, then add a 1-inch piece of fresh gingerroot, 2 or 3 crushed garlic cloves, a few sprigs of parsley, and a small onion, coarsely chopped. Adjust heat to bubble very gently for 2 to 3 hours. Drain through a sieve, discarding the solids. Cool to room temperature and refrigerate until ready to use, then skim off the surface fat before reheating.

• Instead of boiling the soaked rice in water, cook it for 15 minutes by the total absorption method (page 15) in $2\frac{1}{2}$ cups of reduced broth with a little salt. Before baking, put a layer of cooked rice at the bottom of the casserole, then add the chicken, then the onions, then the remaining rice. Serve in the casserole or mix the rice, onions, and chicken on a platter.

• For a sauce to pass at table, put $1\frac{1}{2}$ cups of the broth in a saucepan when you start to fry the marinated chicken. Add 2 onions, peeled and sliced very thin, $\frac{1}{2}$ cup raisins, $\frac{1}{4}$ teaspoon saffron threads, 1 tablespoon butter, $\frac{1}{4}$ teaspoon ground ginger, $\frac{1}{4}$ teaspoon ground cinnamon, and a pinch of salt. Cook covered over very low heat for 45 minutes, then remove the cover and cook about 15 minutes until somewhat reduced and thickened. Pass in a gravy boat to be spooned sparingly over the rice as desired. (If using this sauce, you would probably not want to use the suggested onion or raisin garnishes, which are more typical of Indian service.)

Ground Turkey Chile with Rice

Serves 3 or 4

This contemporary North American chile uses real Mexican chiles, a Central Asian pilav structure, and a native meat that can be relatively low in fat. If you are equipped to grind the meat or can get a butcher to do it, remove the skin and clumps of fat before grinding. For super leanness, use all breast meat; for more flavor, add some dark meat trimmed of fat and skin.

> *$1\frac{1}{2}$ cups long-grain white rice*
> *1 dried mulatto chile*
> *2 small dried pasilla chiles*
> *2 small dried chipotle chiles*
> *3 tablespoons olive or peanut oil*
> *1 large clove garlic, minced*
> *1 small onion, chopped fine*
> *1 pound ground turkey meat*
> *$\frac{1}{2}$ teaspoon dried oregano, preferably Mexican*
> *1 teaspoon cumin seeds, ground in a coffee or spice*
> *   grinder, or 1 teaspoon ground cumin*
> *1 cup crushed plum tomatoes, fresh (if ripe) or canned*
> *2 cups homemade or canned turkey or chicken broth, warm*
> *salt to taste*
> *2 tablespoons chopped cilantro (fresh coriander)*

Bring $1\frac{1}{2}$ cups water to a simmer. Add the rice. Cover, remove from heat, and let soak 1 hour.

Roast the chiles for 1 or 2 minutes in an unoiled skillet over medium heat. This makes them pliable enough to work with. Then cut them open and remove and discard stem, veins, and seeds. Let cool for a few minutes, break into pieces, and grind to a powder in a coffee or spice grinder.

Heat oil in a large heavy skillet. Add garlic and onion and sauté until soft. Add turkey and cook, stirring, until it turns light brown and gives up its water. Continue cooking until the water boils off. Pour off any excess fat. Stir in oregano and cumin.

Add chiles and tomatoes to the skillet. Cook over very low heat for 20 minutes. Pour in the chicken broth and stir. Add salt, turn up heat, and bring to a boil. Drain rice and spread over the turkey and sauce in the skillet. Cover, reduce heat to very low, and cook 20 minutes or until rice is done.

To serve, uncover the skillet and replace the lid with an upside-down platter. Hold the platter down with one hand, grasp the skillet handle with the other hand, and flip, setting platter-side-down on a counter and removing skillet from the top. Sprinkle with chopped cilantro.

Gingered Orange Duck with Rice

Serves 4

This duck recipe, true to no tradition but indebted to a few, flew in from nowhere and composed itself.

> *1 4- or 5-pound duck, with neck, cut into 1 back,*
>   *2 wing tips, and 2 each breast pieces, thighs,*
>   *and drumsticks*
> *salt and freshly ground black pepper*
> *up to 2 tablespoons olive oil*
> *1 large onion, cut in half and then into thin slices*
> *2 cloves garlic, minced*
> *minced fresh gingerroot to equal amount of garlic*
> *1 pound turnips, sliced thin, then cut into matchsticks*
> *1 bunch broadleaf parsley, chopped except for a few sprigs*
>   *(1 cup chopped)*
> *1½ cups long-grain white rice*

$\frac{1}{2}$ *cup sherry*
grated zest and juice 1 orange
juice $\frac{1}{2}$ lemon, freshly squeezed

Remove and discard excess fat from the duck back and wing tips. Put back, wing tips, and neck in a large saucepan with salt, pepper, and 4 cups water. Bring to a boil and simmer gently 2 to 3 hours. Remove and discard the solid pieces and skim off any fat on top. Strain broth back into the saucepan and keep warm.

Remove skin and excess fat from breast and leg pieces. Fry 8 to 10 minutes on each side in a large nonstick skillet over low to medium heat. Remove and set aside.

If you have done a thorough job of removing the duck fat, you might have to add up to 2 tablespoons of rendered fat or olive oil at this point. If there is too much fat in the skillet, pour off the excess.

Add onion, garlic, and ginger to skillet and cook, stirring occasionally, until soft. Spread out to cover bottom of skillet and add turnip sticks in a flat layer. Sprinkle with parsley (reserving a few sprigs), salt, and pepper. Top with duck and rice, then more salt and pepper. Pour sherry, then orange zest and orange and lemon juice, then $2\frac{1}{4}$ cups of the broth around the edges and over all the rice. Push rice off meat to cover with liquid. Bring to a boil, cover, turn heat to low, and cook 20 to 25 minutes or until rice and duck are done, moving the skillet an inch or so a few times during cooking if needed for even cooking.

Uncover skillet. Hold skillet handle with one hand, and with the other hand hold a platter upside down on top of the skillet. Flip skillet and platter together so that the skillet ends up on top and the food ends up on the platter. Scrape any stuck pieces from the skillet and add to platter unless burned black. Top with parsley sprigs and serve.

Meaty Rice Dishes

Maria's Cuban Rice with Pork and Corn

Serves 4 to 6

Pork, once synonymous with fat, is now bred leaner and lighter than most beef. Maria Alvarez uses it with rice and corn for this meal-in-a-dish from her native Cuba. Maria's 1-to-1 rice-and-water ratio is more typical of medium-grain rice cooking, but it's not too chewy in this recipe. If you prefer a softer rice, use 3 cups water to 2 cups rice. If you can't get Cuban bijol (page 55), color the oil with annato seed (page 54) or use ½ teaspoon ground cumin and ½ teaspoon turmeric.

1 pound lean pork, cut into ½- to 1-inch cubes
1 teaspoon paprika, or more to taste
salt to taste
4 tablespoons olive oil
1 large onion, chopped
1 large red bell pepper, cut into 1-inch squares
1 large clove garlic, mashed
2 cups long-grain white rice
1 teaspoon bijol (see headnote above)
1 cup corn, scraped from cob or frozen

Dust pork with paprika and salt. Heat oil in a large heavy saucepan over medium heat. Add pork and cook until browned lightly on all sides. Remove to paper towel. Add onion to pan and sauté 5 minutes until soft, then add red pepper and garlic and cook another 5 minutes. Add rice, reserved pork, bijol, and 2 cups water. Bring to a boil. Cover, reduce heat, and simmer 10 minutes. Stir in the corn, cover, and simmer another 10 minutes. Remove from heat and let sit, still covered, another 10 minutes. Fluff before serving.

Roasted Brown Rice with Wild Rice, Sausage, Chestnuts, and Mushrooms

Serves 4

This is my heretical version of the roasted brown rice casserole on page 229. When I served that vegetarian dish to my neighbor Toby Barton, his wicked comment was "Add sausage." He never thought I'd do it — but here it is, Toby. Brown rice and sausage aren't usually cooked together, because they represent such different if not hostile dietary camps. But here, with just a small amount of sausage, browned separately to leave some fat behind, they combine with the other earthy ingredients for a main dish that is rich in flavor yet relatively low in fat.

6 dried shiitake mushrooms
$2\frac{1}{2}$ cups beef, poultry, or vegetable broth or water
8 chestnuts
$\frac{3}{4}$ cup long-grain brown rice
$\frac{1}{2}$ pound sweet Italian sausage, sliced thin
2 tablespoons olive or walnut oil or butter
2 cloves garlic, minced
1 medium leek, white only, chopped small (about $\frac{1}{2}$ cup chopped)
$\frac{3}{4}$ cup wild rice
1 tablespoon fresh thyme leaves or 1 teaspoon dried
1 tablespoon chopped fresh sage leaves or $1\frac{1}{2}$ teaspoons
   crumbled dried sage
salt and freshly ground black pepper to taste

Soak the mushrooms in $\frac{3}{4}$ cup water for 20 to 30 minutes. Remove mushrooms, discard tough stems, and chop caps. Drain soaking liquid through a sieve lined with cheesecloth or through a coffee filter and add to the broth.

With a small sharp knife, make a long top-to-bottom slit through the shell on the flat side of each chestnut, then a short perpendicular slit to form a cross. Drop chestnuts into boiling water for about 2 minutes. Remove with slotted spoon and, while still warm, peel off shell and inner skin. Chop each chestnut into 6 to 8 pieces.

Heat a large heavy skillet over medium heat. Spread brown rice on the skillet to toast for 5 or 10 minutes, until grains are a deep golden or a light toasty brown color. Stir as needed to prevent uneven roasting. When rice has turned a deep golden or light toasty brown, remove from pan and set aside.

Add sausage slices to skillet and brown lightly on both sides. Remove to paper towel.

Put broth in a small saucepan over low heat and keep warm.

Heat oil or butter over medium heat in a heavy saucepan or Dutch oven. When hot, add garlic and leek and cook 3 to 5 minutes to soften. Add mushrooms and cook another 3 to 5 minutes until soft. Add the sausage, chestnuts, toasted rice, wild rice, thyme, sage, salt, and pepper. Add broth and bring to a boil. Cover, turn heat to low, and cook 45 minutes or until all the water is absorbed.

Tomato Lamb Stew for Chelo

Serves 4 to 6

This stew is derived from the one that Mrs. Mostafavi, my pilau tutor from Iran, served me with the chelo on page 62. I include her french fries here as an interesting authentic touch, but I make the stew without the potatoes. The lemon is my substitute for Mrs. Mostafavi's dried Persian limes, which should be used if you have access to Middle Eastern groceries.

> *4 tablespoons olive oil*
> *10 fresh ripe plum tomatoes, peeled, seeded, and chopped,*
>   *or 1 28-ounce can Italian plum tomatoes, drained,*
>   *seeded, and chopped*
> *1 large or 2 small baking potatoes, peeled and cut into*
>   *sticks for french-frying (optional)*
> *oil for deep-frying (if using potatoes)*
> *1 medium-large onion, minced*
> *2½ pounds lamb shoulder, trimmed of fat and cut into 2-inch cubes*
> *½ cup cooked yellow split peas*
> *¼ teaspoon ground cinnamon*

½ cup chopped broadleaf parsley
salt and freshly ground black pepper to taste
1 lemon, cut into 4 to 6 wedges, seeds removed, plus
   chopped or grated zest of a second lemon

Heat 1 tablespoon olive oil in a medium-size skillet or large saucepan. Add tomatoes and simmer, stirring occasionally, as you proceed with recipe.

If you are including the french fries, heat several inches of oil to between 350° and 360°F, preferably in a deep fryer that has a frying basket with a handle. Drop in the potatoes and fry until golden. (They don't have to be cooked through.) Lift out the basket containing the potatoes and set aside.

Heat 3 tablespoons olive oil in a large heavy skillet over medium heat. Add the onion and cook until golden. Add the lamb and brown lightly on all sides. Add the simmering tomatoes, the split peas, cinnamon, parsley, salt, pepper, lemon wedges, and water just to cover. Reduce heat and cook 1 hour, adding the lemon zest and the potatoes (if using) for the last 10 minutes or so.

Serve the stew and the chelo separately so that everyone can choose to have them side by side (which I prefer) or with the stew on top.

Variation

Mrs. Mostafavi makes a simpler rice dish that can be cooked in with a stew. Wash and soak 2 cups of basmati rice as in the chelo recipe on page 62. Then drain, rinse, and add to the stew after browning the meat. Add the other ingredients and 2 additional cups of boiling water.

Lamb and Eggplant Pilau

Wash and soak 2 cups of basmati rice as in the recipe for chelo on page 62.

While the rice is soaking, peel 1 small to medium eggplant and cut it into strips about ½ inch by 2 inches. Sprinkle with salt and drain 30 to 60 minutes in a colander or wire basket set over a pan or bowl.

Meanwhile, prepare the Tomato Lamb Stew for Chelo, above, but omit the potatoes and the split peas.

While the stew is cooking, rinse the eggplant and pat dry. Heat 4 tablespoons oil, preferably in a nonstick skillet, and cook the eggplant until golden on all sides. Remove, pat dry on paper towel, then add to the stew.

Boil and drain the rice, then lay down the tadig (bottom crust) of your choice, as directed in the chelo recipe and its tadig variations. Top the tadig with a thin layer of rice, then add the stew. (If soupy, use a slotted spoon to transfer the solids, then boil down the liquid until thick and spoon this over the lamb.)

Add remaining rice in a mound and proceed as in the chelo recipe.

Jambalaya

Serves 6

For over a century, compilers of American dictionaries and Louisiana cookbooks have come up with offhand conjecture and hearsay history about the origin of jambalaya — the dish and the name. According to one recent cookbook, "Jambalaya means jumble in the Creole dialect." But jambalaya, it seems, has Old World origins. Culinary historian Karen Hess has turned up references to a pilau titled "jambalaya" (with various spellings) from nineteenth-century Provence. One Provençal writer attributed it to Arab sources, which Hess finds linguistically credible. But whatever the derivation, for longer than any living memory, jambalaya — the name and the dish — has spoken of good times and good eats in the accents of Louisiana's Creole and Cajun cooks.

Strictly as a rice dish, jambalaya is more interesting than gumbo, because the rice here is an integral part of the stew, not just a bed for the real piece of work. But jambalaya, it must be said, is a far less serious affair. My New Orleans contacts, who go back for generations, explain jambalaya as an end-of-the-week kitchen cleanup, a poor people's frugal way of using up ingredients at hand. They never explain how poor people managed to have such a variety of rich ingredients perpetually on hand, but maybe that's why jambalaya always smacks of celebration.

Here, then, is the Big Easy in a pot. Without the roux and rituals of gumbo preparation, it's a forgiving dish that encourages you to do it your way — even if your way is less lavish with the hog fat than bayou hospitality might mandate. This recipe calls for less fat than was the custom and offers some alternatives (even turkey sausage, if you like) for those who want to believe that a prudent jambalaya is not a contradiction in terms.

½ pound andouille or other sausage, sliced
½ cup chopped cooked ham (optional)
2 to 4 tablespoons cooking fat (lard, bacon drippings,
*   butter, or olive oil)*
2 pounds chicken, turkey, or duck parts
½ pound small or medium shrimp, shelled and deveined
*   (1 cup shelled)*
1 medium onion, chopped
1 green bell pepper, chopped
1 stalk celery, chopped
2 cloves garlic, chopped
1 cup fresh ripe or canned tomatoes, peeled, seeded, and chopped
3½ cups chicken, turkey, or duck broth
2 cups long-grain white rice
1 teaspoon fresh thyme leaves or ½ teaspoon dried
¼ teaspoon ground cayenne, or to taste
salt and freshly ground black pepper to taste

Heat a large heavy kettle, Dutch oven, or cast-iron skillet over a medium flame. Add sausage and cook 5 minutes. Add ham to the sausage and cook until ham and sausage are lightly browned on all sides. Remove with slotted spoon and drain on paper towel. Pour off excess fat or add cooking fat, as needed, then add the poultry parts. Cook 15 minutes, turning to brown on all sides and partially cook. Remove to paper towel. Add shrimp and cook, turning, 1 or 2 minutes, until pink on both sides. Remove and set aside. Add more fat if needed. Add onion, pepper, and celery and cook 5 minutes to soften. Add garlic and cook 5 to 10 minutes until onion and garlic are turning golden brown. Stir in the tomatoes and simmer 10 minutes. Return sausage and ham to the pot. Tear poultry meat from the bones, discard skin and bones, and return meat to the pot. Add broth and bring to a boil. Add rice and seasonings. Cover, reduce heat, and simmer 20 minutes. Remove from heat, press shrimp into the rice mixture, replace cover, and let sit 10 minutes.

Louisiana Gumbo

You can't talk about the birth of gumbo without evoking that old American daydream of an ethnic melting pot. Gumbo is not just a metaphor; it *is* a melting pot, a grassroots intermingling of elements from four continents that occurred in early New Orleans. The name *gumbo* comes from a West African word for okra, a principal ingredient and a vegetable unknown in this country until it was carried here by Africans on slave ships. Even earlier, Native Americans were drying and pulverizing sassafras leaves to make a powder that they used for medicine and seasoning. Adopted by the earliest French settlers, who named it *filé*, that too became a signature ingredient in gumbo. The foundation of a classic gumbo is the fat-and-flour roux, a legacy of those same French settlers (who probably didn't know that their ancestors had learned the trick from the Italians). The dish is seasoned with the chile peppers that the French-and-Spanish Creoles took up in the Caribbean before migrating to New Orleans. Other Creole contributions go back to France and Spain — though some, such as green peppers, were New World natives unknown in Spain before the Columbian encounters. The Cajun French exiled from eastern Canada brought their own *trucs* and touches when they settled on the bayous; and I'm sure New Orleans's Italian population has put its stamp on gumbo. Subject all these contributions to long, slow simmering, a practice the slaves brought from Africa, and they blend into one complex, harmonious whole.

Procedure

For all its diverse elements, making gumbo is not a formidable undertaking; but it does require some attention. No two experts fry the vegetables, the okra, and the roux in exactly the same order, and though many do them cumulatively in the same pan, New Orleans home cooks I know agree with me that things progress more smoothly when the roux is done in a separate pot. If you have all your ingredients lined up before beginning, you can easily tend two pots at the same time.

The Roux

A French roux, made by cooking flour in hot fat, can be made white or brown depending on the cooking time and temperature. Gumbo cooks go for a brown roux, achieved by stirring until the color deepens from amber to caramel to russet, nut, or even chocolate brown. Some insist that this process should take up to 1 hour or more over very low heat; others work over medium-high heat for 10 or 15 minutes. All are unforgiving about burned roux: The only remedy is to scrap it and begin anew. This recipe has you start safely on low heat, increase the pace with caution, and finish at a light brown stage in 20 to 30 minutes.

The Cooking Fat

Some traditional gumbo cooks still swear by lard for making the roux and the vegetable sauté. Others achieve a wonderful rich depth of taste using bacon drippings or rendered duck fat. But even in New Orleans, oil mixed with butter or oil alone is gaining favor. If butter were to be used alone, though, it should probably be clarified (page 53) to prevent burning.

The Thickening Agent

Louisiana cooks tend to define a gumbo by its thickening agent. With or without the roux, itself a thickener, there are okra gumbos and there are filé gumbos, and most gumbo cooks and connoisseurs insist that the two should never meet in the same pot, though one or another is essential if you are to call the mixture gumbo. To me, as to others of the okra gumbo persuasion, it's hard to imagine the dish without the background flavor and texture that this modest vegetable provides. If you are turned off by okra's viscous, stringy — okay, slimy — quality, try making gumbo and you will see that very quality transformed into a virtue. Sliced and stirred, and stirred, and stirred, as it is here, the strings gradually disappear and the gumbo becomes one thick soupy substance (though soft but separate pieces of okra will remain).

When filé is cooked in liquid, it has some of the same sticky qualities. The word is from the French for "ropey," a reference to the viscous strings that form when filé is stirred into a boiling pot. Today, though, filé is used mostly as a vestigial "seasoning," stirred into or sprinkled over the cooked gumbo after it's removed from the heat.

The Meat and Seafood

Like Spanish paella, Louisiana gumbo lives in the world's imagination as a giant pot fired up for parties and heaped with all manner of pork, fowl, and shellfish. In local practice, though, home cooks habitually make more manageable gumbos (and paellas), some all meat, some all seafood (or just crab), some mixed, some elegantly restrained as in one old New Orleans restaurant's celestial-sounding duck and oyster gumbo.

The Rice

I have to face it, the rice is a sort of stepchild in a gumbo meal. It's always there but not a focus of attention or even an integral part of the mix. Most recipes I've read call for ridiculously small dollops in each dish. My experience is that generous portions go fast, especially when there is self-service on seconds.

The rice of Louisiana tradition is long grain and white, and it was always rinsed well to wash away the starch. Today it seems that most New Orleans cooks use Uncle Ben's Converted Rice, which doesn't require washing to cook up in separate grains. Any long-grain white rice will do.

Ann Marie's LaRocca Gumbo

Serves 6 to 8

With my apologies for a few procedural changes, this is my sister Ann Marie LaRocca's composite version of her New Orleans in-laws' gumbo variations. Sometimes Ann Marie uses Italian sausage, initially a substitute for the traditional andouille but now a family favorite.

The vegetables:

2 tablespoons butter
2 tablespoons olive oil
1 medium onion, chopped small
1 green bell pepper, chopped small
3 stalks celery, chopped small
3 cloves garlic
1 bunch scallions, white part and first 3 inches of green, minced

The roux:

2 tablespoons butter
2 tablespoons olive oil
4 tablespoons flour

The thickener:

1 pound fresh okra, trimmed and sliced, or 2 10-ounce
    packages frozen sliced okra

The cooking liquids:

2 cups fresh or canned tomatoes, peeled, seeded, and chopped
2 quarts mild chicken broth (or half canned broth, half water)

The meats:

1 pound andouille or other sausage
up to 4 tablespoons olive oil
legs, thighs, wings, and split breast of 1 chicken

The seasonings:

2 teaspoons fresh thyme leaves or 1 teaspoon dried
1 bay leaf, in 1 piece
$\frac{1}{4}$ to $\frac{1}{2}$ teaspoon ground cayenne, or $\frac{1}{2}$ to 1 teaspoon hot
    red pepper flakes, or to taste
salt and freshly ground black pepper to taste

The rice:

4 cups long-grain white rice

The seafood:

1 pound shrimp, shelled and deveined
1 pint container shucked oysters, including liquid (if available)

For the vegetables, heat butter and oil in a large skillet (not cast-iron) over medium-low heat. Add onion, pepper, celery, and garlic. Set aside scallions.

Then start the roux, but stir the vegetables occasionally while you are working on the roux.

To make the roux, heat the butter and oil over low heat in a heavy-bottomed kettle or Dutch oven large enough to hold all the gumbo ingredients. Add the flour and cook, stirring almost constantly, until the roux turns a deep amber or russet brown. This should take 20 to 30 minutes. When the roux is under way, raise the heat cautiously if desired to advance the process, but be careful not to burn the roux.

After the chopped vegetables are soft but not brown (10 to 15 minutes), start stirring in the sliced okra. You will still be switching back and forth between the two pots, stirring the roux with one spoon and stirring the okra and vegetables with another. The okra will be viscous and stringy at first, but after about 20 minutes of stirring the sliminess will be gone.

When the roux has reached the desired russet brown, stir in the tomatoes. (Stand back; it will splatter.) Then, if the okra is ready, stir the vegetables and okra into the roux, then stir in the broth. If the roux is ready before the okra, stir a cup or so of broth into the roux to keep it from burning and hold over very low heat until you can add the vegetables and okra and the rest of the broth. Either way, when this base is all assembled, bring to a boil, reduce heat, and simmer uncovered while you proceed with the recipe.

Heat the vegetable-cooking skillet or another large skillet (cast-iron is fine now) over medium heat. Add the sausage and fry to brown on each side. Remove with slotted spoon and add to the gumbo. Pour off excess fat or add olive oil as needed. Add chicken pieces and fry about 10 minutes on each side. Remove to paper towel. When chicken is cool enough to handle, pull off the skin and pull the meat from the bones. Tear the meat into shreds and add to the gumbo, discarding skin and bones. Add seasonings and scallions.

In a large saucepan or kettle, bring 6 cups salted water to a boil and add the rice. Return to the boil, cover, and reduce heat to simmer 20 minutes. Remove from heat and let sit 10 minutes.

While the rice is resting, add the shrimp to the gumbo. Five minutes later add the oysters with their liquid. Simmer another 5 minutes, still uncovered.

Spoon some rice onto each plate or bowl, then top with gumbo.

Chicken and Sausage Gumbo

Follow directions for Ann Marie's LaRocca Gumbo, above, but omit the shrimp and oysters. If you like, chop up to a half-pound of that leftover cooked ham that Louisiana kitchens always seem to have on hand. Fry and remove the ham to season the skillet before putting in the chopped vegetables, then return it later to the assembled vegetables, roux, and broth. Make duck and sausage gumbo or turkey and sausage gumbo (using 2 or 3 pounds of turkey parts) the same way. Use the duck scrap parts to enhance the stock. Some of the duck fat can go into the roux.

Seafood Gumbo

Serves 6

My brother-in-law Tony LaRocca remembers his mother's crab gumbo as a family Christmas Eve tradition, festively replete with whole crabs. Other versions cater to the effete and use only picked crabmeat. Here is a compromise.

Use all the ingredients listed for Ann Marie's LaRocca Gumbo (page 144) except the chicken broth, chicken, and sausage. Instead of the meats, use a dozen live crabs and increase the amount of shrimp to 2 pounds. If you can, buy shrimp with heads still on, to flavor the stock.

To prepare the crabs: Using tongs, drop a few of the crabs into boiling water and boil until they turn bright red. Remove with the tongs. Repeat until all of the crabs have been boiled. Then throw the shrimp shells and heads into the crab boiling water and cook 20 minutes. Remove with a slotted spoon and discard the shells and heads. Pour the water through a sieve lined with cheesecloth. Save the water.

When each crab is cool enough to handle, pull back the tab, or apron, from the back shell, then pull up and remove the entire shell. Pull off and save the two large claws. From the body, remove and discard the spongy grayish "dead man's fingers" and the solid white intestines. (Don't discard the light green "crab butter" or any bright orange roe. These are choice parts, to be left on the crab or saved and stirred into the gumbo.) Then, using both hands (one on each side of the crab), break the body in half down the middle.

All of this can be done the day before. The crab claws and bodies should be refrigerated until ready to add to the gumbo.

To begin the gumbo, cook the vegetables, roux, and okra, and add the tomatoes and stock (using crab-cooking water for stock), as in the recipe for Ann Marie's LaRocca Gumbo. Add the seasonings and simmer, uncovered, at least 30 minutes. Then put the rice on to cook and add the crab claws and bodies to the gumbo. When the rice is resting, add the shrimp to the gumbo and cook 5 minutes, then add the oysters and their juice and cook another 5 minutes. Spoon the gumbo over the rice for each serving.

FOUR

Paella, Risotto, and Other Spanish and Italian Ways with Medium-Grain Rice

⁊

THE paellas of eastern Spain and the risottos of northern Italy are the prominent exceptions to Europe's general ineptitude in cooking rice, a foreign food still known to many as the sweetened mush of nursery puddings. And these exceptions, like the various pilaf relatives featured in Chapter Three, have their roots in the rice and the rice cooking methods disseminated by the Arabs, who in turn had picked up pilau from the Persians and brought it with them on their conquests and travels.

Soon after Arab conquerors crossed into Spain from North Africa in the early eighth century, they were growing rice along the lakes and rivers near the Iberian peninsula's southern and eastern coasts, especially in Valencia's freshwater marshlands around Lake Albufera. Four centuries later, the Arabs unseated but their grain well entrenched in Valencian and Catalan kitchens, James I of Aragon ruled that rice cultivation in the entire region be limited to the Albufera marshlands. His purpose was to contain malaria, but the lasting effect of the decree was to assure Valencia's status as the center of Spain's rice culture.

True to pattern, soon after the Arabs conquered Sicily in the ninth century they were planting rice on that island and in other spots they occupied in the southern Italian peninsula. According to Mary Taylor Simeti's scholarly and charming *Pomp and Sustenance,* subtitled *Twenty-five Centuries of Sicilian Food,* Sicilians continued to grow rice into the eighteenth century. Certainly they have an impressive repertoire of rice-based specialties to show for it, for all their primary reliance on bread and pasta. But northern Italy, now the center of Italian rice growing and cooking, was influenced more by Spain's rice culture than by Sicily's. And rice cultivation was not established in its modern location, along the Po Valley in the northern regions of Piedmont, Lombardy, Emilia-Romagna, and the Veneto, until the fifteenth and sixteenth centuries — a politically unsettled time when Lombardy and its ruling city Milan, now a risotto capital, came under Spanish domination.

Certainly the rice cooking specialties and traditions of Spain and Italy are two separate and distinct branches of the art; but there is reason enough to consider the two together, and apart from other offspring of the pilau tradition. Unlike the variations that developed under Arab influence elsewhere, the Spanish and Italian specialties are made (respectively) with Spanish and Italian varieties of medium-grain *japonica* rice. And whereas pilau cooks wash off the starch of their fluffier long grains and take pains to make each grain dry and separate, Spaniards and Italians cook their rice unwashed, in ways that take advantage of their shorter grains' starchy, absorbent qualities.

In both paella and risotto, the rice is sautéed (usually with some onion) before the cooking liquid is added; both use broth, not water, as the cooking liquid; and, most distinctively, both are cooked uncovered through the entire process. In both countries, too, the rice dish is served traditionally as lunch or as a first course, though today the more elaborate versions, especially of paella, would seem to make a second course superfluous.

Rice Cooking from Paella Country

Of all the traditional dishes that Americans have appropriated with more enthusiasm than fidelity, paella might be the most widely misrepresented. More than ten years ago Penelope Casas reported in *The Foods and Wines of Spain,* "I recently tasted paellas all over New York City for a New York newspaper, and the results were appalling." After a decade of flying foods and heated culinary exploration, not much has changed. "I've ordered paellas many times in the states but never got a good one," says my Catalan cooking adviser Gabriel Yuc, a Barcelona native famous among D.C.-area friends for his own paellas. And

New York newspapers still run recipes for paella, made in deep pots with Uncle Ben's or other long-grain rice, that might as well be titled Yankee Jambalaya.

Only two of the recipes that follow are for dishes that the Spanish call paellas; and not all are traditional dishes executed exactly as in one or another town or province on Spain's rice-growing eastern coast. But all the dishes featured here are prepared in the manner typical of that entire region. It is this singular cooking style as much as any list of signature ingredients that distinguishes paellas and their culinary kin in Catalonia, Valencia, and farther south.

In cooking any Spanish rice dish (and any Spaniard will tell you that paella is primarily a rice dish), it's important to use European medium-length rice, a type of short-grain *japonica* rice. Spain's own varieties, grown mostly in Valencia, are not widely available here, but some specialty groceries carry them or will order some. Italian arborio rice, very similar in shape, is the best commonly available substitute.

Also essential, as the flavor that the rice grains will absorb, is a good full-bodied homemade broth. Italian risotto is fine made with a mild stock, but we're dealing here with a more robust tradition. Of the stocks in Chapter Two of this book, I use the browned version of the chicken stock or chicken-beef stock, or for seafood dishes a reduced fish stock. Kevin Cahill's lobster stock is excellent with the seafood dishes. The chicken-lamb stock, though not traditional with paella, adds depth of flavor to rice dishes cooked with chicken and meat.

Just as essential is the method of cooking the rice uncovered in a wide, shallow pan. Valencians use a shallow, oval, slope-sided metal pan, usually cast-iron, with a C-shaped handle at each end. The pan itself, also called a paella, is thought to have its origins in the patella, a similar shallow iron pan used by the ancient Romans who occupied Spain's Mediterranean coast about two thousand years ago. In Catalonia the favored vessel is a clay cassola, also wide and shallow. Catalans might layer their rice a little deeper than in Valencia, but the general procedure is the same.

In either vessel, the rice is traditionally cooked out of doors over an open fire of wood or vine cuttings that starts out hot, then gradually subsides as the paella cooks. Coleman Andrews, who discusses Valencian paella in his book *Catalan Cuisine,* explains how "live flames lapping around the edges of the *caldero* [paella pan] actually create a kind of miniatmospheric inversion on the surface of the vessel, flavoring the dish a bit with woodsmoke even as the rice on the bottom of the pan and around the edges takes on the *socarrat* or dark brown crust so prized by paella lovers."

Indoors, today's Spaniards use their paella pans on the stovetop, sometimes finishing in the oven. American cooks, lacking large paella pans and oversized burners, have to scale their paella to what can be accommodated in a large cast-iron skillet. Paella pans with more capacity are available here in specialty houseware shops but require a bigger heat source than our standard stovetop burner, so some compromises are required either way.

To cook a paella main dish for 4 to 6 on my small gas burners, I use a cast-iron skillet labeled 12 inches that actually measures 10 inches across the bottom and $11\frac{3}{4}$ inches across the top. I might have to move the skillet a bit now and then to keep the rice around the edges cooking evenly, and the inconstant heat might stretch out the cooking time by a few minutes. However, the heavier the pan, the better the heat distribution will be. To feed more people, I'd make two paellas in two large skillets. A 15-inch paella pan makes for better distribution of the rice but, on most stoves, worse heat distribution, even when placed over two adjacent burners, as some suggest.

Another approach, and possibly the only choice if your stove burners are electric, is to transfer the skillet or paella pan to a preheated 375°F oven after pouring on the boiling broth. Immediately reduce the oven temperature to 350°F, cook 10 minutes, then reduce the heat further to 325°F, and cook another 10 to 15 minutes. Remove from the oven, cover with a dish towel, and let rest 10 minutes.

The recipes that follow call for stovetop cooking over a gradually lowered flame (I turn it down two or three times during the 20 to 25 minutes) but allow for the oven finish if preferred. Some cook the paella for 10 minutes on the stove, then transfer to a 325°F oven for the remaining cooking time.

To induce a bottom crust, I keep the pan over the lowest possible heat, instead of turning off the heat, for the final 10-minute resting period. This doesn't guarantee a perfect crust like the tadig in the Persian pilau featured earlier, but it can make for some good scrapings.

Rice Cooked in Fish Stock

Serves 4 to 6

This simple side dish for fish gets its character from a good homemade fish stock made with fresh fish heads and bones, usually available cheap from fish stores, and from the strong garlic sauce spooned on at table.

In the fishermen's classic arroz abanda, a whole fish or a mix of fish is used to make the broth, then eaten separately as a second course after the rice.

The stock:

head and bones 2 fresh fish
1 onion, coarsely chopped
1 leek, white and light green parts, trimmed and washed
3 cloves garlic, crushed
1 small bunch parsley, stems and all
1 teaspoon dried thyme or oregano
1 cup dry white wine

The rice:

4 tablespoons olive oil
2 cloves garlic, minced
2 fresh ripe tomatoes, peeled, seeded, and chopped,
    or 4 canned Italian plum tomatoes, seeded and
    chopped, without juice from can
2 tablespoons parsley, minced
1 teaspoon paprika
$\frac{1}{4}$ teaspoon hot red pepper flakes (optional)
$1\frac{1}{2}$ cups Valencian or Italian arborio rice
$\frac{1}{4}$ teaspoon saffron threads, crumbled
salt and freshly ground black pepper to taste

The alioli:

4 cloves garlic, flattened and very finely minced
salt to taste
up to $\frac{1}{2}$ cup extra-virgin olive oil

1 lemon, quartered lengthwise

Put all the stock ingredients in a large stockpot with 6 cups water. Bring to a boil, cover with the lid slightly ajar, and adjust heat to simmer 30 minutes. Strain through a sieve, discard solids, and return stock to the pot. Boil another 30 minutes to reduce to $3\frac{1}{2}$ or 4 cups.

To make the rice, heat oil in a paella pan or large heavy skillet over medium heat. Add garlic and tomatoes and cook, stirring occasionally, until very thick. Stir in parsley, paprika, and optional pepper flakes. Add rice and cook, stirring, to coat. Add 3½ cups hot stock. Crumble the saffron and add with salt and pepper. Cook uncovered 20 to 25 minutes, beginning over medium-high heat and gradually reducing heat to very low. During cooking time, move the skillet back and forth a bit now and then if needed for even cooking. (See page 152 for electric stove and oven alternatives.) Remove from heat, cover with a dish towel, and let sit 10 minutes.

While the rice is resting, make the alioli (oil and garlic sauce): Put the garlic in a mortar, sprinkle with salt, and grind with a pestle to a thick paste. Add the oil a few drops at a time, all the while grinding with the pestle in a circular motion, until the garlic appears to be blended into the oil. You might not need all the oil. Pass the alioli and the lemon wedges at table.

Vegetable Rice in Fish Stock

Serves 6 to 8

With a few added ingredients, rice cooked in fish stock becomes a more substantial first course or side dish with fish. The dish works as well with eggplant or artichokes or both or neither, depending on how simple or elaborate you want it.

> *all the ingredients for the fish stock in Rice Cooked in*
> *   Fish Stock (preceding recipe)*
> *½ pound eggplant, peeled and cut into 1-inch dice, or 3*
> *   or 4 small artichokes, or both*
> *3 to 6 tablespoons olive oil*
> *1 onion, chopped*
> *1 pound fresh ripe tomatoes, peeled, seeded, and chopped,*
> *   or 1 cup canned Italian plum tomatoes, seeded and*
> *   chopped, without juice from can*
> *3 cloves garlic, minced*
> *½ cup parsley, chopped fine*
> *⅓ pound fresh green beans, trimmed and cut into 2 or 3 lengths*
> *1 red bell pepper, cut into thin strips*

2 cups Valencian or Italian arborio rice
2 teaspoons paprika
½ teaspoon hot red pepper flakes (optional)
2 teaspoons fresh or 1 teaspoon dried oregano or thyme
salt and freshly ground black pepper to taste
4 cloves garlic, flattened and very finely minced
up to ½ cup extra-virgin olive oil
2 lemons, quartered lengthwise

Put all the stock ingredients in a large spaghetti pot with 6 cups of water. Bring to a boil, cover with the lid slightly ajar, then adjust heat to boil gently 30 minutes. Strain through a sieve, discard solids, and return stock to the pot. Boil another 30 minutes to reduce to 4½ cups.

If using eggplant, spread the cubes in a colander placed over a plate or bowl. Sprinkle with salt and allow to drain 30 to 60 minutes. Then rinse with cold water and dry between layers of paper towel.

If using artichokes, remove and discard the outer, bottom layer of leaves. Slice off the pointed leaf tips at the top and cut off the tips of the other leaves. Cut the artichokes in half lengthwise, if small, or in quarters lengthwise, if medium-size.

Heat 3 tablespoons oil in a large nonstick skillet over medium heat. Add eggplant, if using, and cook, stirring occasionally, until lightly browned, about 10 minutes. Remove with slotted spoon and set aside on paper towel.

Add up to 3 more tablespoons oil (if pan is dry) and heat. Add onion and cook, stirring occasionally, over medium-low heat about 20 minutes, until brown but not burned. Add tomatoes and cook, stirring, until very thick. Add garlic, parsley, green beans, and red bell pepper. Cook, stirring, for 5 minutes. Add rice and stir to coat with oil and tomatoes. Return eggplant to the pan. Add artichokes if using. Stir in paprika and optional pepper flakes. Add stock with oregano or thyme, salt, and pepper. Bring to a boil. Cook uncovered 20 to 25 minutes, beginning over medium-high heat and gradually reducing heat to very low. During cooking time, move the skillet back and forth a bit now and then if needed for even cooking. (See page 152 for electric stove and oven alternatives.) Remove from heat, cover with a dish towel, and let sit 10 minutes. (Or rest over very low heat as suggested on page 152.)

While the rice is resting, make the alioli (oil and garlic sauce) as directed in the previous recipe. Pass the alioli and the lemon wedges at table.

Rice with Bacalao, Eggplant, and Peppers

Serves 3 or 4

Bacalao is Spanish for salt cod, enjoyed in Mediterranean Europe for more than one thousand years. If unfamiliar with salt cod, see page 115 for directions on soaking, which should begin a day before you plan to cook it.

> *1 medium or 2 or 3 small eggplants (1 pound total),*
>   *unpeeled, cut into strips about 3 inches long and*
>   *½ inch wide*
> *3½ cups fish stock (page 153), bottled clam juice mixed*
>   *with water, or Vegetable Stock (page 28)*
> *½ teaspoon hot red pepper flakes*
> *½ teaspoon saffron threads, crumbled*
> *4 to 6 tablespoons olive oil*
> *1 medium-large onion, cut in half lengthwise, then sliced thin*
> *3 large cloves garlic, chopped*
> *1 green and 1 red bell pepper (or 3 small bell peppers,*
>   *1 green, 1 red, and 1 yellow), seeded, cored, and*
>   *cut into thin strips*
> *½ pound boneless, skinless salt cod, soaked, drained, and*
>   *cut into ½-inch squares*
> *6 canned Italian plum tomatoes, without juice*
> *1 tablespoon fresh thyme leaves or 1 teaspoon dried*
> *1½ cups Valencian or Italian arborio rice*

Sprinkle eggplants with salt and spread in a colander placed over a plate or bowl. Allow to drain 30 to 60 minutes. Then rinse and dry between layers of paper towel.

Heat stock or clam juice in a small saucepan and stir in the pepper flakes and saffron. Keep hot but not boiling.

Heat 3 tablespoons oil in a large nonstick skillet. Add eggplant and cook, stirring often, until slightly browned. Remove with slotted spoon to drain on paper towel. Add more oil as needed. When hot, add onion and cook over medium heat 5 minutes. Add garlic and peppers and cook, stirring often, until soft, about 5 minutes. Add fish and cook on both sides, 5 minutes in all. Add tomatoes and break up with a wooden spoon. Stir in thyme and cook 5 minutes. Add rice, stir to coat, and cook 5 minutes. Bring broth to a boil and pour evenly over the mixture. Cook uncovered 20 to 25 minutes, beginning over medium-high heat and gradually reducing heat to very low. During cooking time, move the skillet back and forth a bit now and then if needed for even cooking. (See note on page 152 for electric stove and oven variations.) Remove from heat, cover with a dish towel, and let rest 10 minutes. (Or rest over very low heat as suggested on page 152.)

Arroz Negro I
Catalan Black Rice

Serves 4 as a first course

This version of the Barcelona classic makes a dramatic opening for a seafood dinner.

My Barcelona sources say the cuttlefish used for black rice in Spain has more and stronger-flavored ink than does the squid available here, which can't be counted on to yield much ink. My solution is to have a few packets of squid ink, sold in specialty groceries, to supplement what the squid on hand supply. The packets contain about 1 teaspoon of ink apiece. Even with 2 packets the rice still won't be really black, but it will have a decided black cast. Buying cleaned squid and getting all the ink from packets simplifies the preparation considerably.

> *all the ingredients for the fish stock in Rice Cooked in*
>   *Fish Stock (page 152), but with head and bones of*
>   *only 1 fish*
> *1½ pounds squid*
> *1 or 2 packets squid ink*
> *1 red bell pepper*
> *1 dried mild red chile such as New Mexico or ancho*
> *3 tablespoons olive oil*
> *1 medium-large onion, chopped*
> *1 pound fresh ripe tomatoes, skinned, seeded, and*
>   *chopped, or 1 cup canned Italian tomatoes, seeded*
>   *and chopped, without juice from can*

1¼ cups Valencian or Italian arborio rice
¼ teaspoon hot red pepper flakes (optional)
¼ teaspoon saffron threads, crumbled
salt and freshly ground black pepper to taste
4 cloves garlic, flattened and very finely minced
up to ½ cup extra-virgin olive oil
1 lemon, quartered lengthwise

Put all the stock ingredients in a large pot with 6 cups water. Bring to a boil, then cover pot with the lid slightly ajar. Adjust heat to boil gently 30 minutes. Strain through a sieve, discard solids, and return stock to the pot. Boil another 30 minutes or so to reduce to 3 cups.

To clean the squid, grab the outer body with one hand and the tentacles and head with the other hand; pull the tentacles, head, and innards from the body. Cut off and reserve the tentacles, leaving the eyes connected to the innards. Cut the tentacles into shorter lengths. Look for two long silvery ink sacs on the sides of the innards. Carefully remove the sacs to a small sieve held over a small bowl. Discard head and innards. From the body pull out and discard the long transparent quill-like bone. Rinse body under running water, cleaning out and discarding any stuff left inside the body. Peel off the pink skin and slice the body into rings. Break the ink sacs and push the ink through the sieve into the bowl. Pour ½ cup warm water through the sieve into the bowl with the ink. Unless all or most of the sacs were intact and filled with ink, stir in 1 or 2 packets of squid ink.

Roast and peel the red pepper as directed on page 49. Discard core and seeds and cut the pepper into strips.

Roast the dried chile 2 minutes on each side in a small unoiled frying pan over medium heat. Remove from heat, cut open, and remove and discard seeds, veins, and stems. Break into pieces and grind to a powder in a coffee or spice grinder.

Heat the oil in a paella pan or a large heavy skillet over medium-low heat. Add the onion and cook, stirring occasionally, about 20 minutes, until brown but not burned. Add tomato and cook, stirring, until very thick. Add most of the red pepper (reserving a few strips to decorate the top) and cook, stirring, 2 or 3 minutes. Add the squid rings and tentacles and cook, stirring, 2 or 3 minutes. Add rice and stir to coat with oil and tomato. Stir in all the ink and water, using a rubber spatula to scrape it from the bowl. Add hot stock, then the ground chile, the optional pepper flakes, and the saffron, salt, and pepper. Cook 20 to 25 minutes, beginning over medium-high heat and gradually reducing heat to very low. During cooking time, move the skillet back and forth a bit now and then if needed for even cooking. (See page 152 for electric stove and oven alternatives.) Remove from heat. Arrange reserved pepper strips over the rice. Cover with a dish towel and let sit 10 minutes. (Or rest over very low heat as suggested on page 152.)

While the rice is resting, make the alioli as directed on page 154. Pass the alioli and lemon wedges at table.

Arroz Negro II
Catalan Black Rice

Serves 8 as a first course; 4 or 5 as a main dish

This expansive arroz negro, a specialty of Barcelona, takes some time to prepare but very little to consume as a one-dish meal.

The stock:

all the ingredients for the fish stock in Rice Cooked
in Fish Stock (page 152)

The seafood:

16 littleneck clams or mussels, or 8 of each
½ pound shrimp, with heads if possible
1½ pounds squid
up to 3 packets squid ink
½ pound monkfish or halibut fillets, cut into 1½-inch squares

The rice:

1 red bell pepper
1 dried mild red chile such as New Mexico or ancho
3 tablespoons olive oil
1 medium-large onion, chopped

1 pound fresh ripe tomatoes, skinned, seeded, and
chopped, or 1 cup canned Italian plum tomatoes,
seeded and chopped, without juice from can
2¼ cups Valencian or Italian arborio rice
¼ to ½ teaspoon hot red pepper flakes (optional)
¼ to ½ teaspoon saffron threads, crumbled
salt and freshly ground black pepper to taste
1 cup shelled fresh green peas, if available, or 1 cup
any fresh peas in pods (such as sugar snap peas
or snow peas)

The alioli:

4 cloves garlic, flattened and very finely minced
salt to taste
up to ½ cup extra-virgin olive oil

2 lemons, quartered lengthwise

Put all the stock ingredients in a large pot with 7 cups of water. (If you are shelling the shrimp, add shells to the stock.) Bring to a boil and cover, leaving lid slightly ajar. Adjust heat to boil gently for 30 minutes. Strain through a sieve, discard solids, and return stock to the pot. Boil another 20 to 30 minutes to reduce to 4½ cups.

Put the clams in cool salted water with a handful of cornmeal for 1 to 3 hours, to draw out the sand. Then scrub the clams, discarding any that have opened, and refrigerate until ready to use.

Debeard and scrub the mussels, discarding any that have opened.

Shell and devein the shrimp if you prefer, or have them the Catalan way with shells and heads attached.

Clean and slice the squid and mix the ink with water, adding extra packets of ink as needed, as directed in the preceding recipe. (Or buy cleaned squid and ink packets.)

Roast and peel the red pepper as directed on page 49. Discard core and seeds and cut pepper into strips.

Roast the dried chile for 2 minutes on each side in a small unoiled frying pan over medium heat. Remove from heat, cut open, and remove and discard seeds, veins, and stems. Break into pieces and grind to a powder in a coffee or spice grinder.

Heat the oil in a paella pan or a large, heavy, nonstick skillet over medium-low heat. Add shrimp and cook 1 minute on each side. Remove and set aside. Add the onion and cook, stirring occasionally, about 20 minutes, until brown but not burned. Add tomato and cook, stirring, until very thick. Add most of the red pepper (reserving a few strips to decorate the top) and cook, stirring, 2 or 3 minutes. Add the squid rings and tentacles and cook, stirring, 2 or 3 minutes. Add the monkfish and cook about 1 minute on each side. Add rice and stir to coat with oil and tomato. Stir in all the ink and water, using a rubber spatula to scrape it from the bowl. Add stock, then the ground chile and optional pepper flakes. Crumble and add the saffron. Add salt and pepper. Cook uncovered over medium-high heat for 10 minutes. Stir in the peas. Press clams and/or mussels, hinged side down, into the rice mixture. Reduce heat to simmer steadily, still uncovered, 10 to 15 minutes, moving the skillet now and then if needed for even cooking. (See page 152 for electric stove and oven alternatives.)

Remove from heat. (Or leave on burner and turn heat as low as possible as suggested on page 152.) Spread the shrimp and the reserved pepper strips over the rice mixture. Cover with a dish towel and let sit 10 minutes. Then, if any clams or mussels have failed to open, boil or steam them for a few minutes in broth or water. Discard any that still won't open and return the others to the rice.

While the rice is resting, make the alioli as directed on page 154. Pass the alioli and lemon wedges at table.

Arroz con Pollo

Serves 4 or 5 as a main dish

Versions of this chicken with rice are popular in North America, where the dish is known by its Spanish name but usually cooked in a deep casserole using long-grain rice. Here the familiar ingredients are cooked with Spanish rice and in the Spanish manner.

Because Spanish-style arroz con pollo lacks the taste-intensive accents common in Caribbean dishes of the same name, it depends for flavor on a good strong homemade broth. You might use the chicken stock on page 29 but with the reduced or browned variations described on pages 28 and 32.

1 chicken, cut up as directed
salt and freshly ground black pepper to taste
1 tablespoon paprika
5 tablespoons olive oil
1 red bell pepper, chopped
1 green bell pepper, chopped
1 medium onion, chopped
2 large cloves garlic, minced
2 fresh tomatoes, skinned, seeded, and chopped, or 1 cup
  canned Italian plum tomatoes, seeded and chopped,
  without juice from can
2 cups Valencian or Italian arborio rice
½ cup dry white wine
4 cups hot chicken stock
½ teaspoon saffron threads, crumbled
1 teaspoon fresh thyme leaves or ½ teaspoon dried
salt and freshly ground black pepper to taste

Cut the chicken (or have it cut) into 2 drumsticks, 2 thighs, 4 breast pieces, a back, 2 wings, and 2 wing tips. Then cut the thighs in half and cut the knobby bone ends off the drumsticks. Reserve back, wing tips, and neck for making stock. Sprinkle remaining pieces with salt, pepper, and paprika.

Heat the oil over medium heat in a paella pan or a large heavy skillet. Add chicken legs and cook 10 minutes, turning to brown on both sides. With the legs still in the pan, add remaining chicken pieces and cook 10 minutes, turning to brown on both sides. Remove chicken pieces and set aside. Add peppers, onion, and garlic to pan and cook, stirring occasionally, until soft. Add tomatoes and cook 5 minutes. Add rice and stir to coat. Add wine and cook until absorbed. Add stock, then saffron and thyme. Add salt and pepper. Return chicken to pan and bring to a boil.

Cook uncovered 20 to 25 minutes, beginning on medium-high heat and gradually reducing heat to very low. During cooking time move the skillet a bit now and then if needed for even cooking. (See page 152 for electric stove and oven alternatives.) Remove from heat, cover with a dish towel, and let rest another 10 minutes. (Or rest over very low heat as suggested on page 152.)

A Paella Valenciana

Serves 5 or 6 as a main dish

In Valencia, where the dish was born, paella is a pristine affair. Traditionalists like to point out that the original paellas were merely rice from the local marshlands mixed with two or three kinds of beans and seasoned with some local land snails. Some would allow eels from a local lagoon on the short list of founding ingredients. Today, some Valencians are giving in to what purists call baroque extravagance, and restaurants indulge huge parties with paellas made in giant pans far bigger than the average New York kitchen. But most would add to "true" paella Valenciana only a little chicken or rabbit, perhaps a bit (but not too much) of each, perhaps one or the other with some pork or duck or frog meat. Valencians advise foreigners who can't get their fresh land snails to substitute rosemary, because that's the flavor that the snails give off from their wild rosemary diet. Along the coast another paella, made with seafood, has been long established, but Valencians still look askance at mixing fish and shellfish with chicken and meat — "a very common mistake" made by outsiders, chides Alicia Rios in *The Heritage of Spanish Cooking*.

Still, outsiders to whom paella wouldn't be paella without "the works" can find some precedent in the equally serious rice cooking of Catalonia, Valencia's neighbor to the north and the source of the mixed paella given on page 164.

In both of the following paella recipes, the amount of rice is limited by the size of our standard large skillets and our standard stovetop burners. If you choose to use two pans, or use a large paella pan over two burners and then in the oven, you could use $2\frac{1}{2}$ to 3 cups of rice and 5 to 6 cups of stock without increasing the amounts of other ingredients.

> *1 dried mild red chile such as New Mexico or ancho,*
>   *if available, or 1 teaspoon paprika*
> *3 tablespoons olive oil*
> *3 to 4 pounds chicken, rabbit, duck, or any combination,*
>   *cut into a total of 10 to 12 pieces*
> *3 cloves garlic, minced*
> *2 tablespoons parsley, minced*

1 large fresh tomato, peeled, seeded, and chopped as
directed on page 48, or 3 canned Italian plum
tomatoes, seeded and chopped, without juice from can
½ pound fresh green beans, trimmed and cut in half
2 cups Valencian or Italian arborio rice
1 cup peeled fresh fava beans or 1 cup cooked dried
white beans such as great northern
4¼ cups browned or reduced chicken or duck or
chicken/duck stock, hot
¼ to ½ teaspoon saffron threads, crumbled
2 or 3 sprigs fresh rosemary
salt and freshly ground black pepper to taste

Roast the dried chile, if using, 2 minutes on each side in a small unoiled frying pan over medium heat. Remove from heat, cut open, and remove and discard seeds, veins, and stems. Break into pieces and grind to a powder in a coffee or spice grinder.

Heat oil in a paella pan or a large heavy skillet over medium-high heat. In two batches, add the chicken, rabbit, and/or duck pieces and cook 10 minutes on each side. Prick duck pieces to drain off as much fat as possible. Remove to paper towel.

Remove all but about 3 tablespoons of fat from the pan. Add garlic, parsley, and tomato and cook, stirring, until tomato is almost dry. Stir in the green beans, then the rice, and cook, stirring, to coat. Stir in the favas or white beans, then the hot stock. Add the saffron, rosemary, ground chile or paprika, salt, and pepper. Cook 20 to 25 minutes, beginning over medium-high heat and gradually reducing heat to very low. Shift skillet back and forth a bit during the cooking time if needed for even cooking. (For electric stove and oven alternatives see page 152.) Remove from heat, cover with a cloth dish towel, and let rest 10 minutes. (Or rest over very low heat as suggested on page 152.)

Catalan Mixed Paella

Serves 6 as a main dish

"Valencian paellas don't mix meat and seafood," admits my Catalan rice adviser Gabriel Yuc, who does. "In Barcelona we put in lots of things, but only a little bit of any one thing. In Spain the rice is the important thing. In America, the important thing is lots of things."

For this mixed paella, geared to the capacity of a large cast-iron skillet, I have tried to balance American expectations of lots of things with a respectable portion of rice, the important thing. Thus most of the seafood is cooked separately, then set on top of the paella. Still, if you are making this in a paella pan, you could use up to 3 cups of rice and 6 cups of stock without increasing amounts of the other ingredients.

The recipe begins with the fried onion-and-tomato sofrito (sofregit in Catalan) that is a mark of Catalan cooking. Gabriel cooks the onion until it's "almost burnt" and the tomato until it's "almost dry."

18 to 24 littleneck clams or mussels, or some of each

*2 dried mild red chile peppers such as New Mexico
     or ancho*

3 to 6 tablespoons olive oil

6 jumbo shrimp or prawns, unshelled, with heads if possible

*1 chicken, duck, or rabbit cut into small pieces as in the
     recipe for Arroz con Pollo (page 161)*

*½ pound short pork ribs, cut into separate ribs and
     trimmed of fat, or ⅓ pound lean pork, chopped*

1 medium-large onion, chopped (about 1½ cups chopped)

*1 pound fresh ripe tomatoes, peeled, seeded, and chopped
     (page 48), or 1 cup canned Italian plum tomatoes,
     seeded and chopped, without juice from can*

*½ pound squid, cleaned and cut into rings as directed
     on page 158 (optional)*

3 cloves garlic, minced

4 tablespoons broadleaf parsley, minced

*1 roasted and peeled red bell pepper (page 49), cut into
     thin strips*

½ pound fresh green beans, trimmed and cut into 2 or 3 lengths

*½ pound fresh peeled fava beans or 1 cup cooked dried
     white beans such as great northern*

2¼ cups Valencian or Italian arborio rice

4¾ cups browned or reduced Chicken Stock (page 29)

½ teaspoon saffron threads, crumbled

*1 tablespoon chopped fresh rosemary or 1½ teaspoons
chopped dried rosemary needles
salt and freshly ground black pepper to taste
½ pound sugar snap peas or crisp fresh snow peas,
in pods, or 1 cup shelled fresh green peas*

Soak the clams in cool salted water and scrub the clams and mussels as directed in the recipe for Arroz Negro II, page 159. Discard any that are cracked or opened.

Roast chiles 1 or 2 minutes on each side in a small unoiled skillet over medium heat. Remove from heat, cut open, and remove and discard seeds, veins, and stems. Break into pieces and grind to a powder in a coffee or spice mill.

Heat 3 tablespoons oil in a paella pan or a large cast-iron skillet over medium heat. Add shrimp or prawns and cook 2 to 3 minutes on each side. Remove and set aside. Add chicken, duck, or rabbit pieces. Cook 10 minutes on each side or until well browned. Remove from pan.

Add pork and cook a few minutes on each side to brown. Remove with slotted spoon.

Pour off excess fat or add oil as needed. Add onion and cook over medium-low heat 15 to 20 minutes, until brown but not burned. Add tomatoes and cook until very thick. Add squid and cook, stirring, 5 minutes. Add garlic, parsley, red pepper strips, green beans, and fava beans, if using. Cook, stirring, 5 minutes. Return chicken and pork to the skillet. Add rice and stir to coat. Stir in the ground chiles. Add the stock, saffron, rosemary, salt, and pepper. Bring to a boil, then adjust heat to boil moderately 10 minutes. Reduce heat to a simmer. Stir in fresh peas and cooked dried white beans, if using. Cook, still uncovered, 10 to 15 minutes, moving the skillet a bit now and then if needed for even cooking of the rice. (See page 152 for electric stove and oven alternatives.)

Arrange shrimp or prawns over the paella. Remove from heat. Cover with a dish towel and let rest 10 minutes. (Or rest over very low heat as suggested on page 152.)

While the rice is resting, steam the clams and mussels over broth or water until they open. Discard any that do not open. Arrange on the paella, pressing hinged sides into the rice.

Risotto

To me, stirring risotto can be a blissful way to unwind after work, and having a second helping of risotto can be more satisfying than giving it up for a meat course.

The arbiters of such matters are constantly reminding us that Italians have risotto (or pasta) as a first course only; but that doesn't mean that risotto is a lesser dish and must be followed by a grander one. It's just that Italians don't have a "main dish"; an Italian meal is more like a parade of separate but equal dishes, in contrast to the simultaneous three-ring circus of American custom. As far as I'm concerned, then, an Italian first course can just as well be an American side dish or everyday main dish.

Risotto in any case is not the ideal dish to cook for a crowd. It's hard to work with more than 1½ to 2 cups of dry rice, enough for 6 to 8 as a first course or 3 or 4 as a main dish, though to serve more people a practiced risotto cook can do two risottos side by side in separate pans without much difficulty.

Although I would serve any of these risottos to guests, I usually have risotto (or pasta for that matter) as the main dish at an everyday dinner. I suspect that lots of ordinary Italian families do too. And because I have risotto often, I tend to avoid the more elaborate, meat-fatted, and expensive versions in favor of vegetable risottos with full tastes and strong accents.

Among the risottos that follow, then, the traditional ones have been lightened, but not enough to compromise their essential qualities. (Let's face it, you can't make a risotto worth its name to suit a Pritikin diet.) All hew to the following principles of contemporary-traditional risotto making.

The Rice

All the recipes require Italian medium-grain rice with a firm, pearly-white center that remains slightly chewy even when the risotto is cooked to a creamy consistency and a translucent outer portion that absorbs the cooking liquid and softens to produce the creamy texture. Italian arborio is the variety called for here because it is most widely available in this country, but connoisseurs in Italy praise a newer hybrid, carnaroli, that might be coming to our neighborhoods soon. A third type, vialone nano, is preferred by Venetians who like their risotto looser, or, as they say, "wavy" (*all'onde*), but with a harder center to the grain.

The Cooking Liquid

Unlike its lustier Spanish cousin, paella, risotto does not demand a hefty stock. Although a mild beef broth is traditional with many risottos, most of the recipes included here call for a light chicken stock, often with vegetable stock as an alternative. Seafood risottos can be made with a mild fish stock or a vegetable stock, or with lobster stock, which gives excellent results. Recipes for all these stocks can be found in Chapter Two. Homemade stocks are always tastier than the canned ones available, but I feel that risotto (unlike paella) is well worth making even with canned chicken stock, especially when reinforced with a little dry white wine or mushroom-soaking water.

You can never be sure exactly how much broth or other liquid any given risotto will require; amounts listed in the recipes are approximate. You might have a little left over or you might have to finish with a little more white wine or with water.

The Cooking Fat

A traditional risotto begins by sautéing chopped onion and then the rice in a few tablespoons of butter, sometimes with the addition of chopped pancetta or other Italian ham; then more butter is added for the finish. Today, though, many risotto cooks begin with more heart-sparing olive oil or with some combination of butter and olive oil. I follow their precedent, and usually make the traditional finish of a tablespoon of butter an option where I feel it adds to the dish.

The Cheese

Whenever Parmesan cheese is called for, using genuine Parmigiano-Reggiano imported from Italy pays off enormously in flavor and fragrance. Buy it in wedges, grate the amount needed just before using, and keep it in the refrigerator, tightly double-wrapped in the cheese-store paper and in plastic or aluminum foil or both. For some recipes that call for a sharper flavor, I use the Italian sheep-milk cheese Romano pecorino.

Timing and Texture

Many Italian cookbooks say that the process of stirring in the broth should take 18 to 20 minutes. However, Italian cooking authority Marcella Hazan, who never steers you wrong, advises tasting after 20 but admits to preferring a risotto cooked for 25 to 30 minutes, which I have found more realistic. Still, the cooking should be stopped when the grains are still a bit resistant, since they will continue to cook in the pot for a minute or so.

Risotto with Saffron

Serves 6 as a first course or side dish

Made with a tablespoon or two of chopped bone marrow sautéed at the start, this dish becomes the classic risotto alla milanese traditionally served with the equally classic veal preparation, osso buco. It's the one often cited exception to the rule that risotto is served only as a first course. But with or without the marrow or the osso buco, saffron risotto is an inspired combination.

> *5 cups chicken broth*
> *½ teaspoon saffron threads, crumbled*
> *1 or 2 tablespoons unsalted butter*
> *2 tablespoons olive oil*
> *1 small onion, chopped small*
> *1½ cups arborio rice*
> *½ cup dry white wine*
> *⅓ cup freshly grated Parmigiano-Reggiano cheese*
> *salt and freshly ground black pepper to taste*

Heat the broth in a saucepan. When warm, ladle ½ cup of broth into a cup and add the saffron. Keep the remaining 4½ cups broth warm over a low flame.

On the next burner, heat 1 tablespoon butter and the oil in a large heavy saucepan over medium heat. Add onion and sauté until soft but not brown. Add rice and cook, stirring, 2 or 3 minutes. Add wine and cook, stirring, until liquid is evaporated. Add saffron broth and cook, stirring, until liquid is evaporated. Ladle a half-cup broth into the cup that held the saffron broth and pour that into the rice. (This helps pick up any precious saffron left behind in the cup.) Continue to add broth $\frac{1}{2}$ cup at a time, stirring constantly and wiping the sides and bottom of the pot to prevent sticking. As each addition of broth is absorbed, add the next. After the rice has cooked for a total of 20 or 30 minutes and is creamy on the outside but still a bit firm in the center of each grain, remove from heat. Stir in the cheese, the remaining tablespoon butter, if using, and the salt and pepper.

Risotto with Fresh Mushrooms

Serves 6 as a first course, 3 or 4 as a main dish

The depth of flavor from good mushrooms, fresh or dried, enhances a risotto. For a recipe using dried porcini mushrooms, see the Risotto with Roasted Vegetables and Smoked Mozzarella on page 178.

> *4 tablespoons olive oil*
> *1 or 2 tablespoons unsalted butter*
> *$\frac{1}{2}$ pound mixed fresh mushrooms such as shiitake,*
> *   cremini, and portobello, chopped*
> *$\frac{1}{2}$ cup dry white wine*
> *1 small onion, chopped small*
> *2 cloves garlic, minced*
> *$1\frac{1}{2}$ cups arborio rice*
> *5 cups hot chicken or vegetable broth*
> *1 tablespoon fresh thyme leaves or 1 teaspoon dried*
> *$\frac{1}{4}$ cup chopped parsley*
> *$\frac{1}{3}$ cup freshly grated Parmigiano-Reggiano cheese*
> *salt and freshly ground black pepper to taste*

Heat 1 tablespoon olive oil and 1 tablespoon butter in a medium-size nonstick skillet. Add mushrooms and cook until soft. Add $\frac{1}{4}$ cup wine. Reduce heat to very low and cook 5 minutes. Remove from heat and set aside.

Heat 3 tablespoons oil in a large heavy saucepan over medium heat. Add onion and cook until soft but not brown. Add garlic and cook until soft, 1 or 2 minutes. Add rice and cook, stirring, 2 or 3 minutes. Add the remaining $\frac{1}{4}$ cup wine and cook, stirring, until liquid is absorbed. Begin stirring in the chicken broth $\frac{1}{2}$ cup at a time, stirring constantly and wiping the sides and bottom of the pan to prevent sticking. As each addition of broth is absorbed, add the next. When almost done, stir in the thyme, then the mushrooms, then the parsley. Add more broth, stirring as before, until rice is done, creamy on the outside but still a bit firm in the center of each grain. Remove from heat and stir in the cheese, the remaining tablespoon butter, if using, and the salt and pepper.

Red Pepper Risotto

Serves 6 as a first course, 3 or 4 as a main dish

Smooth, flavorful pureed roasted pepper or bright red accents of diced fresh pepper? I refuse to choose between them.

> *2 medium red bell peppers plus $\frac{1}{2}$ medium or 1 small one*
> *3 tablespoons olive oil*
> *1 large clove garlic, minced*
> *1 small onion, chopped small*
> *1$\frac{1}{2}$ cups arborio rice*
> *5 cups hot chicken or vegetable broth*
> *$\frac{1}{3}$ cup freshly grated Parmigiano-Reggiano cheese*
> *salt and freshly ground black pepper to taste*

Roast and peel the two medium peppers as directed on page 49. Chop and puree to a paste in a food processor. Cut the remaining pepper into small dice.

Heat the oil in a large heavy saucepan over medium heat. Add garlic and onion and sauté until soft. Add diced pepper and cook, stirring, 1 minute. Add rice and cook, stirring, until liquid is absorbed. Continue adding the broth $\frac{1}{2}$ cup at a time, stirring constantly and wiping the sides and bottom of the pan to prevent sticking. As each addition of broth is absorbed, add the next. After 20 to 25 minutes, when the risotto is almost done, stir in the red pepper puree. Continue to stir in the broth until the grains of rice are creamy on the outside but still a bit firm in the center. Remove from heat. Stir in the cheese, then the salt and pepper.

Variation

For a colorful variation on Red Pepper Risotto, use 3 small bell peppers, 1 red, 1 yellow, and 1 green. Roast and peel all the peppers as directed on page 49, then remove and discard the stems, cores, veins, and seeds and cut the peppers into thin strips. Proceed with the recipe but omit the diced pepper and instead of the pureed pepper, stir in the pepper strips.

Risotto with Squash

Serves 6 as a first course, 3 or 4 as a main dish

Some squash risotto recipes have the cook puree the squash to pervade the risotto; others chop it and scatter it through in discrete bits. This one, like the Red Pepper Risotto, on page 171, has it both ways.

1 very small butternut squash (about 1 pound) or a
1-pound piece, peeled, seeded, cleaned, and chopped
into $\frac{1}{4}$-inch to $\frac{1}{2}$-inch dice (about 3 cups diced)
2 tablespoons olive oil
1 or 2 tablespoons unsalted butter
1 medium leek, white and light green parts, chopped
small (about $\frac{1}{2}$ cup chopped)
1$\frac{1}{2}$ pounds arborio rice
$\frac{1}{2}$ cup dry white wine
5 cups hot chicken broth
3 tablespoons chopped fresh sage leaves or 1 tablespoon
dried crumbled (not powdered) sage leaf
$\frac{1}{3}$ cup freshly grated Parmigiano-Reggiano cheese
salt and freshly ground black pepper to taste

Set aside 1 cup of the diced squash. Steam or boil the other 2 cups until very soft, then mash with a fork or potato masher or puree in a food processor.

Heat the oil and 1 tablespoon of the butter in a large heavy saucepan over medium heat. Add leek and cook 2 or 3 minutes. Add the uncooked cup of diced squash and cook 5 minutes, stirring occasionally. Stir in the rice and cook 2 or 3 minutes. Add wine and cook, stirring, until absorbed. Add $\frac{1}{2}$ cup of broth and cook, stirring, until liquid is absorbed. Continue to add the broth $\frac{1}{2}$ cup at a time. As each addition is absorbed, add the next, stirring constantly and wiping the sides and bottom of the pot to prevent sticking. When nearly done, stir in the sage, then the mashed squash. Add more broth until the rice has cooked 20 to 30 minutes and is creamy on the outside but still a bit firm in the center. Remove from heat. Stir in the cheese, the optional tablespoon butter, and the salt and pepper.

Risotto Primavera

Serves 6 to 8 as a first course, 3 or 4 as a main dish

Now that fresh vegetables from somewhere are available all year, this risotto needn't be restricted to the primavera season. However, if fresh asparagus and fresh peas are not to be had, cook a different vegetable risotto and wait for spring.

> *$\frac{1}{2}$ pound fresh asparagus*
> *$\frac{1}{2}$ pound fresh green beans, cut into $1\frac{1}{2}$-inch lengths*
> *$\frac{1}{3}$ cup pine nuts*
> *2 tablespoons olive oil*
> *2 tablespoons butter*
> *1 small leek or 3 large scallions, white and light green
>   parts, chopped small, or 2 tablespoons minced
>   shallots*
> *1 small or $\frac{1}{2}$ medium zucchini, diced*
> *$1\frac{1}{2}$ cups arborio rice*
> *$\frac{1}{2}$ cup dry white wine*
> *5 cups homemade vegetable broth or freshly extracted
>   carrot and celery juice or light chicken broth, hot*

1 cup shelled fresh peas
3 fresh plum tomatoes, skinned, seeded, and chopped (page 48)
¼ cup coarsely chopped fresh basil leaves
¼ cup heavy cream (optional)
⅓ cup freshly grated Parmigiano-Reggiano cheese
salt and freshly ground black pepper to taste

Snap off the stem ends of the asparagus stalks and discard or save for stock. Cut off tips and set aside. If stalks are not very thin, peel them with a vegetable peeler. If they are thick, peel them and blanch them in boiling stock or water for 3 or 4 minutes. Cut all stalks into 1½-inch lengths.

If you like the beans very tender, blanch them in boiling water for 4 or 5 minutes. (I don't.)

Toast pine nuts on an unoiled pan in a preheated 350°F oven or toaster oven 5 minutes, until golden but not dark brown.

Heat oil and 1 tablespoon butter over medium heat in a large heavy-bottomed saucepan. Add leek, scallions, or shallots and cook, stirring, 5 minutes. Add zucchini and cook 5 minutes or until soft. Add rice and cook, stirring, 2 or 3 minutes. Add wine and stir until liquid disappears. Add ½ cup broth and cook, stirring, until liquid is absorbed. Continue adding broth ½ cup at a time, stirring up from the bottom of the pan to prevent sticking. As each ½ cup of broth is absorbed, add the next. After the first 7 or 8 minutes, stir in the green beans, then the asparagus stalks but not the tips. Stir in more broth, then stir in the peas. After another 10 minutes, or when the risotto is almost done, stir in the asparagus tips, then the tomatoes, then the basil. After about 2 minutes remove from heat. Stir in the cream, if using, then the butter, then the cheese, salt, and pepper.

Risotto with Asparagus and Peas

Serves 6 as a first course or side dish, 3 or 4 as a main dish

This is risotto primavera at its most pristine and, arguably, its most delicious.

1 pound fresh asparagus
2 tablespoons olive oil

2 tablespoons minced shallots or scallions
1½ cups arborio rice
½ cup dry white wine
¼ teaspoon saffron threads, crumbled
5 cups steaming-hot homemade vegetable broth or
*   freshly extracted carrot and celery juice or*
*   light chicken broth*
1 cup shelled fresh peas
2 tablespoons chopped fresh basil leaves
1 tablespoon butter
¼ cup freshly grated Parmigiano-Reggiano cheese
salt and freshly ground black pepper to taste

Snap off the stem ends of the asparagus stalks and discard or save for stock. Cut off tips and set aside. If stalks are not very thin, peel them with a vegetable peeler. If they are thick, peel them and blanch them in boiling stock or water for 3 or 4 minutes. Cut all stalks into 1½-inch lengths.

Heat oil over medium heat in a large heavy-bottomed saucepan. Add shallots or scallions and cook, stirring, 5 minutes. Add rice and cook, stirring, 2 or 3 minutes. Add wine and stir until liquid disappears. Drop saffron into the broth, then add ½ cup broth to the risotto and cook, stirring, until liquid is absorbed. Continue adding broth ½ cup at a time. As each ½ cup of broth is absorbed, add the next. After the first 7 or 8 minutes, stir in the asparagus stalks but not the tips. Stir in more broth, stirring rice up from the bottom to prevent sticking, then stir in the peas. Continue stirring in the broth for another 10 to 12 minutes, until the risotto is almost done, then stir in the asparagus tips. Cook 2 minutes, or until tips are soft and rice is creamy on the outside but a bit al dente. Remove from heat and stir in the basil, then the butter, then the cheese. Add salt and pepper as needed.

Variation

After cutting up the asparagus, marinate briefly in ¼ cup lemon juice until ready to add. To transfer to the risotto, remove from the juice with a slotted spoon. Splash some of the residual lemon juice into the risotto just before stirring in the cheese.

Golden Vegetable Risotto

Serves 6 as a first course, 3 or 4 as a main dish

I've borrowed the fresh, naturally sweetish carrot and celery juices used in this vegetable risotto from the Risotto d'Oro that executive chef Michael Romano made famous at Manhattan's Union Square Cafe and once demonstrated for a crowd of shoppers at Macy's Cellar at Herald Square. For those who don't have a juicer, he suggests buying bottled juice at a natural-foods store or specialty grocery. But it's really the fresh extraction that gives a juice-bathed risotto its vibrancy and mystique.

> *3 cups carrot juice, freshly extracted*
> *2 cups celery juice, freshly extracted*
> *3 tablespoons olive oil*
> *3 or 4 scallions, sliced thin*
> *1 clove garlic, minced*
> *1½ cups arborio rice*
> *½ cup white wine*
> *1 small carrot, peeled and diced*
> *½ orange, yellow, or red bell pepper, diced*
> *1 small or ½ medium zucchini or yellow summer squash, diced*
> *¾ cup small broccoli florets*
> *½ cup freshly grated Parmigiano-Reggiano cheese*
> *salt and freshly ground black pepper to taste*
> *1 tablespoon chopped broadleaf parsley*

Heat carrot and celery juice in a small saucepan and keep warm over a low flame.

On the next burner, heat the oil in a large heavy saucepan over medium heat. Add scallion whites and garlic and cook, stirring, until well coated with oil. Add rice and cook, stirring, until well coated with oil. Add wine and cook, stirring, until liquid is absorbed. Stir in the carrot. Add the warm juice ½ cup at a time, stirring constantly to prevent sticking. As each addition of juice is absorbed, add the next. After about 12 minutes, stir in the pepper and zucchini. About 5 minutes later add the broccoli. Continue adding juice and stirring as before. After a total of about 25 minutes, when the grains of rice are creamy on the outside but still slightly al dente in the center, remove from heat. Stir in the cheese, salt, pepper, scallion greens, and parsley.

Risotto with Mozzarella and Hot Red Pepper Flakes

Serves 6 as a first course, 3 or 4 as a main dish

Use the full teaspoon of hot pepper flakes to make what Italians would call a risotto *arrabbiata*, or *angry*. The fresh mozzarella mellows the mood.

> 3 tablespoons olive oil
> 2 cloves garlic, minced
> 1 small onion, minced
> 1½ cups arborio rice
> 5 cups hot chicken broth
> 1 tablespoon tomato paste
> 4 or 5 tablespoons sun-dried tomatoes, cut into thin strips
> 3 tablespoons pitted and chopped black olives, such as
>   gaeta or oil-cured Sicilian (about 12 olives)
> ½ red pepper, roasted and peeled as directed on page 49,
>   or from a jar of roasted red peppers, cut into thin
>   2-inch-long strips
> ½ to 1 teaspoon hot red pepper flakes
> 6 ounces mozzarella, fresh if possible, shredded or diced
> ½ cup chopped broadleaf parsley
> salt and freshly ground black pepper to taste
> 2 tablespoons freshly grated Parmigiano-Reggiano cheese

Heat the oil in a large heavy saucepan over medium heat. Add garlic and onion and cook, stirring, until soft but not brown. Add rice and cook, stirring, 2 or 3 minutes. Add ½ cup hot broth and cook, stirring, until broth is absorbed. Continue adding the broth ½ cup at a time, stirring constantly and wiping the bottom and sides of the pan to prevent sticking. As each addition of broth is absorbed, add the next. After using about ⅔ of the broth, stir in the tomato paste mixed with a little broth, then the sun-dried tomatoes, olives, pepper strips, and pepper flakes. Continue stirring and adding broth until the rice is done, creamy on the outside but still slightly chewy in the center of each grain. Turn off the heat and stir in the mozzarella, then the parsley. Add salt and pepper. Sprinkle with the grated cheese. Allow to sit 2 or 3 minutes before serving.

Risotto with Roasted Vegetables and Smoked Mozzarella

Serves 6 to 8 as a first course, 4 as a main dish

This aromatic, earthy, and full-flavored risotto makes a substantial informal dinner with Italian bread, a tossed green salad, and a bottle of Italian wine.

> *4 or 5 dried porcini or shiitake mushrooms ($\frac{1}{2}$ ounce)*
> *6 tablespoons extra-virgin olive oil*
> *1 green Italian pepper, cored, seeded, and coarsely chopped*
>   *into 1- to 1$\frac{1}{2}$-inch pieces*
> *1 large red bell pepper, cored, seeded, and coarsely*
>   *chopped into 1- to 1$\frac{1}{2}$-inch pieces*
> *2 medium onions, peeled and cut into 8 pieces each*
> *1 tablespoon chopped fresh rosemary needles*
> *6 to 8 whole unpeeled cloves garlic*
> *1$\frac{1}{2}$ cups arborio rice*
> *1 tablespoon chopped fresh oregano or 1 tablespoon fresh thyme leaves*
> *5 cups hot vegetable or chicken broth*
> *6 ounces smoked mozzarella, shredded or diced*
> *$\frac{1}{4}$ cup freshly grated Parmigiano-Reggiano cheese*
> *salt and freshly ground black pepper to taste*

Soak mushrooms in $\frac{1}{2}$ cup warm water for 20 to 30 minutes. Remove and pat dry on paper towel. Cut off and discard tough stems (if using shiitake) and cut smaller caps in half, large ones into quarters. Strain mushroom-soaking water through a coffee filter and reserve.

While mushrooms are soaking, preheat oven to 400°F. Use 2 tablespoons of olive oil to coat a shallow baking pan large enough to hold the vegetables without crowding. Add the green and red pepper pieces to the pan and toss them in the oil to coat. Mince about $\frac{1}{4}$ of the onion pieces and set aside. Add the remaining onion pieces to the roasting pan and toss to coat with oil. (Don't worry if the pieces fall into smaller pieces.) Sprinkle half the rosemary over vegetables in pan. Put the garlic cloves on a piece of aluminum foil. Pour 1 tablespoon oil over the garlic, then fold up the foil to wrap the garlic in a sealed bundle. Add this to the roasting pan. Roast for 20 minutes, then toss the vegetables with a spatula. Add mushrooms to the pan and toss to coat with oil. Roast another 10 minutes. When done, onions should be starting to turn an amber color and both onions and peppers will be starting to turn black around the edges. Remove from oven. Remove the garlic from the foil and peel and smash the softened cloves. Scrape up with a knife and hold on the knife blade until needed.

Heat 3 tablespoons oil in a large heavy saucepan over medium heat. Add the minced onion and cook 3 to 5 minutes until soft. Add rice and cook, stirring, 2 or 3 minutes. Add reserved mushroom-soaking broth and cook, stirring, until liquid is absorbed. Stir in the oregano and remaining rosemary. Add $\frac{1}{2}$ cup hot vegetable or chicken broth and cook, stirring, until liquid is absorbed. Continue adding broth $\frac{1}{2}$ cup at a time, stirring constantly and wiping the sides and bottom of the pot to prevent sticking. When nearly done, scatter garlic around the top and stir it in; garlic should disappear into the risotto. Then stir in the roasted vegetables. When the grains are creamy on the outside but still slightly firm in the center, 20 to 30 minutes after adding the rice, remove from heat. Stir in the mozzarella, then the grated cheese, then the salt and pepper. Let sit 1 or 2 minutes before serving.

Scallop Risotto

Serves 6 to 8 for a first course, 3 or 4 as a main dish

Here is the French scallop dish coquilles St. Jacques reborn as a risotto.

> *5 cups light fish stock*
> *1 cup dry white wine*
> *$\frac{1}{2}$ cup heavy cream at room temperature*
> *$\frac{1}{4}$ teaspoon plus a pinch saffron threads, crumbled*
> *4 tablespoons extra-virgin olive oil*
> *1 or 2 tablespoons butter*
> *4 medium cremini or cultivated mushrooms*
>   *(about 1 ounce each), chopped*

¾ pound small bay scallops, rinsed
3 to 4 tablespoons minced shallots
1½ cups arborio rice
2 tablespoons chopped broadleaf parsley
salt and freshly ground black pepper to taste

Bring stock to a simmer, add ½ cup wine, and keep warm on the stove.

Put the cream in a cup and add ¼ teaspoon saffron.

Heat 2 tablespoons oil and 1 tablespoon butter in a large skillet. Add mushrooms and cook, stirring, about 3 minutes until no longer dry. Add scallops and toss with the mushrooms and cooking fat. Add ¼ cup wine, bring to a simmer, and cook another 3 to 5 minutes until scallops give up their liquid and turn from shiny to dull white. Pour liquid from the skillet (there will be about ½ cup) into the cup with the cream and saffron. Set aside the scallops and mushrooms.

Heat 2 tablespoons oil in a large heavy saucepan over medium heat. Add shallots and cook, stirring, 2 or 3 minutes until soft. Add rice and cook, stirring, 2 or 3 minutes. Add remaining ¼ cup wine. When liquid has been absorbed or evaporated, add ½ cup stock and cook, stirring, until liquid disappears. Continue adding stock ½ cup at a time, stirring constantly and waiting until each addition is absorbed before adding the next. After about 15 minutes, when the rice is not yet done, stir in the cream and scallop liquid ½ cup at a time. Continue stirring in more stock ½ cup at a time (or ¼ cup at the end), until the rice is done, creamy on the outside but still a little firm in the center of each grain. (Add the last stock amounts judiciously, since you will not be adding cheese to soak up excess liquid.) Stir in the optional tablespoon butter. Remove from heat and stir in the parsley, the mushroom-scallop mixture, salt, pepper, and the extra pinch saffron. Allow to sit 1 or 2 minutes before serving.

Kevin Cahill's Risottos at Pronto Cena

It is owner-manager Charles Moschini whose Tuscan roots and family visits to the old country inspired Pronto Cena restaurant, an oasis of good eating on Jersey City's Hudson River waterfront. But it's Pronto Cena chef Kevin Cahill, however he came by the talent, who cooks risotto like one born with a wooden stirring spoon in his hand. One off-peak Saturday afternoon he demonstrated several of his specialties in Pronto Cena's kitchen, simultaneously stirring and composing different risottos at different stages of completion.

The three examples that follow are among the Pronto Cena favorites that can be made with easily acquired ingredients. Kevin serves each portion on or beside a cuplike leaf of radicchio, endive, or other green — a nice touch to borrow for a first-course risotto.

Although the other risotto recipes in this book begin with 1½ cups of rice, Kevin works with a pound (about 2¼ cups) of rice at a time and apportions the other ingredients accordingly; I have kept his numbers, since you'll probably want to invite guests to share these big risottos.

Kevin Cahill's Salmon Risotto with Asparagus

Serves 6 to 8 as a first course, 4 as a main dish

> ½ pound fresh asparagus
> 2 tablespoons olive oil
> 1 pound salmon, cut into 1- to 1½-inch pieces
> 1 bunch scallions, trimmed, using white parts sliced
>   crosswise and first 3 inches of green cut into thin strips
> 2 cups arborio rice
> ½ cup dry white wine
> 6 cups hot lobster or vegetable stock
> 2 tablespoons butter
> 2 tablespoons freshly squeezed lemon juice
> salt and freshly ground black pepper to taste

Snap off and discard tough stem ends of the asparagus stalks. Blanch remaining asparagus in hot water for 4 or 5 minutes or more, depending on thickness of stalks. Cut off tips and cut stalks into thick slices.

Heat the oil in a large heavy saucepan over medium heat. Add salmon and sauté briefly until almost done. Remove with slotted spoon and set aside. Add scallions and sauté until clear. Add rice and sauté 1 minute until fully coated. Add wine and cook, stirring, until liquid is absorbed. Add stock ½ cup at a time, stirring constantly and wiping sides and bottom of pan to prevent sticking. As each addition of broth is absorbed, add the next. When risotto is almost done, stir in the asparagus. Cook until al dente, with a stiff but creamy texture. Return salmon to the pot, then whisk in the butter. Add lemon juice. Season with salt and pepper.

Kevin Cahill's Tuna Risotto

Serves 6 to 8 as a first course, 4 as a main dish

> 2 tablespoons olive oil
> 1 pound fresh tuna steak, cut into 1- to 1½-inch pieces
> 1 medium onion, chopped small
> 2 cups arborio rice
> 6 cups hot fish stock
> 1 or 2 tablespoons butter
> ½ teaspoon hot red pepper flakes
> 2 tablespoons freshly squeezed lemon juice
> salt and freshly ground black pepper to taste

Heat the oil in a large heavy saucepan over medium heat. Add tuna and cook briefly until browned on all sides. Remove with slotted spoon and set aside. Add onion to the pan and sauté until clear. Add rice and sauté 1 minute until fully coated. Add ½ cup stock and cook, stirring, until the liquid is absorbed. Continue adding stock, stirring constantly and wiping the sides and bottom of the pan to prevent sticking. As each addition of stock is absorbed, add the next. When almost done, stir in the tuna. Continue adding broth and stirring until al dente, with a stiff but creamy texture. Then whisk in the butter, stir in the pepper flakes and lemon juice, and season with salt and pepper.

Kevin Cahill's Chicken Liver Risotto

Serves 6 to 8 as a first course, 4 as a main dish

> 2 tablespoons olive oil
> 2 leeks, trimmed, well washed, and cut into narrow 3-inch strips

2 cups arborio rice
6 cups hot chicken stock
4 ounces Chicken Liver Pâté (following recipe), or to taste
2 tablespoons butter
4 tablespoons freshly grated Parmigiano-Reggiano cheese
salt and freshly ground black pepper to taste

Heat the oil in a large heavy saucepan over medium heat. Add leek and sauté until clear. Add rice and sauté 1 minute until well coated. Add $\frac{1}{2}$ cup stock and cook, stirring, until liquid is absorbed. Continue adding stock $\frac{1}{2}$ cup at a time, stirring constantly and wiping the sides and bottom of the pan to prevent sticking. As each addition of stock is absorbed, add the next. Cook until al dente, with a stiff but creamy texture. Stir in the pâté, then the butter, then the cheese. Season with salt and pepper.

Chicken Liver Pâté

This recipe makes more pâté than you will need for the risotto, but you should have no trouble using it up as a spread on toast or crackers.

1 tablespoon butter or olive oil
1 medium red onion, minced
5 anchovy fillets, chopped
1 tablespoon capers, chopped
1 pound chicken liver, duck liver, or a combination,
    washed, trimmed, and chopped
salt and freshly ground black pepper to taste
1 tablespoon cognac, if you have some, or dry vermouth

Heat butter or oil in a medium-size skillet over medium-low heat. Add onion and anchovies and cook 5 minutes until the onion is soft. Add capers, then chicken liver, and cook gently 10 to 15 minutes, until liver is light brown throughout and falls apart when pressed with the back of a wooden spoon. Add salt, pepper, and cognac or vermouth. Mash by hand or in a food processor.

Leftover Risotto Pancake

True, in my house leftover risotto is something of a contradiction in terms. Still, it's worth making a little extra in the first place in order to enjoy this lunch or breakfast the next day. This amount serves 2.

> *1 egg, beaten*
> *2 cups leftover risotto*
> *8 teaspoons olive oil*
> *4 teaspoons freshly grated Parmigiano-Reggiano cheese*

Mix the egg with the risotto. Heat 2 teaspoons oil in a nonstick 6-inch frying pan (or oil a 6-inch circle in a larger nonstick pan). Add half the risotto mixture, flatten to form a 6-inch pancake, and cook over low to medium heat for 5 minutes, or until a nice golden crust forms on the bottom of the rice. Lightly oil a plate and set it upside down over the pancake, then flip the plate and frying pan so that the pancake is transferred, crust up, to the plate. Scrape up any crust that might have stuck to the pan. Add another 2 teaspoons oil to the pan. Slide the pancake onto the oiled pan and cook 5 minutes to crust the other side. Slide onto plate and sprinkle with 2 teaspoons cheese. Repeat with the remaining risotto mixture.

To make lunch for 1 with just 1 cup of leftover risotto, I use only half the beaten egg and discard the rest. If you prefer, use the whole egg; the result will fall somewhere between a risotto pancake and a risotto frittata.

Boiled Italian Rice

Boiling rice spaghetti-style in large pots of water has long been standard practice wherever rice is an everyday food and cooking water is readily available. Often the boiling is just the first step in a more complicated process involving steaming or baking with a sauce or stew. But northern Italians also make the immediate most of plain boiled rice by tossing it in Parmigiano-Reggiano and butter, just as their southern compatriots might dress spaghetti for a quick and simple first course or light meal. And just as plain boiled pasta can be infinitely varied according to the cheeses, herbs, or sauces tossed with it before serving, arborio rice proves at least as responsive to a similar range of flavor-infusing partners. These suggestions are among the simplest, which might also be the most appropriate.

Boiled Italian Rice with Parmigiano-Reggiano and Butter

Serves 4 as a first course or side dish, 2 or 3 as a main dish for lunch or light supper

> *1 cup arborio rice*
> *½ cup freshly grated Parmigiano-Reggiano cheese*
> *2 tablespoons unsalted butter, at room temperature*
> *salt and freshly ground black pepper to taste*

Pour the rice into 2 quarts boiling salted water, stirring briefly with a wooden spoon to prevent sticking on the bottom. When the water returns to a boil, adjust heat to boil steadily until the rice is tender but still a bit al dente, 15 to 18 minutes. Drain through a sieve, then dump into a serving bowl. Stir in the cheese, then the butter, slicing with a knife for faster melting as you mix it in. Season with salt and pepper.

Variations

• Stir in 4 ounces of diced or grated fresh mozzarella with the Parmigiano-Reggiano cheese. Reduce butter to 1 tablespoon.
• After stirring in the cheese, stir in chopped fresh herbs such as 4 tablespoons parsley or basil or 2 tablespoons sage or 1 tablespoon thyme.
• While the rice is cooking, steam 1 cup fresh shelled peas for 10 minutes. Stir into the cooked rice and cheese.
• Omit the butter and stir in 1 cup warm tomato sauce prepared as on page 49.

Boiled Italian Rice with Romano and Garlic

Serves 4 as a first course or side dish, 2 or 3 as a main dish for lunch or light supper

> 1 cup arborio rice
> 2 tablespoons olive oil
> 2 cloves garlic, minced
> ¼ cup freshly grated Romano pecorino cheese
> salt and freshly ground black pepper to taste

Boil, drain, and turn out the rice as directed in the recipe on page 185. When the rice is cooking, heat the oil in a small saucepan over very low heat. Add the garlic and cook very slowly until golden. If the garlic threatens to burn before the rice is done, remove from heat and add more oil to cool. When the rice is done, stir in the oil and garlic, the cheese, and the salt and pepper.

Boiled Italian Rice with Red Pepper Puree

Serves 4 as a first course or side dish, 2 or 3 as a main dish for lunch or light supper

> 1 cup arborio rice
> 1 roasted, peeled red pepper (see page 49)
> 1 tablespoon unsalted butter
> 1 tablespoon olive oil
> 2 scallions, white and some green, trimmed and sliced thin
> 1 clove garlic, minced
> 2 tablespoons freshly grated Parmigiano-Reggiano or
>   Romano pecorino cheese
> salt and freshly ground black pepper to taste

Boil, drain, and turn out the rice as directed in the recipe on page 185. While the rice is cooking, puree the pepper in a food processor. Melt the butter in a frying pan with the oil, then add scallions and garlic and cook until soft. Add pureed pepper and keep over low heat until rice is ready. Then mix all ingredients together in the serving bowl.

Rice Balls

Among the charms of southern Italy's (and Italian America's) rice cooking are her deep-fried rice balls. When I worked in Brooklyn in the mid-1980s, my favorite lunch was a softball-size rice ball, similar to Cosimo's version, below, topped with tomato "gravy." It cost $1.50 at a tiny neighborhood lunchroom.

Arancini, a stuffed Sicilian version named for the golden fried balls' resemblance to little oranges, can require a little or a lot more effort and are often made at home and filled with whatever savory goodies the resident cook has made her specialty. Some stuff the balls with tiny, painstakingly homemade meatballs long simmered in tomato sauce. The Italian ham and cheese combination called for here, a common choice in Sicily as well, is far less time consuming. For a good meatless version, omit the ham and add some chopped cooked spinach. A similar mozzarella-stuffed rice ball identified with Rome and its environs is called *suppli al telefono* because the cheese strings out like telephone wires when the balls are pulled apart.

Cosimo's Rice Balls

Serves 6 as a first course, side dish, or light lunch

Cosimo Manzoni from Bari, Italy, cooks these easily prepared rice balls at Lisa's Italian Deli in Hoboken. I top them with a plain tomato sauce such as the one on page 49.

> *1½ cups arborio rice*
> *¾ cup freshly grated imported Romano pecorino cheese*
> *¾ cup dry bread crumbs*
> *½ cup chopped broadleaf parsley*
> *1 tablespoon chopped fresh oregano or 1 teaspoon dried*
> *salt and freshly ground black pepper to taste*
> *3 eggs, beaten*
> *cooking oil for deep-frying*

Drop the rice into 3 quarts boiling water and cook 12 to 15 minutes or until tender but slightly al dente in the center. Drain through a sieve, shake dry, then dump into a large bowl. Stir in the cheese, bread crumbs, parsley, oregano, salt, and pepper, then mix in the beaten eggs. Form into 6 baseball-size balls.

In a small saucepan, heat 2 to 2½ inches of oil to 325°F. Deep-fry the balls one at a time by lifting with a slotted spoon and placing in the fat to brown the bottom, then turning with the spoon to brown the other half. Remove to paper towel. The browning takes only about 1 minute per ball.

Arancini

Serves 4 to 6 as a first course, side dish, or light lunch

I mix some nontraditional orange zest into these Sicilian rice balls to extend the "little orange" motif and add a fragrant, flavorful dimension to the rice. The stuffing can be changed to suit your inclination, as suggested on page 187.

Arancini can be served plain or with a homemade tomato sauce, which can be as simple as the one on page 49.

> ¼ teaspoon saffron threads, crumbled
> 2¼ cups chicken stock or water
> 1 cup arborio rice
> salt and freshly ground black pepper to taste
> ½ cup freshly grated Romano pecorino or Parmigiano-
>   Reggiano cheese, or ¼ cup each
> oil for deep-frying, 2 inches deep in a saucepan
> 1 or 2 beaten eggs for the coating, plus 1 for the rice balls
> ¾ cup to 1½ cups bread crumbs
> 1 tablespoon finely minced orange zest (optional)
> 2 very thin slices imported prosciutto (about 1½ ounces),
>   chopped very small
> 4 ounces fresh mozzarella, chopped very small
> 8 to 12 large fresh basil leaves, minced (optional)

Drop the saffron into the chicken stock and bring to a boil. Add the rice, salt, and pepper. When the stock returns to a boil, cover the pot, reduce the heat to very low, and cook about 18 minutes or until all the liquid is absorbed and the rice is tender but still a bit al dente. Transfer to a large bowl and mix in the grated cheese. Let cool to room temperature.

When ready to make the rice balls, put the oil in a saucepan to heat. Set out two small flat bowls. Put 1 or 2 beaten eggs in one of the bowls and $\frac{3}{4}$ to 1 cup bread crumbs in the other. (Amounts needed will depend on the consistency and number of the rice balls; the more you make, the more coating you need. I start at the low end and add more egg and bread crumbs if needed.)

Mix the rice and grated cheese combination with the orange zest and 1 beaten egg, then form into 6 to 8 stuffed balls. As you form each ball, poke a hole in it with your finger; insert bits of prosciutto, cheese, and optional basil; and pinch the rice to close the hole, adding a bit more rice if needed to cover.

As each ball is stuffed and formed, roll it in the bowl of beaten egg and then the bread crumbs. Set aside on a plate or cookie sheet. (Balls can be refrigerated at this point for up to a few hours. Because of the uncooked eggs, I wouldn't hold them for days as some suggest.)

When all the balls are made and the oil has heated to 325°F, drop a few balls into the oil. Fry until golden brown all around, turning bottom-up once if necessary for even frying. This might take only 1 minute for each group of balls.

Once fried, the balls can be held for an hour or so or refrigerated for a day or so and reheated in a 350°F oven. I prefer to cook and consume them straight off.

Baked Italian Rice

Italy's big baked rice dishes — sometimes layered like lasagna, sometimes filled and crusted like savory "pies" — tend to be extravagant preparations made especially for Christmas or other holidays or feasts. Naples's Sortu di Riso and Sicily's Tummàla, the latter said to be of Arab origin and named for an eleventh-century Emir of Catania, are layered casseroles, typically replete with meatballs, sausage, ham, *and* chicken, along with a similar profusion of cheeses and vegetables and tomato sauce, that seem designed to compensate in one lavish dish for an entire season of fasting. My meatless entry here is less elaborate, though admittedly still too rich in butter for everyday consumption.

Then there are northern Italy's splendid crusted rice casseroles. Parma is famous for its bomba di riso, made with a rich rice crust and filled with wine-braised pigeon. In Tuscany, where its Emilia-Romagna origin is acknowledged, the bomba of Parma is given different fillings and called timballo di riso for its drumlike shape and its resemblance to a classic pastry-shelled timballo (timbale in France). Bomba or timballo, this casserole has two advantages over the baked rice "pies" or "cakes" of other cultures: the rice is flavored with delicious Parmesan cheese and sometimes a rich broth as well, and the buttered baking dish it's cooked in has a light dusting of bread crumbs, a low-tech nonstick coating that guarantees one beautiful unbroken golden crust.

The three crusted casseroles here have been scaled for three different casserole sizes, from $1\frac{1}{2}$ to 4 quarts. As a variation on the drum shape, any of them could be baked in a ring mold of the appropriate size. A sauce, such as red pepper puree, might be streaked over the turned-out rice; however, I wouldn't want to completely cover the impressive crust.

Italians recommend a bomba or timballo as a first course; I make it the centerpiece of an evening meal. My fillings are also fairly free and streamlined improvisations. In different seasons and on different occasions, I might dream up other fillings. In this, I second the advice of Harriott Pinckney Horry, the eighteenth-century Carolina author of the "rice pye" recipe cited on pages 21–22. Mrs. Horry did not bother with directions for any specific filling but called simply for "a rich fill . . . of beef or veal or any thing you please."

Baked Layered Rice and Eggplant

Serves 4 to 6

Try this as a sophisticated alternative to lasagna, with its eggplant, rice, and balsamella in place of the standard Italian-American noodles, meat, and cheeses. As for that funny spelling, according to Italian cooking authority Giuliano Bugialli, Italians were making balsamella long before the French named it *béchamel* in the eighteenth century.

> *2 medium eggplants*
> *olive oil for coating eggplants*

The marinara sauce:

4 tablespoons olive oil
2 cloves garlic, minced
3 medium onions, chopped fine (2 cups chopped)
1 large carrot, chopped fine
2 stalks celery, chopped fine
1 35-ounce can Italian plum tomatoes
$\frac{1}{2}$ teaspoon salt (if tomatoes are unsalted)
$\frac{1}{4}$ teaspoon freshly ground black pepper
$\frac{1}{8}$ teaspoon sugar
$\frac{1}{8}$ teaspoon ground cinnamon

$1\frac{1}{2}$ cups arborio rice
3 tablespoons butter
$\frac{1}{2}$ teaspoon saffron threads, crumbled
$\frac{1}{4}$ cup finely chopped Italian parsley

The balsamella sauce:

6 tablespoons unsalted butter
6 tablespoons flour
3 cups milk
salt and freshly ground black pepper to taste
$\frac{1}{4}$ teaspoon nutmeg

$\frac{1}{2}$ cup freshly grated Parmigiano-Reggiano cheese

Preheat oven to 350°F. Cut eggplants crosswise into $\frac{1}{2}$-inch slices. Brush on both sides with olive oil and bake 20 to 30 minutes on an oiled baking sheet, turning after 15 minutes.

To make the marinara sauce, heat oil in a large heavy skillet. Add all the vegetables and cook, stirring occasionally, 10 minutes without browning. Push tomatoes through a sieve to remove seeds and add with juice to the skillet. Add seasoning. Simmer 30 minutes.

Drop rice into 2 quarts salted boiling water and cook 15 minutes. Drain and return to cooking pot. Melt 3 tablespoons butter with the saffron threads in a small saucepan. Stir in parsley and pour over the drained rice.

To make the balsamella, melt butter in a saucepan over low heat. Add flour, stir well, and remove from heat. In another saucepan heat milk to just below a boil. Return butter and flour to low heat and add the milk all at once. Stir 10 minutes. Stir in salt, pepper, and nutmeg and remove from heat.

Raise oven temperature to 375°F. Oil a 9-inch × 13-inch baking pan. Coat lightly with marinara sauce. Add in layers one-third of the rice, half the eggplant, and half the remaining marinara sauce. Repeat with half the remaining rice, all the remaining eggplant, and all the remaining marinara sauce. Top with remaining rice, then the balsamella sauce. Sprinkle with grated cheese. Put the uncovered dish in the oven, reduce heat to 350°F, and bake 30 minutes.

Spring Vegetable Timballo

Serves 4 or 5 as a first course, 2 or 3 as a main dish

With Italian bread, a salad, and white wine, this makes a charming springtime supper.

The filling:

3 tablespoons olive oil
1 medium leek, white and light green parts, chopped fine
2 large cloves garlic, minced
½ cup shelled fresh fava beans (8 or 10 pods)
4 to 6 caps fresh cremini, shiitake, or other mushrooms,
*   or 1 or 2 caps portobello mushrooms, chopped*
12 baby zucchini (3 or 4 inches long), quartered,
*   or 1 small zucchini, cut into 3-inch strips*
2 sprigs fresh fennel feather, chopped (4 tablespoons
*   chopped), or other chopped fresh herbs to taste*
½ cup chopped fresh parsley
½ cup dry white wine
1 pound fresh plum tomatoes, skinned, seeded, and
*   chopped (page 48), or 1 cup canned Italian plum*
*   tomatoes, seeded and chopped*
salt and freshly ground black pepper to taste

The shell:

1⅓ cups arborio rice
1 egg, beaten
⅓ cup freshly grated Parmigiano-Reggiano cheese

The coating:

2 tablespoons butter, very soft
2 tablespoons fresh bread crumbs

For the filling, heat the oil in a large skillet over medium-low heat. Add leek and cook to soften. Add garlic, fava beans, mushrooms, and zucchini. Cook until all the vegetables are soft and garlic and zucchini are turning golden. Add fennel, parsley, and wine. Increase heat to medium and cook until wine is reduced. Add tomatoes and cook uncovered over medium heat about 15 minutes or until sauce is no longer watery. Add seasoning.

For the shell, drop the rice into 3 quarts boiling water. Return to a boil, and boil about 12 minutes or until almost done but still a little too chewy. Drain through a strainer. Let sit in the strainer for a few minutes, then mix with the egg and the cheese.

Preheat the oven to 375°F. Coat the sides and bottom of a 1½-quart casserole with the butter, then dust with bread crumbs. Make a shell of the rice mixture by smoothing a layer onto the bottom of the pan, then pressing a thin but solid wall of rice around the sides. Spoon in the filling and top with the remaining rice, pressing against the sides to complete the shell. Bake 30 to 35 minutes until a golden or light brown crust forms around the edges. (To check, slide a table knife between the side of the casserole and the wall of rice.) Remove from oven and let rest for a few minutes. Then, wearing oven mitts, hold a serving platter upside down on top of the casserole and flip so that the platter sits right side up on a countertop and the casserole is upside down on top. Tap the sides and bottom of the casserole and lift it up, leaving the timballo on the platter.

Timballo with Ratatouille, Chicken, and Olives

Serves 8 as a first course, 4 or 5 as a main dish

I've borrowed the French name for the Mediterranean vegetable melange that gives this filling a sumptuous feel without the usual profusion of meats. If serving as a first course, you might leave out the chicken breast.

The ratatouille:

1 medium eggplant, peeled and cut into $\frac{1}{2}$-inch $\times$
    2-inch strips
salt as needed
4 to 5 tablespoons olive oil
1 medium-large onion, sliced thin
1 green bell pepper, cut into thin strips
2 small or medium zucchini, cut into strips
3 large cloves garlic, minced
2 cups fresh plum tomatoes, skinned and seeded
    (page 48), or 2 cups Italian canned tomatoes,
    pushed through a sieve to remove seeds
$\frac{1}{2}$ cup chopped fresh parsley or basil or a combination
salt and freshly ground black pepper to taste

The remaining filling:

1 pound skinned, boned, sliced chicken breast
up to 1 tablespoon olive oil
15 to 18 Mediterranean black olives (e.g., Spanish,
    Italian, or Greek), pitted and coarsely chopped

The shell:

2 cups arborio rice
2 eggs
$\frac{1}{2}$ cup freshly grated Parmigiano-Reggiano cheese

The coating:

2 tablespoons butter, very soft
2 tablespoons dry bread crumbs

For the ratatouille, sprinkle the eggplant with salt and drain 30 to 60 minutes in a colander or wire basket over a plate or bowl.

Heat 2 tablespoons oil in a large skillet. Add onion and cook about 5 minutes until soft. Add pepper and cook another 5 minutes until soft. Remove with slotted spoon and set aside on a slightly tilted plate (to drain off the oil). Add another tablespoon of oil to the pan, then add the zucchini and garlic. Cook 5 to 10 minutes until turning golden. Remove with slotted spoon to plate with onion and pepper. Pour any oil that has drained from the vegetables back into the pan and add another tablespoon or so of oil as needed. Add eggplant and cook, stirring occasionally, until coated and softened. Return sautéed vegetables to pan and add the tomatoes, herbs, salt, and pepper. Cook uncovered over medium-low heat about 15 minutes, until vegetables are done or almost done and sauce is no longer watery. (If sauce threatens to dry up, add a little more tomato or a little water, lower heat, and cover for remaining cooking time. The ratatouille should end up very moist but not so soupy as to make the rice soggy.)

Meanwhile, for the remaining filling, cook the chicken briefly on both sides until no longer pink in another skillet sprayed or smeared with olive oil. Remove from pan. When cool enough to handle, cut or tear into strips or shreds. Set aside with the chopped olives.

For the shell, drop the rice into 3 or 4 quarts boiling salted water. Return to a boil, and boil about 12 minutes or until almost done but still a little too chewy. Drain through a strainer. Let sit in the strainer for a few minutes, then mix with the eggs and cheese.

Preheat oven to 375°F. Coat the sides and bottom of a $2\frac{1}{2}$-quart casserole with the butter, then dust with bread crumbs. Make a shell of the rice mixture by smoothing a layer of rice onto the bottom of the pan, then pressing a thin but solid wall of rice around the sides. Add, in layers, the chicken, then the ratatouille, then the olives. Top with the remaining rice, pressing the edges of the top rice layer against the sides of the pan to complete the shell. Bake 30 to 35 minutes or until a golden or light brown crust forms around the edges. (To check, slide a knife between the side of the casserole and the wall of rice.) Unmold as directed in the preceding recipe, for Spring Vegetable Timballo.

Variation

Make the same ratatouille filling but use Spanish green olives instead of black ones and add $\frac{1}{2}$ cup dry sherry with the tomatoes. Instead of the chicken breast, use the breast and leg meat from 1 duck. Make a stock of the duck bones and scrap pieces, and use that to cook the rice in broth as in the recipe for Party Timballo that follows, using 2 cups of rice and $4\frac{1}{4}$ cups of stock to fit the $2\frac{1}{2}$-quart casserole of this recipe. Omit the grated cheese from the rice mix.

Party Timballo

Serves 12 as a first course or as part of a party buffet, 6 to 8 as a main dish

Cooking the rice in broth, somewhat in the Spanish manner, makes a richly flavored shell for this festive timballo.

The filling:

$1\frac{1}{2}$ ounces dried porcini mushrooms
$\frac{1}{2}$ pound Italian sausage (sweet, hot, or a mixture)
3 tablespoons olive oil
1 chicken, cut up
1 large onion, chopped
3 large cloves garlic, minced
1 cup fresh plum tomatoes, skinned, seeded, and
    crushed (page 48), or 1 cup canned crushed
    tomatoes, seeded
up to 1 cup mushroom-soaking water
1 cup chicken broth
$\frac{1}{2}$ cup chopped fresh broadleaf parsley
$\frac{1}{2}$ cup chopped fresh basil leaves
1 tablespoon chopped fresh oregano or 1 teaspoon dried
salt and freshly ground black pepper to taste

The rice:

3 tablespoons olive oil
3 cups arborio rice
6 cups chicken broth, such as the browned chicken
    stock on page 29, hot
3 eggs, beaten
$\frac{3}{4}$ cup freshly grated Parmigiano-Reggiano cheese

The coating:

3 to 5 tablespoons butter, very soft
3 to 5 tablespoons dry bread crumbs

For the filling, soak mushrooms for 30 minutes in $1\frac{1}{2}$ cups warm water. Remove, wipe clean, pat dry, and chop. Strain mushroom-soaking liquid through a coffee filter and set aside.

Remove casing from sausage and remove and discard any large chunks of pure fat. Heat oil in a large skillet. Add chicken pieces and brown on all sides, about 15 minutes. Remove and set aside. Add onion and cook 5 minutes. Add garlic and cook 5 minutes. Add sausage, break up into chopped-meat form, and brown lightly. Add remaining filling ingredients. Bring to a boil, then adjust heat to simmer gently, uncovered, until chicken is cooked, about 30 minutes. Remove chicken. If liquid is too soupy, turn up the heat and continue cooking to reduce. When chicken is cool enough to handle, tear meat from bones and into shreds. Discard skin and bones and return meat to the sauce, off heat.

While chicken is cooking, make the rice. Heat 3 tablespoons oil in another large deep skillet. Add the rice, stir to coat, and cook, stirring, 3 to 5 minutes. Add the broth, bring to a boil, then lower heat to bubble gently, uncovered, 15 to 18 minutes or until the liquid is entirely absorbed and the rice is almost done but still a little chewy. You might have to move the skillet a bit now and then to keep the rice cooking evenly all around the edges. If rice is soupy, pour into a strainer to drain before proceeding. Let cool for a few minutes, then mix with the eggs and cheese.

Preheat oven to 375°F. Coat the sides and bottom of a 4-quart casserole or Dutch oven with 3 tablespoons of the butter, then dust with 3 tablespoons of bread crumbs. Make a shell of the rice mixture by smoothing a 1-inch layer onto the bottom of the pan, then pressing a solid $\frac{1}{2}$-inch wall around the sides. Spread the filling over the bottom rice layer, then top with the remaining rice, pressing the edges of the top rice layer against the sides of the pan to complete the shell. If you like, sprinkle the top with the remaining 2 tablespoons bread crumbs, then dribble with the remaining 2 tablespoons butter. This won't show when the timballo is turned out, but it makes a nice bottom crust on the platter. Bake 35 minutes or until a golden or light brown crust forms around the edges of the shell. Unmold as directed in the recipe for Spring Vegetable Timballo on page 192.

FIVE

Some Asian Ways with Rice

⸕

THE first rice farmers were Asian; and in the seven thousand or more years since they domesticated the grain, entire Asian cultures have risen from the rice fields. Today Asian farmers still grow 90 percent of the world's rice crop, and almost all of it is consumed in the country where it is grown. China alone produces more than one-third of the world's rice and exports less than 0.5 percent of its production. According to leading Chinese-food historian K. C. Chang, the people of southeastern China get more than three-quarters of their calories from rice.

A typical family in southeastern China or the Southeast Asian countries might start the day with soup and rice or with a thin rice porridge, then fry up the previous night's leftover rice for lunch or a snack. For dinner the family will sit down to individual bowls of plain boiled rice; any other dishes at the table will be set out in serving bowls for sharing as condiments or toppings for the rice.

When bits of meat or fish are not stir-fried for topping rice, they might be wrapped in paper-thin rice-flour pancakes and flavored with a dipping sauce containing rice wine vinegar. When soup is on the menu, at breakfast time or later, rice is there somewhere: it might be cooked plain and served in separate individual bowls or roasted raw and ground to a powder, then stirred in to thicken the broth. Leftover rice from an earlier meal or noodles made from fine rice flour might be added to the soup pot. Or the crisp bottom crust from a pot of cooked rice might be deep-fried in oil, then dropped into hot broth to make the beloved sizzling soup set down on page 209.

Farther north, both Korea and Japan have their own versions of the pan-Asian rice porridge, their own breakfasts of soup and rice, their own rice-with-leftovers for family lunch, and their own toppings for plain boiled rice. A major difference is that whereas southern Chinese and Southeast Asians grow and eat mostly long-grain varieties, Koreans and Japanese are exclusively devoted to short-grain rice.

So close is the association between the Japanese and the stubby rice varieties of their fields and tables that all short-grained rice, including the somewhat longer varieties sometimes labeled "medium grain," is known officially as *japonica* (as distinct from the long-grain *indica* type grown in India). But short-grain rice did not originate in Japan. According to anthropologist E. N. Anderson, an authority on Chinese food history, both long-grain and short-grain rices were grown in China before 5000 B.C. But it was only about two thousand years ago that rice made its way into southern Japan, probably through Korea. Since the short-grain type has a shorter growing season, it was the rice that took hold in these relatively northern lands. Even that famously Japanese rice specialty, sushi, had its ancient origins around northern Thailand or southeastern China, though the Japanese have undoubtedly advanced the art. And only in the past few hundred years has rice become a staple food for the average Japanese.

Today McDonald's golden arches coexist with Shinto arches in Japan, and new take-out fried chicken chains are swamped with orders on American Thanksgiving. Beef mania, previously an upper class affliction, rages in Japan and Korea. Asians everywhere are taking up toast for breakfast, sandwiches for lunch, and potatoes with the evening meal. As a result, they eat less rice. Yet rice is still by far the leading staple, and the old rice standbys are still basic fare in the old rice-growing regions.

It is these enduring everyday dishes, homey comfort food accomplished without much expense or fuss, that are featured in this chapter. In that spirit I've limited the recipes to dishes that are easily accomplished here as well; some Asian favorites had to go in deference to North American tastes and pantries. It's easy, though, to expand your everyday Asian rice repertoire by serving plain rice, as Asians most often have it, with toppings and condiments from Chapter Two.

One Asian country not represented in this chapter is India, the continent's second biggest rice producer after China and the home of several regional rice cuisines of surpassing splendor and variety. But the qualities of northern India's native long-grain rice and the influence of centuries of Moghul rule are such that India's most glorious rice dishes, and those most easily incorporated into a Western meal, fit within the pilaf family sampled in Chapter Three of this book.

Asian Home Cooking

Zosui

Serves 4

The Japanese eat zosui for breakfast, lunch, light family supper, or midnight snack. This recipe is for the zosui that Kathy Nakajima Hyman prepared for me in her Weehawken, New Jersey, kitchen. But Kathy emphasizes that there is no one rigid formula for zosui, and as she cooked she suggested the various additions and alternatives that I have listed at the end.

When done, zosui should have the consistency of a thick soup or a soupy porridge.

2 chicken thighs, skinned
4 to 6 dried shiitake mushrooms
3 or 4 cups leftover cooked short-grain rice (or see Variations below)
1 small to medium carrot, cut into thin julienne strips
3 or 4 stems Asian broccoli or broccoli rabe, sliced
2 scallions, trimmed and sliced thin
small handful wakame (a seaweed) (optional)
½ teaspoon instant dashi
1 tablespoon light soy sauce
fresh gingerroot for grating

Cook the chicken in 6 cups of simmering water for 20 minutes. Remove pan from heat and remove chicken from the water. Tear meat from the bones and return bones to the cooking water. Shred meat and set aside. When the cooking water has cooled to warm, drop mushrooms in to soak 30 minutes. Then remove mushrooms. Cut off and discard tough stems. Slice caps and set aside. If needed to filter out any grit from the mushrooms, remove bones from the cooking water and pour the water through a cheesecloth-lined sieve or a drip coffee holder with filter.

Bring the strained water to a boil in a large saucepan or spaghetti pot. Add rice, breaking up any lumps as you put it in. Adjust heat to a simmer, add carrot, and cook 10 minutes. Add the shredded chicken, sliced mushroom caps, broccoli stems, scallion whites, and wakame (not too much wakame; it swells considerably). Simmer another 10 minutes. Season with dashi and soy sauce. Ladle into individual bowls and top each bowl with scallion greens and freshly grated ginger.

Variations and Additions

• If you have no leftover rice, begin by cooking 2 cups short-grain rice in 2 cups water as directed for Japanese short-grain rice on page 17.

• Instead of raw chicken thighs, use any leftover cooked chicken meat, shredded. Start with 6 cups homemade (page 35) or instant dashi or chicken broth instead of water. Soak mushrooms in the broth and proceed as directed, omitting the instant dashi at the end.

• Instead of adding soy sauce at the end, mix 1 tablespoon of miso with a little hot water and stir it into the pot for the last 10 minutes of cooking.

• Instead of or in addition to the carrot, dice or julienne $\frac{1}{2}$ to 1 cup zucchini, eggplant, potato, squash, yam, or daikon.

• Add $\frac{1}{2}$ cup fresh peas with the vegetables.

• Add diced tofu for the last 2 or 3 minutes.

• Swirl in a lightly beaten egg with the soy sauce at the end.

Donburi

Like paella in Spain, the term *donburi* in Japan refers to both a particular rice-based food preparation and the special container associated with it. Here the container is not a cooking pot but a special bowl, larger than an individual plain rice bowl, used for serving individual portions of donburi. Donburi the food is a meal-in-a-bowl, presented with rice on the bottom and some dashi-simmered meat, fish, egg, or vegetables on top. It's an unpretentious dish enjoyed at home for family lunches or gobbled at fast-food donburi chains in the course of a busy Japanese day.

Chicken Donburi

Serves 2 for lunch

This to me is the basic and best donburi. Sometimes sliced shiitake mushroom caps are dropped in with the chicken. Eggs are another common addition, as in the Oyako Donburi that follows.

> *1 cup short- or medium-grain white rice*
> *1 cup Dashi (page 35)*
> *2 tablespoons soy sauce*
> *2 tablespoons mirin (Japanese sweet rice wine) or*
> > *2 tablespoons sake and 2 teaspoons sugar*
> *½ chicken breast, skinned, boned, and cut into*
> > *small strips, or 1 to 2 cups leftover chicken*
> *2 scallions, green part only, trimmed and sliced thin*
> *Roasted Seaweed and Sesame Seeds (page 39)*

Rinse rice under cold running water until water runs clear. Drain and add to 1¼ cups water in a saucepan. Soak 30 minutes. Then bring to a boil in the same water, cover, reduce heat, and simmer 15 minutes. Remove from heat and let rest 10 minutes.

Meanwhile, in another saucepan make the dashi and add the soy sauce, mirin, and chicken to the simmering dashi. Cook until the chicken is done, about 5 minutes.

Fluff rice and spoon into individual bowls. Top each portion with some chicken, then spoon the broth onto the rice. Top with scallion greens and roasted topping.

Oyako Donburi

Serves 2 or 3 for lunch

When Japanese moms add eggs to chicken donburi, they call the combination oyako donburi, meaning "parent and child," a reference to the chicken and egg.

There are various ways to incorporate the eggs, but they are always added at the very end and barely set, as they will continue cooking over the hot rice.

> *1 recipe Chicken Donburi (page 202), plus 1 or 2 eggs,*
> *stirred just to mix whites and yolks*

Follow the recipe for Chicken Donburi. When rice and broth are done, ladle the rice into individual bowls, then quickly swirl the egg into the broth. In seconds, when the egg is lightly set, remove pot from heat and spoon chicken, egg, and broth over individual rice mounds. Roast and add the sesame seed–seaweed topping if desired.

Beef Donburi with Shiitake

Serves 2 for lunch

This modern-day donburi uses the stir-fry technique, uncommon in Japan's traditionally fat-free cooking.

> *all the ingredients for Chicken Donburi (page 202)*
> *without the chicken or scallions*
> *2 tablespoons cooking oil*
> *½ onion, sliced very thin, then cut in half to form half-moons*
> *4 to 6 ounces beef, cut into thin strips*
> *2 or 3 shiitake mushroom caps, cut into strips*

Cook the rice, make the dashi, and add the soy sauce and mirin as in the recipe for Chicken Donburi.

While the dashi is simmering, heat the oil in a frying pan and stir-fry the onion, beef, and mushrooms until the onion and mushrooms are soft and the beef is no longer red. Then lift out with slotted spoon and drop into the broth. Simmer 5 minutes. Serve mixture over rice as in Chicken Donburi, then add the sesame seed–seaweed topping.

Chirashi-Zushi
Scattered Sushi

Serves 4 or 5 for a meal, 8 to 10 as part of a buffet or party spread

To me sushi, like cappuccino, is more fun to have at an establishment devoted to its preparation than to make at home. The Japanese seem to agree; they rarely make formally shaped sushi at home. As Sonoko Kondo explains in her Japanese cookbook *The Poetical Pursuit of Food,* they know they can get better at a sushi bar, where the chef in charge has trained in his profession for eight or ten years. Shizuo Tsuji, who trains professional chefs in Japan, says in his book *Japanese Cooking: A Simple Art* that by some accounts "when [rolled sushi is] done properly, all the rice grains face the same way." Both authors also warn that the raw fish essential to most sushi must be exceptionally fresh, so that care and skill are even more critical in its selection and preparation than in the forming of the rolls.

For all their caveats, both authors end up offering good instructions for presentable rolled sushi. But as sushi bars now thrive in North America, and especially as the fish available at most North American markets is unlikely to be this morning's catch, I prefer to emulate the Japanese and leave formed and raw-fish sushi to the experts.

However, there is one kind of sushi that the Japanese do make at home. It is called scattered sushi because the additions are simply scattered over the rice, but it is made with the same vinegar-and-sugar-flavored sushi rice as the more carefully formed styles. This "dressing" and the various colorful and taste-intensive toppings make chirashi-zushi a sensational everyday meal or party platter. It's endlessly interesting to eat because each bite is a little different from the last.

There is no prescribed combination of toppings for chirashi-zushi. Use as many as you like. I recently threw Japanese restraint to the winds and made a dazzling platter using all the toppings listed below plus some lime-marinated chiles (page 47) I happened to have left over from a Mexican meal.

The sushi rice:

*2½ cups Japanese-type short- or medium-grain white rice,
    washed and drained
5 tablespoons rice wine vinegar*

4 tablespoons sugar
1½ teaspoons salt

The toppings:

1 recipe Soy-Marinated Cucumber (page 39)
½ pound shrimp, cooked and shelled, tails on
Egg Strips (page 38) made with 2 eggs and 2 tablespoons
    cooking oil
2 or 3 tablespoons pickled ginger (available at Asian
    groceries and natural-food stores)
5 or 6 Soy-Simmered Mushrooms (page 38)
3 or 4 tablespoons chopped umeboshi plum (available
    at Japanese and natural-food stores)
1 large or 2 medium scallions, trimmed and sliced thin
½ pound crisp, fresh sugar snap peas or snow peas
1 small or ½ large red bell pepper, cut into thin strips
½ large mild green chile, cut into very thin strips
2 sheets toasted nori and 2 tablespoons Roasted Seaweed
    and Sesame Seeds (page 39)

Put the rice in a saucepan with 2¾ cups cool water and let soak 30 minutes, off heat. Bring to a boil. Cover the pot and reduce heat to very low. Cook 15 minutes. Remove from heat and let rest, covered, 5 or 10 minutes.

Mix the vinegar, sugar, and salt. (To ensure blending, mix in a small saucepan over low heat, then allow to cool to room temperature.)

While the rice is soaking and cooking, prepare the toppings. The peas and the red pepper and green chile strips should be steamed or (nontraditionally) stir-fried for 3 minutes just before tossing onto the rice.

While the rice is still steaming hot, spread it onto a platter and begin gradually sprinkling on the vinegar-sugar mixture, stirring it in with a damp, flat spoon using a sideways motion. (The Japanese use a special wooden rice paddle.) At the same time, the rice being sprinkled should be fanned vigorously, to prevent clumping and to give the grains a desirable sheen. (In sushi parlors the fanning is a job for an apprentice — or a team of them. A home cook can use an electric fan or enlist a helper to fan with a magazine.)

If all the toppings are not done before the rice is finished, just add them as they are ready. Sushi rice should not be served steaming hot and can easily wait a half hour or so, or even 2 or 3 hours when held under a damp cloth.

Southeast Asian Coconut Rice

Serves 4 as a side dish

This pleasing side dish, rich and fragrant but easy to make, is less homey than others in this section: It's often served on special occasions throughout Southeast Asia. It's good with fish, pork, duck, or chicken and is usually accompanied by condiments such as minced Thai chiles, chopped cucumber, and fish sauce.

> *1 cup Thai jasmine rice*
> *2 cups fresh coconut milk (page 52) or 1 cup canned*
> *   coconut milk and 1 cup chicken stock or water*
> *1 tablespoon soy sauce*
> *1 teaspoon minced fresh gingerroot*
> *1 teaspoon turmeric*
> *3-inch stem lemongrass, bruised, cut into 1-inch lengths,*
> *   or 1 teaspoon grated lemon or lime zest*
> *1 curry leaf, if available*
> *2 tablespoons whole small basil leaves, or large basil*
> *   leaves cut into thin strips*

Rinse the rice in a sieve under cold running water until the water runs clear. Shake sieve and rake with your fingers to remove water.

Combine rice with all other ingredients except basil in a heavy-bottomed saucepan. Bring to a boil, then adjust heat to bubble steadily about 10 minutes, or until surface liquid disappears and small steam holes appear on top of the rice. Cover, reduce heat to very low, and cook 10 minutes. Remove from heat and let rest another 10 minutes. Sprinkle with basil to serve.

Chinese Rice with Cabbage

Serves 3 or 4

This humble but tasty Chinese dish makes a good everyday dinner with only bottled soy sauce and a simple stir-fry.

1½ cups long-grain rice
salt to taste
1 tablespoon peanut oil
½ onion, sliced thin
2 cloves garlic, minced
½ pound Chinese napa or other cabbage (see Note, below), sliced thin

To wash away the starch, as is traditional, rinse the rice in a sieve under cold running water until the water runs clear. Shake to drain off water. (This step is optional.)

In a saucepan, add rice and salt to 2½ cups water. Bring to a boil, then adjust heat to bubble gently until surface water is absorbed, about 10 minutes after turning on the heat.

Meanwhile, heat the oil in a wok or nonstick skillet over medium-high heat. Cut onion slices in half and add to the oil. Stir-fry 1 minute. Add garlic and stir-fry 1 minute. Add cabbage and stir-fry 1 minute or until coated and soft.

Make a hole in the center of the rice and push the stir-fried vegetables into the hole. Cover with rice from around the edges. Cover pot, reduce heat to very low, and cook 10 minutes. Remove from heat and let rest, still covered, another 5 minutes.

Note: If you can't get napa, a lovely delicate Chinese cabbage, try bok choy, savoy cabbage, or regular green cabbage. Regular green cabbage should be stir-fried a bit longer than the others, until no longer stiff.

Rice with Chinese Sausage

Serves 4 or 5

In this humble Chinese classic, sausage is steamed over cooking rice, so that the fat trickles down and flavors the rice. It makes a satisfying everyday dinner with 1 or 2 vegetable dishes and some Chinese condiments.

1½ cups long-grain rice
2 links Chinese sweet sausage (lop chong)

To conform with Chinese tradition, put the rice in a strainer and rinse under cold water until the water runs clear. Drain well. (This step is optional with American rice.)

Add rice to $2\frac{1}{2}$ cups boiling water. Return to a boil, then reduce heat to a low boil and leave to cook uncovered.

While the rice is bubbling, cut the sausage into $\frac{1}{4}$-inch slices, but leave the slices standing as if the sausage were still intact.

When the rice has cooked for 5 or 10 minutes and the surface water has disappeared, slide a knife blade under each sliced sausage and transfer the slices to the top of the rice. The slices should fall over like dominoes. (Don't worry if they don't line up beautifully.) Press gently to partially embed in the rice.

Cover the pot, then reduce heat to very low and cook 15 minutes. Remove from heat and let steam another 10 minutes.

Chinese Rice Cake

Rice cake is a Chinese term for the crust of rice that sticks to the bottom of the pan when it is left to cook after the rice is done. To make rice cake, put 1 cup of long-grain white rice in a heavy-bottomed saucepan with $1\frac{3}{4}$ cups of water and bring to a boil over medium-high heat. Then cover the pot, reduce the heat to very low, and cook another 30 minutes. Without removing from the heat, uncover and scoop out most of the rice, leaving about $\frac{1}{2}$ inch in the bottom. The soft rice you remove can be eaten immediately with a sauce or topping or refrigerated to be stir-fried a day or two later. The remaining $\frac{1}{2}$ inch will cook further to form the crust.

There are various ways to obtain and remove the crust, but in my experience the most successful is the method described by Craig Claiborne and Virginia Lee in their *Chinese Cookbook.* Lee lets the bottom layer cook uncovered for a full hour after scooping out the soft rice. Somehow with the longer cooking — leave it even longer if it's not yet crisp and golden on the bottom — the crust will lift right out without scraping, in one intact piece.

Allow the crust to dry and cool at room temperature several hours or overnight. It can then be nibbled as is or with a dipping sauce. Some soften it in tea, though that seems to me to defeat the whole purpose. Better in my view is to "puff" the crust by deep-frying, as in the following recipe. You can also save up crusts in a tightly sealed jar in the refrigerator until you have several to fry and share for a snack.

Puffed Rice Cake

Puffed rice cake is made by deep-frying the crust from the bottom of the rice pot. First make the crust, or cake, as directed in the preceding recipe for Chinese Rice Cake, and let it dry at room temperature for several hours or overnight. A few days will not hurt. The cake can be fried whole or broken into a few pieces.

In a deep heavy-bottomed pot, heat a few inches of corn or vegetable oil for deep-frying. When almost smoking (about 425°F), drop in the rice cake or the first piece of crust. It will puff up immediately. Push it down into the oil with the back of a slotted spoon to puff further, until slightly browned. This should take no more than 1 minute. Remove from oil and repeat with remaining pieces. Cool to finger tolerance on a paper towel, then sprinkle with salt or sugar or serve with a soy-based dipping sauce. Or drop it into Sizzling Rice Soup, as described in the following recipe.

Sizzling Rice Soup

Serves 4

Kids love it. This traditional Chinese tempest in a soup pot puts Rice Krispies to shame in the snap-crackle-and-pop department. Have it as a first course or as a family lunch with plain cooked rice and condiments.

> *1 ounce Chinese, shiitake, or other earthy dried mushrooms*
> *2 tablespoons soy sauce*
> *2 teaspoons Asian sesame oil*
> *1 tablespoon rice wine vinegar*
> *½ teaspoon (or to taste) Asian garlic chile paste*
> *8 ounces tofu, cut into ½-inch cubes*
> *4 cups homemade Chicken Stock (page 29), strained and defatted*
> *1 tablespoon slivered fresh gingerroot*
> *½ pound Chinese napa or savoy cabbage, shredded*
> *3 or 4 scallions, trimmed and sliced thin*
> *1 tablespoon chopped cilantro (fresh coriander)*
> *salt to taste if needed*
> *corn or vegetable oil for deep-frying*
> *rice cake for deep-frying (see Puffed Rice Cake, preceding recipe)*

Soak the mushrooms for 30 minutes in 2 cups warm water. Remove and pat dry. Discard tough stems and cut the caps into thin strips. Pour the soaking water through a sieve lined with cheesecloth and reserve.

While the mushrooms are soaking, combine the soy sauce, sesame oil, vinegar, and chile paste. Add the tofu, toss, and leave to marinate.

Combine the mushroom-soaking water with the chicken stock and bring to a simmer. Add ginger, mushrooms, and cabbage and cook 10 minutes. Add the tofu with marinade and cook 10 minutes. Stir in the scallions and cilantro and cook 5 minutes. Add salt if needed.

While the soup is simmering, heat the oil in a separate pot and deep-fry the rice cake as directed in Puffed Rice Cake, using 1 piece per serving. To serve, remove rice cake from the oil and drop immediately into the individual bowls of soup, or drop into empty bowls and immediately ladle the soup over the rice cake. When the spitting and sizzling die, enjoy the soup.

Variation

Substitute ½ pound diced raw or leftover cooked pork or chicken for the tofu. If raw, add with the mushrooms.

Rice Noodles

Thin Asian rice noodles, variously labeled rice sticks, mi fun, sen mee, bihon, or rice vermicelli, among other names, can be found dried in Asian markets and some grocery shops and supermarkets. Most are crinkly and come bent into long skeins. They require no cooking. Instead of being boiled like Italian pastas, they are simply covered with water at a warm room temperature and soaked until softened. This can take from only a few minutes for the very thin noodles comparable to angel hair pasta to twenty to thirty minutes or more for others. (Some rice noodle packages give soaking times and temperatures; others don't. Wider noodles, not as common here and not called for in these recipes, might require soaking in boiling water or brief cooking.) Once soaked, the noodles can be drained and tossed with a sauce, such as the Sesame Chile Soy Sauce on page 37, or mixed at the last minute into stir-fries or soups, as in some of the following recipes.

Another way to prepare rice noodles is to drop them unsoaked into hot oil for deep-frying. They will immediately puff up. Turn them with a slotted spoon to puff the other side and remove immediately. This makes a crunchy noodle good for serving under or sprinkling on top of stir-fries.

Rice noodles can be a boon to anyone who is allergic to wheat, since they can substitute for Italian pasta with any sauce desired. The recipes included here, though, are limited to Asian dishes.

Miso Noodle Soup

Serves 4 to 6 as a first course, 2 or 3 as a light meal

This light, clear, delicate soup is fat free and rich in vitamins, minerals, and protein, with a fresh gingery taste you don't get from sautéed ginger. With the sautéed vegetables it makes a balanced light meal.

Japanese and Koreans enjoy miso soup with rice or noodles at any meal, including breakfast. I've stretched some boundaries here to accommodate the rice noodles common to southeastern China and Southeast Asia.

> $\frac{1}{4}$ *pound thin rice noodles*
> *6 cups Dashi (page 35), Seaweed Stock (page 34), or water*
> *1 tablespoon minced fresh gingerroot*
> *4 scallions, trimmed and sliced thin*
> *1 cup diced root vegetables such as daikon, turnips,*
>   *carrots, or parsnips (optional)*
> *leaves from $\frac{1}{2}$ pound kale or spinach, cut into thin strips*
>   *about $2\frac{1}{2}$ inches long*
> $\frac{1}{2}$ *pound tofu (2 squares), diced*
> *4 tablespoons barley or hatcho miso*
> *a few sprigs cilantro (fresh coriander), separated into*
>   *individual leaves (optional)*

Cover the noodles with warm water and leave to soak 20 to 30 minutes, or as directed on package. Drain.

Meanwhile, bring dashi, stock, or water to a boil. Add ginger, white and light green parts of scallions, and diced vegetables. Cook 10 minutes. Add kale, if using, and tofu. Cook 10 minutes. Scoop out ½ cup of the water and mix it with the miso, then stir it back into the soup pot. Cook 10 minutes. If using spinach, add it for the last 5 minutes. When done, add noodles, stir, then remove from heat and ladle into individual bowls. Sprinkle each bowl of soup with slices of scallion greens and optional cilantro.

Cold Rice Noodles with Sesame Sauce

Serves 2 for a light meal, 4 as a first course

Cold sesame noodles are a summer favorite at Chinese take-out restaurants in this country. Since rice noodles don't have to be cooked, they are a good choice for a hot day in a home kitchen. I add the matchstick vegetables for cool, fresh flavor, color, and a little crunch.

> ½ pound thin rice noodles (page 210)
> 4 tablespoons soy sauce
> 3 tablespoons rice wine vinegar
> 4 tablespoons Asian sesame oil
> 4 teaspoons Chinese pepper oil
> 1 tablespoon sugar
> 1 6-ounce piece daikon, sliced thin and cut into tiny matchsticks
> ½ carrot, peeled and cut into tiny matchsticks
> 2 large cloves garlic, sliced thin and cut into tiny strips
> 1 piece fresh gingerroot, about 1 inch × 1½ inches,
>   sliced thin and cut into tiny matchsticks
> 1 kirby cucumber, seeded and cut into thin 2- to 3-inch strips
> ½ to 1 jalapeno pepper, seeded, cored, and cut into thin strips
> 2 scallions, trimmed
> 5 tablespoons Chinese sesame paste

Put the noodles in a large bowl with warm water to cover. Soak 20 to 30 minutes while preparing the sauce. Drain and leave in sieve or colander to dry.

Mix soy sauce, vinegar, oils, and sugar, then toss in the daikon, carrot, garlic, ginger, cucumber, and jalapeno pepper to marinate 10 minutes or longer.

Cut scallion whites into very thin slices, break slices into rings, and cut green parts into thin 2- to 3-inch strips.

With a slotted spoon, remove vegetable strips from marinade and add to scallions.

In the empty noodle-soaking bowl or another large bowl, mix sesame paste with 5 tablespoons water. Add marinade and stir to make a smooth sauce. Return noodles to the bowl and toss to coat the noodles with the sauce. Sprinkle with the scallions and marinated vegetable sticks.

Noodles with Herb Paste

Serves 3 or 4 as a main dish for lunch or with other dishes

This recipe derives from an herb paste in *Bruce Cost's Asian Ingredients,* a shopping guide with recipes by the California-based Asian food authority. Cost calls the mixture "Asian Pesto" and recommends using Asian basil and Asian mint, if available. I add more Asian flavors, among them sesame oil. I like to mix straight and hot sesame oil; proportions depend on the tolerance of the diners and the hotness of the oil.

> $\frac{1}{2}$ *pound thin rice noodles (page 210)*
> *4 tablespoons chopped raw, unsalted peanuts*
> *2 large cloves garlic, smashed flat and cut crosswise*
> *1 tablespoon fresh gingerroot, chopped*
> *4 tablespoons peanut oil*
> *1 tablespoon Asian sesame oil (see headnote above)*
> $\frac{1}{2}$ *cup tightly packed fresh basil (Asian if available)*
> $\frac{1}{4}$ *cup tightly packed fresh mint (Asian if available)*
> $\frac{1}{4}$ *cup tightly packed cilantro (fresh coriander)*
> *2 tablespoons freshly squeezed lime juice*
> *1 tablespoon soy sauce*
> $\frac{1}{2}$ *teaspoon sugar*
> *salt and freshly ground black pepper to taste*

Soak the noodles for 20 to 30 minutes in a large bowl with warm water to cover. Drain. Toast the peanuts on an unoiled surface in a 350°F toaster oven for 5 minutes, until lightly browned. Turn half the nuts into a food processor with all the other ingredients and process to a paste. Toss paste with noodles in a large bowl and stir to mix well. Sprinkle with remaining nuts.

Thai-Style Fish and Noodles

Serves 4 for lunch, 2 or 3 for dinner

Here is a simple meal-in-a-noodle-dish that can be varied to suit your inclination, pantry, and occasion. For example, shrimp can substitute for the fish. The red pepper and peas, or other vegetables, might be separately steamed or stir-fried and served on the side instead of being mixed in, as here. Or instead of poaching in coconut milk, the fish can be marinated and stir-fried as in the variation following the basic recipe.

> $\frac{1}{2}$ *pound thin rice noodles (page 210)*
> *3 tablespoons Thai fish sauce (nam pla)*
> *3 tablespoons freshly squeezed lime juice*
> *1 teaspoon sugar*
> *1 teaspoon Asian garlic chile paste or $\frac{1}{2}$ teaspoon*
>   *chopped dried red chile*
> *1 teaspoon turmeric*
> *1 cup coconut milk*
> *1 pound fish fillet, cut into bite-size pieces*
> *3 tablespoons peanut oil*
> *1 tablespoon sesame oil*
> *1 bunch scallions, trimmed and cut into thin 1- to*
>   *$1\frac{1}{2}$-inch-long shreds*
> *3 large cloves garlic, sliced thin and cut into thin strips*
> *$1\frac{1}{2}$-inch cube fresh gingerroot, sliced thin, then cut*
>   *into thin strips*
> *1 medium red bell pepper, cored, seeded, and cut into*
>   *thin strips (optional)*

½ pound snow peas or sugar snap peas, trimmed (optional)
2 tablespoons basil leaves, cut into thin strips
2 tablespoons mint leaves, cut into thin strips
2 tablespoons cilantro (fresh coriander), chopped
1 small fresh Thai red chile or other small fresh chile,
    seeded, cored, and cut into thin strips
3 or 4 tablespoons unsalted roasted peanuts, crushed with
    a rolling pin
1 lime, cut lengthwise into 4 wedges

Soak noodles in warm water to cover for 20 to 30 minutes or until soft. Drain through a large strainer and hold in strainer until needed.

Mix fish sauce, lime juice, sugar, and chile paste or chopped chile. Reserve.

Stir turmeric into coconut milk in a medium-size frying pan over medium-low heat. Add fish and poach 5 minutes or until just done. Remove from heat.

Heat oils in a wok or large heavy skillet over medium-high heat. Add white and light green scallion parts. Add garlic and ginger and cook, stirring, 1 or 2 minutes (5 minutes if not using pepper strips and peas). Add red pepper strips, if using, and cook, stirring, 2 or 3 minutes. Add peas, if using, and cook, stirring, 2 or 3 minutes. Stir in the drained noodles, then the fish sauce mixture. Add fish and coconut milk. Stir in half the chopped herbs.

Remove to a serving platter and sprinkle with scallion greens, remaining chopped herbs, fresh chile strips, and peanuts. Serve with lime wedges.

Variation

Omit the coconut milk. In a food processor, make a paste of the scallion white, garlic, ginger, turmeric, and sesame oil. Rub paste on fish and marinate 1 hour at room temperature or several hours in the refrigerator. Heat the peanut oil in the wok or skillet. Add fish and all the marinade. Cook briefly on both sides until done, then remove and set aside. Stir-fry the vegetables as above, then stir in the drained noodles and the fish sauce mixture. Remove to serving platter, top with the fish, and garnish as above.

Pad Thai

Serves 4 as a lunch or first course

This most famous of Thailand's several rice noodle specialties is often called the country's national dish. My tasters prefer this version to the local Thai takeout's sweeter version.

> ½ pound thin rice noodles (page 210)
> ¼ cup strained tamarind pulp (page 50)
> 3 tablespoons Thai fish sauce (nam pla)
> 1 teaspoon sugar
> 1 tablespoon freshly squeezed lime juice
> 1 teaspoon Asian garlic chile paste or ½ teaspoon
>   hot red pepper flakes and 2 cloves garlic, minced
> 4 tablespoons vegetable or peanut oil
> 3 scallions, trimmed and cut into thin, 1- to 1½-inch-long shreds
> ½ pound small or medium shrimp, shelled and deveined
> 2 eggs, beaten
> 4 tablespoons unsalted roasted peanuts, crushed fine with
>   a rolling pin
> 1 tablespoon ground dried shrimp (available at Southeast
>   Asian markets), optional
> 1½ cups fresh bean sprouts, rinsed
> 3 tablespoons chopped cilantro (fresh coriander)
> 1 lime, cut lengthwise into 4 wedges

Soak the noodles in warm water to cover 20 to 30 minutes. Drain.

Put the tamarind in a small dish. Stir in the fish sauce, sugar, lime juice, and chile paste or pepper flakes.

Heat the oil in a wok or large heavy skillet over medium-high heat. Reserving a few green scallion shreds to sprinkle over the top, add the scallions and stir-fry 1 minute. Add minced garlic, if using, and stir-fry 1 minute. Add shrimp and cook 1 minute on each side or until pink on both sides. Do not overcook. Pour in the beaten eggs, stirring quickly in a swirling motion as soon as the eggs hit the pan. Immediately dump in the noodles and stir to heat and mix with the eggs. Pour the tamarind–fish sauce mixture over the noodles and stir to mix. Add a few more dashes of fish sauce if too dry. (There will be no loose liquid sauce but there should be enough to color all the noodles.) Stir in half the peanuts, all the ground dried shrimp, if using, and 1 cup bean sprouts. Cook, stirring, until bean sprouts are warm and slightly wilted.

Pour contents of the pan onto a serving platter and top with remaining peanuts, remaining bean sprouts, the reserved scallion greens, and the chopped cilantro. Serve with lime wedges.

Singapore Noodles

Serves 4 as a main dish

I've encountered wildly different versions of this dish, named for those sold on the streets of Singapore but popular in southern China as well, in numerous Asian cookbooks and at several Chinese take-out restaurants in my neighborhood. Common to all are rice noodles, curry paste or powder, a few vegetables cut into tiny julienne, and some mixture of shrimp, pork (especially Chinese barbecued pork), and chicken. (The take-out versions boast all three.) In place of barbecued pork, I use a taste-intensive marinade for the shrimp and chicken.

½ pound small shrimp, shelled and deveined
1 whole skinless, boneless chicken breast, cut into small strips

The marinade:

2 large cloves garlic, smashed flat and minced as
*   small as possible*
1 tablespoon fresh gingerroot, grated or minced
*   as small as possible*
¼ teaspoon ground cayenne
1 teaspoon curry powder
2 tablespoons Japanese rice wine
2 tablespoons rice wine vinegar
2 tablespoons soy sauce
1 tablespoon Asian sesame oil
½ teaspoon sugar

½ pound thin rice noodles (page 210)
4 tablespoons peanut oil
1 egg, beaten
2 cloves garlic, cut into tiny sticks
1 medium-small onion, cut lengthwise into thin strips
½ green bell pepper, cut crosswise and then into very thin strips
1 or 2 red Thai chiles or small green chiles, seeded and
  cut into very thin strips
1 medium carrot, cut into matchstick-size strips
½ medium zucchini, cut into matchstick-size strips
small handful fresh mung bean sprouts
2 teaspoons curry powder
½ cup chicken broth
salt to taste if needed
2 tablespoons chopped cilantro (fresh coriander)

Put the shrimp and the chicken in separate wide-bottomed bowls. Mix the marinade and divide between the shrimp and the chicken, tossing to coat. Marinate 30 minutes at room temperature.

Put the noodles in a large bowl with warm water to cover. Soak 20 to 30 minutes or until soft. Drain.

Heat 1 tablespoon peanut oil in a small frying pan. Add egg and tip pan to spread the egg. In seconds, when the egg is set, slide it onto a plate, then turn back into the pan for a few seconds to set the other side. Remove and cut into small strips. Set aside.

Heat remaining 3 tablespoons oil in a wok or large skillet over medium-high heat. Add garlic and onion and stir-fry 1 minute. Remove chicken from the marinade with a slotted spoon. Add to wok and stir-fry 1 minute or until no longer pink on any surface. Add green pepper, chiles, carrot, and zucchini. Stir-fry 1 minute. Remove shrimp from marinade with a slotted spoon. Add to wok and stir-fry 1 minute. Stir in bean sprouts, marinade, and curry powder. Reduce heat, add chicken broth, and cook 1 minute or until vegetables are slightly softened and chicken and shrimp cooked through. Add egg, then the noodles, and mix well to coat the noodles. Add salt if needed. Sprinkle with cilantro to serve.

Fried Rice

Here is humanity's most inspired solution to leftover cooked rice. To southern Chinese and Southeast Asians, fried rice is not a serious meal; it's a quick snack to whip up from odds and ends of food on hand. But because the ingredients they have on hand are not always accessible here, I've tried to strike a balance between fidelity to irreplaceable authentic flavors, such as Southeast Asia's lemongrass, and fidelity to the spirit of fried rice, which might dictate using other items such as lemon zest, handier to us and as flavorful in its own way. Unlike my Asian sources, I'll have fried rice for a weekday dinner, with only a steamed vegetable on the side and fresh fruit for dessert.

Fried rice is most easily accomplished in a wok or nonstick skillet, with cold, dry rice that has been cooked at least a day ahead; a week's refrigeration won't hurt. Any clumps should be separated between thumb and fingers as the rice is added to the pan.

Egg-Fried Rice

Serves 2 to 4 as a snack or side dish

This simplest of fried rice dishes, common in China and in Southeast Asian countries, can be made with ingredients on hand for a lunch or midnight munch. The technique of stirring in the egg can also be incorporated into more complex fried rice dishes.

> *2 tablespoons corn oil*
> *2 medium scallions, trimmed and sliced very thin*
> *2 cups leftover cooked long-grain white rice*
> *1 or 2 beaten eggs*
> *handful fresh mung bean sprouts (optional)*
> *2 teaspoons soy sauce*

Heat the oil in a wok or large nonstick skillet. Add white and light green scallion parts and cook 2 minutes. Stir in the rice. Clear a space in the middle of the wok, or on one side of the pan, and drop in the beaten egg. In a few seconds, as it just begins to set, start stirring vigorously with large circular or swooping motions to fold the egg into the rice and bring the rice back over into the egg. Stir in the bean sprouts, if using, and sprinkle with soy sauce and a scattering of dark green scallion pieces.

Shrimp Fried Rice with Peas

Serves 2 as a main dish, 3 or 4 with other dishes

Lemongrass, available in markets carrying Southeast Asian produce and increasingly in specialty groceries here, gives this Vietnamese-style recipe a delightful fragrance and flavor. Spanking-fresh sugar snap peas, sweeter, plumper, and often fresher than available snow peas, harmonize deliciously. If you can't get either, use shelled fresh green peas or, as a last resort, thawed frozen peas. If lemongrass is unavailable, add 2 teaspoons of lime juice to the finishing sauce mix.

The finishing sauce:

1 tablespoon soy sauce
1 tablespoon Thai fish sauce (nam pla)
1 tablespoon oyster sauce
1 teaspoon Asian sesame oil
1 teaspoon sugar

2 to 3 tablespoons vegetable oil
1 stalk lemongrass, trimmed of tough outer layer and
    minced very fine
2 cloves garlic, cut into very thin sticks
1-inch × 2-inch piece fresh gingerroot, cut into very thin sticks
3 scallions, trimmed, white parts sliced very thin and
    green parts cut into 2-inch-long strips
1 fresh chile, such as jalapeno, seeded and cut into very thin strips
½ red bell pepper, cut into thin strips
2 cups sugar snap peas or snow peas or 1 cup fresh or
    frozen green peas

½ pound medium shrimp, shelled and deveined
2 to 2½ cups leftover cooked long-grain white rice
1 tablespoon chopped cilantro (fresh coriander)
1 tablespoon chopped fresh mint

For the finishing sauce, combine all the ingredients and set aside.

Heat the vegetable oil in a wok or large nonstick skillet over medium-high heat. Add lemongrass, garlic, ginger, and the white and light green scallion pieces. Stir-fry 2 minutes. Add chile and red pepper and stir-fry 2 or 3 minutes. Add peas and stir-fry 1 minute. Add shrimp and stir-fry 1 minute. Add more oil if necessary and stir to heat. Add rice and stir-fry 3 minutes. Stir in the sauce mixture and cook, stirring, 1 or 2 minutes. Top with chopped fresh herbs and dark green scallion pieces.

Chicken Fried Lemon Rice

Serves 2 as a main dish, 3 or 4 with other dishes

Anyone familiar with Thai foods knows the fermented fish sauce nam pla as an almost ubiquitous ingredient. Curry powder, the world's great misappropriation of Indian spicing, has also found its way into real Thai stir-fries. Lemon zest is not a Thai ingredient, but it adds a bright sprightly note to this improvisation.

2 tablespoons chopped raw, unsalted peanuts or 2 table-
*   spoons raw, unsalted cashew pieces*
2 to 3 tablespoons peanut, canola, or corn oil
2 cloves garlic, minced
2 or 3 scallions, trimmed, white part sliced thin and
*   green part cut into thin 2-inch-long strips*
2 teaspoons commercial Indian curry powder
*   (or 1 teaspoon curry powder, ½ teaspoon ground*
*   cumin, and ½ teaspoon ground coriander)*
¼ teaspoon ground cayenne, or to taste
½ pound boned, skinned chicken breast, cut into thin
*   2- to 3-inch-long strips*
slivered zest ½ lemon

> *2 to 2½ cups leftover cooked rice*
> *1 tablespoon soy sauce*
> *2 tablespoons Thai fish sauce (nam pla)*
> *1 teaspoon freshly squeezed lemon juice*
> *¼ teaspoon sugar*
> *1 tablespoon chopped cilantro (fresh coriander)*

Toast the peanuts or cashews on an unoiled surface in a 350°F degree oven or toaster oven for 5 minutes, until lightly browned.

Heat the oil in a wok or large skillet over medium-high heat. Add garlic with the white and lightest green parts of the scallions and stir-fry 2 minutes. Stir in the curry powder and cayenne, then add chicken and stir-fry about 3 minutes, until no longer pink on any surface. Stir in the lemon zest, then the rice, stirring 1 or 2 minutes to coat the rice with the curry. Add the soy sauce, fish sauce, lemon juice, and sugar. Stir-fry 3 minutes. Stir in the scallion greens and the toasted nuts. Sprinkle with chopped cilantro to serve.

Os's Yellow Rice from Bangladesh

Serves 2 or 3 as a snack, light lunch, or side dish

"You want a quick recipe for leftover rice?" asks Os Ahmad, whose mom's Bangladeshi dal and rice recipe appears on page 106. "Here's something you would give the kids for a late morning snack. It's easy and quite delicious."

Os warns, though, that cooking hot dried chiles in very hot oil, as they do in Bangladesh, can make a kitchen uninhabitable. "As soon as it starts to smoke," Os says, "I pick up the pan and walk out the back door." More timid American cooks might opt to keep the oil temperature below the smoking point.

> *2 tablespoons mustard or soy oil or other cooking oil*
> *1 teaspoon turmeric*
> *salt to taste*
> *3 or 4 whole dried cayenne (small hot red) chiles, to taste*
> *1 small onion, chopped small*
> *1 large clove garlic, minced*
> *2 cups leftover cooked rice*

Heat the oil in a skillet over medium-high heat. Stir in turmeric and salt. Add chiles and fry about 1 minute on each side. Remove and set aside. Add onion and garlic and sauté 5 or 10 minutes until turning brown. Add the rice, breaking up any lumps as you put it in. Stir to coat the rice with oil and seasoning, then stir-fry 5 or 10 minutes. Return chiles and toss.

Nasi Goreng
Indonesian Fried Rice

Serves 3 or 4

"Oh, nasi goreng! Very simple," said the accommodating clerk at the Indonesian Consulate in New York. "Just fry some onion and garlic. You can put a little meat, or make very small meat balls. . . . Yes, you can put some shrimp. Then ketjup." Ketchup? Not soy sauce? "You can. Ketjup or soy sauce; they're the same."

After a few more such conversations, a sampling of New York's Indonesian restaurants, and a review of a dozen recipes extracted from my own kitchen library, I can only agree that this most famous of Indonesian dishes is indeed a flexible affair. One distinguishing ingredient is a sweet Indonesian soy sauce called *ketjup manis,* or just *ketjup.* (It's pronounced like *ketchup,* which might explain the presence of tomato ketchup or tomato paste in some English-language recipes.) Even so, "If you don't have that, don't worry," says I. Nyoman Soedirka, who cooks at the Indonesian Mission to the United Nations and owns the Bali Burma restaurant in Manhattan. Another Indonesian ingredient that is "sometimes" used but usually left out at restaurants here is shrimp paste, which can strike the unaccustomed Westerner as unpleasantly strong. You can find ketjup and shrimp paste at Indonesian and some Thai and Chinese markets — or use the substitute ingredients suggested below.

All of which is a very long introduction for a recipe that is, indeed, very simple.

> 4 tablespoons peanut oil
> 2 eggs, beaten
> ½ pound small or medium shrimp, shelled and deveined
> 2 cloves garlic, minced

4 to 6 scallions, trimmed and sliced very thin
2 small fresh chiles, red if possible, seeded and minced
1 chicken breast, skinned and boned and cut into thin
    strips, or ½ pound raw beefsteak or pork, cut into
    small strips
2 cups cold cooked white rice
1 tablespoon ketjup manis (sweet soy sauce), or 1 table-
    spoon dark Chinese soy sauce mixed with 1 tea-
    spoon molasses
½ teaspoon shrimp or anchovy paste, or 1 teaspoon
    Thai fish sauce (nam pla), ground dried shrimp,
    or Chinese oyster sauce
salt to taste if needed
a few sprigs cilantro (fresh coriander)
accompaniments: chopped peanuts, cucumbers, and
    chiles; shredded coconut; lime wedges

Heat 1 tablespoon oil in a large nonstick skillet over medium-high heat. Coat the pan with the beaten eggs to form a large thin omelet. Tip and turn for even cooking. Remove at once when no longer runny and cut into thin strips. Set aside.

Clean the skillet for reuse or use a wok or another large skillet. Heat remaining 3 tablespoons oil over medium-high heat. Add shrimp and cook 1 minute on each side. Remove with slotted spoon and set aside. Add garlic, scallions (reserving dark green pieces), and chiles to the wok or skillet and stir-fry 1 minute. Add chicken, beef, or pork and stir-fry until no longer red on the outside. Add rice, breaking up any clumps as you do. Stir-fry to mix and coat with oil. Return shrimp to the mixture and stir in ketjup and shrimp or anchovy paste or substitute ingredients. Remove from heat but continue stirring for 1 minute before turning out onto serving platter. Salt to taste if needed. Garnish with scallion greens, egg strips, and cilantro sprigs. Serve other accompaniments in small bowls.

East-West: The Brown Rice Cuisine

These recipes, inspired by Asian models or incorporating Asian ingredients, derive from an eclectic brown-rice-based cuisine born more than a generation ago when young Americans dissatisfied with commodity culture and overprocessed foods turned to the East for righteous alternatives and latched onto Japanese diet guru George Ohsawa, founder of Zen macrobiotics. Certainly the American countercuisine of the 1960s and 1970s had many other roots and precedents and independent sources. But Ohsawa's teachings had enormous influence well beyond the corps of macrobiotics' true believers. Largely because the regimen and recipes of Ohsawa and his cookbook-author wife Lima sprang from the cuisine they knew best, the already fat-free diet of their native Japan, shoppers in our proliferating natural-food stores were buying such exotica as seaweed, miso, and pickled plums long before our supermarkets even acknowledged the existence of brown rice.

In this country, as macrobiotics became a movement and an industry, it spawned a foundation, a journal, bookstores, and restaurants, all incorporated under the name "East-West." When I use the term here, though, I refer to a broader range of alternative eaters who came together in places like natural-food co-ops and organic communes, appropriating elements of Asian cooking without much care for purist authenticity. As a sometime fringe member of that company, I've tested these recipes on food co-op potlucks, affinity groups assembling for sit-ins, an alternative high school's volunteer fix-up crew, and other committed connoisseurs of right eating.

The few brown rice recipes that follow are just a fraction of those scattered through the book (and listed in the index). All but one of the others are vegetarian, and all are by nature eclectic; but the few placed here have a particularly heavy East-West accent.

Brown Rice with Miso

Serves 2 to 4

Use this fresh-tasting, fat-free brown rice as a side dish with fish or as a partner to a substantial vegetable dish such as butternut or spaghetti squash with an

Asian sauce. The nutritious miso paste contributes minerals and complementary protein as well as depth to the stock.

> *2 cups Vegetable Stock (page 28), Seaweed Stock (page 34), or water*
> *1 tablespoon miso*
> *1-inch cube fresh gingerroot, sliced*
> *1 to 2 teaspoons freshly squeezed lemon juice, to taste*
> *grated zest 1 lemon*
> *1 cup brown rice (short- or long-grain)*
> *salt to taste*
> *1 tablespoon sesame seeds*

Heat stock in a saucepan and add the miso, smashing and stirring miso to dissolve in the stock. Bring to a boil and add the ginger, lemon juice, lemon zest, rice, and salt. When the stock returns to a boil, cover the pot, reduce heat to very low, and cook 40 minutes. Remove from heat and let stand another 10 minutes before lifting the cover.

While the rice is resting, toast sesame seeds in a small unoiled frying pan over medium heat until they begin to darken and pop. Pour over the rice to serve.

East-West Rice and Greens

Serves 3 or 4

This brown rice and miso adaptation of the Chinese Rice with Cabbage on page 206 makes a substantial side dish to tofu, tempeh, or fish or a nutritious one-dish meal.

> *½ pound leafy greens such as napa cabbage, bok choy,*
> *savoy cabbage, regular green cabbage, Asian broccoli,*
> *Italian broccoli rabe, kale, or spinach*
> *1 tablespoon miso*
> *1½ cups brown rice (short- or long-grain)*
> *1 tablespoon peanut oil*
> *½ onion, sliced thin*
> *2 cloves garlic, minced*
> *salt to taste*

If using cabbage, kale, or spinach, cut the leaves into 1-inch-wide strips. Cut longer strips in half. If using broccoli, discard tough bottom stems and cut leaves, flowers, and remaining stems into 2-inch lengths.

In a saucepan, smash and stir the miso into 3 cups water. Add rice. Bring to a boil, cover, reduce heat to very low, and cook for a total of 40 minutes, adding ingredients during the cooking as specified below.

Meanwhile, heat the oil in a wok or nonstick skillet over medium-high heat. Cut onion slices in half and add to the oil. Stir-fry 1 minute. Add garlic and stir-fry 1 minute. Add greens and stir-fry until somewhat softened (1 minute for spinach or napa cabbage, 2 or 3 minutes for other greens). After the rice has cooked 10 minutes (if using kale) or 30 minutes (for other greens, except spinach), lift the lid from the rice, make a hole in the center, and push the stir-fried greens into the rice. Add salt. Cover with some rice from around the edges, return the lid to the pot, and continue cooking over very low heat until the rice has cooked for 40 minutes. Remove from heat and allow to rest, covered, another 10 minutes. (If using spinach, add for the final 10-minute resting period.)

East-West Stir-Fry

Serves 3 or 4 as a one-dish meal

I've known vegetarians who practically lived on this flexible, forgiving one-dish diet, a free amalgamation of Chinese, Japanese, and American elements. Since almost any vegetable can be tossed into the mix, this ingredient list is deliberately fluid. Because brown rice doesn't really stir-fry well, I mix it in after the liquid.

> *8 ounces tofu, cut into 1-inch cubes*
> *4 tablespoons corn, safflower, or peanut oil*
> *3 cloves garlic, chopped*
> *1½ tablespoons fresh minced gingerroot*
> *1 small onion, sliced very thin, with slices cut in half*
> *½ green, red, or yellow bell pepper, seeded, cored, and*
>   *cut into thin strips*
> *1 small carrot or small white turnip or small zucchini*
>   *or a 4-inch length of daikon, peeled and sliced*
>   *very thin*

$\frac{1}{2}$ *jalapeno or other fresh chile pepper, seeded and cut*
    into thin strips, or $\frac{1}{2}$ teaspoon hot red pepper flakes,
    or 1 teaspoon Asian garlic chile paste
3 or 4 shiitake or other mushroom caps, sliced
$\frac{1}{2}$ *pound Asian broccoli or broccoli rabe, cut into 2-inch-*
    long pieces, or 1 stalk broccoli (about $\frac{1}{2}$ pound), cut
    into florets, or 2 cups sliced bok choy or fresh
    spinach leaves
small handful bean sprouts (optional)
2 tablespoons soy sauce
2 teaspoons Asian sesame oil
2 teaspoons freshly squeezed lemon juice (optional)
$\frac{1}{2}$ *teaspoon sugar*
2 cups leftover cooked brown rice
1 tablespoon sesame seeds, preferably black

Dry the tofu by spreading cubes between layers of a kitchen towel. Heat oil over medium heat in a wok or large nonstick skillet. Add tofu and stir-fry 1 or 2 minutes, until golden brown. Remove with slotted spoon to paper towel. Add garlic, ginger, and onion to the pan and stir-fry 2 minutes. Add pepper strips, sliced vegetables, and fresh chile, if using, and stir-fry 2 minutes. Add mushrooms and stir-fry 2 minutes, stirring well to coat with oil. Add broccoli and stir-fry 5 minutes, or add bok choy or spinach and stir-fry 1 minute. Stir in bean sprouts, then the soy sauce, sesame oil, optional lemon juice, sugar, and pepper flakes if using. If using chili paste, clear a space in the bottom of the wok and mix the paste with the pooled liquid, then stir into the vegetable mixture. Return tofu to the pot. Stir in the rice, then cover, reduce heat to very low, and cook 2 or 3 minutes until vegetables are soft but not soggy.

Heat a small unoiled frying pan over medium-high heat. Add the sesame seeds and toast briefly until they are jumping, then pour over the stir-fry and serve.

Baked Roasted Brown Rice with Chestnuts and Mushrooms

Serves 2 as a main dish, 4 as a side dish

This wonderful cold-weather casserole makes a delicious Thanksgiving side dish, yet it's simple enough for an everyday meal. We have it with a salad and baked sweet potatoes.

Chestnuts as well as shiitake mushrooms are often cooked with rice in Japanese and macrobiotic cooking. A bit of oil rounds out all the nutty, earthy flavors.

> *7 or 8 chestnuts*
> *1 cup long-grain brown rice*
> *2 tablespoons walnut or peanut oil*
> *1 clove garlic, minced*
> *1 medium leek, white only, chopped small (about ½ cup chopped)*
> *5 or 6 fresh shiitake mushrooms (about 2 ounces), chopped*
> *1 teaspoon fresh thyme leaves*
> *salt and freshly ground black pepper to taste*

Preheat oven to 450°F. With a small sharp knife, make a long top-to-bottom slit through the shell on the flat side of each chestnut, then a short perpendicular slit to form a cross. Spread chestnuts on a pizza pan or baking sheet and heat in oven 5 or 10 minutes, until the shell curls away from the slits. Remove from oven and reduce oven temperature to 400°F. While chestnuts are still warm, remove shells and inner peel with knife or fingers. Chop each chestnut into 6 or 8 pieces.

Spread rice on an unoiled baking sheet and put in the oven to roast for 10 or 15 minutes, checking every few minutes to reposition if the grains around the edges are browning faster than the ones in the center. When color has deepened to golden or light toasty brown, remove from oven and from baking sheet and set aside.

Reduce oven temperature to 375°F.

Heat 2 cups of water in a small saucepan and keep hot.

Heat oil in a heavy Dutch oven or flameproof casserole. When hot, add garlic and cook 1 minute. Add leek and cook 3 to 5 minutes to soften. Add mushrooms and cook another 3 to 5 minutes until soft. Add rice, chestnuts, thyme, salt, and pepper. Bring the hot water to a boil and pour over the rice mixture. Cover and bake 40 to 45 minutes until rice is soft and all the water is absorbed. The rice grains will probably burst and fluff up, which is fine. However, if you can manage to remove the casserole when the rice is tender but not yet burst, the flavor will be even more intense.

Baked Brown Rice and Tempeh Teriyaki

Serves 6 as a one-dish meal

This hearty vegetarian dinner is "meaty" enough for the most unreconstructed carnivore. Look for tempeh, a fermented soy product from Indonesia, in natural-food stores.

The teriyaki sauce:

4 tablespoons dark soy sauce
1 tablespoon sesame oil
1 tablespoon rice wine vinegar
4 tablespoons sherry or sake

1 8- or 10-ounce package of soy tempeh, cut into 1-inch squares
3 cups vegetable broth or water
up to 6 tablespoons peanut oil
6 ounces fresh shiitake mushrooms, coarsely chopped
1 teaspoon mustard seeds
1 teaspoon cumin seeds
4 cloves garlic, chopped
2 tablespoons chopped fresh gingerroot
1½ cups short-grain brown rice
1 teaspoon turmeric
¼ or ½ teaspoon ground cayenne
1 large onion, coarsely chopped
about 2½ pounds winter vegetables, peeled and cut into
    1-inch pieces, such as the following combination:
      2 medium carrots

> *12-ounce piece butternut squash or calabaza*
> *1 medium sweet potato*
> *1 large white turnip or 1 parsnip or 1 12-ounce piece daikon*
> *½ pound kale or spinach, coarsely chopped*
> *½ cup raisins (optional)*
> *salt to taste if needed*

Mix the teriyaki sauce in a nonreactive bowl or pan and put the tempeh in it to marinate for 1 hour. Then, reserving the marinade, remove the tempeh and pat dry with paper towel.

Heat broth or water in a small saucepan and keep warm.

Preheat oven to 350°F.

Heat 4 tablespoons oil in a large, heavy Dutch oven or flameproof casserole. Add tempeh, sauté a few minutes on each side, and remove to paper towel. Add mushrooms and cook a few minutes until soft. Remove to paper towel. Add more oil to make 2 tablespoons in the pot. Add mustard and cumin seeds. When they begin to sizzle and pop, add garlic and ginger. Sauté a few minutes until soft. Add rice and cook, stirring, until well coated with oil. Stir in turmeric and cayenne. Add broth, bring to a boil, and stir in reserved teriyaki marinade. Return tempeh and mushrooms to the pot and add all remaining ingredients (unless using spinach, which should be pushed in after stew has baked for 30 minutes). When liquid returns to a boil, stir the pot, cover, and bake 45 minutes or until rice is cooked.

SIX

Simple Sweets

❧

DON'T look here for sinfully luscious drop-dead desserts. Although elaborate sweet rice dishes have attained festival status here and there, more often sweetened rice cooked soft in milk or coconut milk serves as a soothing, satisfying comfort food, enjoyed at home by people who have rice with every meal and by those who know it only in Grandma's puddings. The familiar favorites in this small sampling use different rices and different basic means to achieve the smooth, soft texture that defines rice pudding. All are good for breakfast, for snacks, and for everyday dessert; and some, especially the Indian Kheer on page 236, serve beautifully as chaste and lovely endings to more sumptuous meals.

Baked Rice with Blueberries

Serves 6 to 8

The fruits and flavoring ingredients in this baked pudding and the next can be interchanged, and either can be made with leftover cooked rice. This one gets a lift from blueberries and lemon. For breakfast, try it with maple syrup.

> *¾ cup long-grain white rice*
> *⅛ to ¼ teaspoon salt, to taste*
> *1 tablespoon butter and more for greasing baking dish*
> *4 large eggs*
> *4 to 6 tablespoons sugar, to taste*
> *1½ cups milk*
> *1 teaspoon freshly squeezed lemon juice*
> *grated zest 1 lemon*

1 cup fresh blueberries
1 flat sweet biscuit or butter wafer, crushed with a
  rolling pin, or 1 to 2 tablespoons fine dry
  bread crumbs
4 tablespoons maple syrup (optional)

Put rice, salt, and butter in a saucepan with $1\frac{1}{2}$ cups water. Bring to a boil. Cover, reduce heat to very low, and cook 15 minutes. Remove from heat and let stand, covered, another 15 minutes. Remove lid and cool a few minutes until no longer steaming. (Or use 2 to $2\frac{1}{4}$ cups leftover cooked rice, at room temperature.)

Meanwhile, beat the eggs in a large bowl. Stir in sugar and beat until lightened. Stir in milk, then lemon juice and lemon zest, then the rice, then the blueberries.

Preheat the oven to 325°F. Butter a round 6-cup ($1\frac{1}{2}$-quart) casserole and dust lightly with crumbs. Fill with the rice mixture. Bake 45 to 50 minutes until set. Serve warm, either plain or with maple syrup, or cold.

Oven-Steamed Rice Pudding

Serves 6

The old practice of baking pudding in a pan of steaming water results in smooth, even cooking.

$\frac{1}{2}$ cup long-grain white rice
$\frac{1}{8}$ to $\frac{1}{4}$ teaspoon salt, to taste
1 tablespoon butter and more for greasing baking dish
2 eggs
6 tablespoons sugar
2 cups milk, warm
1 teaspoon vanilla extract
$\frac{1}{8}$ teaspoon nutmeg
$\frac{1}{4}$ teaspoon ground cinnamon
$\frac{1}{2}$ cup golden raisins
1 flat sweet biscuit or butter wafer, crushed with a
  rolling pin, or 1 to 2 tablespoons fine dry bread
  crumbs

Put rice, salt, and butter in a saucepan with $1\frac{1}{4}$ cups of water. Bring to a boil. Cover, reduce heat to very low, and cook 15 minutes. Remove from heat and let stand, covered, another 15 minutes. Remove lid and cool a few minutes until no longer steaming. (Or use $1\frac{1}{2}$ cups leftover cooked rice at room temperature.)

Meanwhile, beat the eggs in a large bowl. Stir in the sugar and beat until lightened. Stir in milk, then the vanilla, nutmeg, half the cinnamon, and the raisins. Add the rice.

Preheat the oven to 325°F. Coat a 6-cup ($1\frac{1}{2}$-quart) casserole with butter and crumbs, as in the previous recipe, and fill with the rice mixture. Dust with remaining cinnamon and any leftover cookie crumbs. Fill a large flat baking pan with about 1 inch of hot tap water. Put the casserole containing the rice in the pan of water and put the pan on a rack in the oven. Bake $1\frac{1}{2}$ hours or until set. Serve warm or cold.

Variation

When adding the spices and raisins, stir in 1 large tart apple, peeled, cored, and cut into small dice. The texture of the pudding will not be as smooth, but the apple taste complements the custardy rice.

Italian Rice Pudding with Ricotta

Serves 8

This makes a delicious dessert when served beside a bowl of whole fresh figs.

> 1 cup arborio rice
> 6 cups milk
> $\frac{1}{4}$ teaspoon nutmeg
> $\frac{1}{4}$ teaspoon ground ginger
> $\frac{1}{4}$ teaspoon ground cinnamon
> $\frac{1}{3}$ cup sugar
> grated zest 1 large or 2 small oranges
> 1 cup ricotta
> 2 teaspoons vanilla extract
> 3 tablespoons sliced almonds

Bring 4 quarts salted water to a boil. Add rice, return to a boil, and boil 7 to 8 minutes. Drain through a strainer. Bring milk to a boil in a large saucepan. Add spices, sugar, orange zest, and rice. Cook over low heat, stirring frequently, 1 hour or until the milk is absorbed. Cool for 2 hours, then whip the ricotta and stir it into the rice with the vanilla. Smooth the top and garnish with the almonds.

Crusted Rice Tarts

These sweet nibbles apply the Italian way of baking timballo (pages 189–197) to a simpler, sweet snack baked in muffin tins.

> $\frac{1}{8}$ *teaspoon saffron*
> *2 tablespoons milk*
> *1 tablespoon golden raisins*
> *1 cup arborio or other medium-grain rice*
> *1 egg, beaten*
> *butter for greasing muffin cups*
> *1 flat sweet biscuit or butter wafer*
> *1 tablespoon pine nuts*
> *4 tablespoons sugar*
> *grated zest 1 lemon*

Preheat oven to 375°F.

Put saffron in a small dish with the milk. Add raisins.

Pour the rice into 3 quarts boiling water, then adjust heat to boil steadily about 15 minutes, until tender but not mushy. Drain and mix with the egg.

While the rice is boiling, butter the insides of 8 muffin cups, each of $\frac{1}{3}$-cup capacity. Smash the cookie with a rolling pin and sprinkle crumbs into the buttered muffin cups. (You will not use all the crumbs.)

Toast pine nuts on an unoiled sheet in the oven 4 or 5 minutes or until golden but not dark brown.

Pack a thin layer of the rice-egg mixture into the cups to form a shell on the bottom and sides. Mix remaining rice-egg mixture with the saffron-milk-raisin mixture and the pine nuts, sugar, and lemon zest; fill muffin cups with this mixture. Sprinkle with remaining crumbs.

Bake 25 to 30 minutes or until a golden-brown crust forms around the edges of the "muffins." Remove from the oven and set muffin tin for 1 minute in an inch or so of cold water in a sink or large pan. Remove from water and scoop out the muffins with a knife blade or small spoon handle.

Kheer
Slow-Cooked Milk with Rice

Serves 4

Any long-grain rice will work here, but the thin, elongated, delicate grains of real Indian basmati help to make this elegantly low-keyed Indian rice pudding a truly regal dessert. Reducing milk for a creamy effect is a classic Indian practice.

> *8 cups milk*
> *4 tablespoons Indian basmati rice, washed and drained*
> *10 green cardamom pods, bruised, or 1 teaspoon ground cardamom*
> *½ teaspoon saffron threads, crumbled*
> *4 tablespoons sugar*
> *pinch salt*
> *2 teaspoons rose flower water (optional)*
> *1 tablespoon blanched, peeled, slivered almonds*
> *1 tablespoon shelled, slivered, unsalted pistachio nuts*

Put the milk in a heavy-bottomed saucepan with the rice and the cardamom pods, if using. Bring to a boil, then adjust heat to a moderate boil. Put 1 tablespoon of the milk in a small cup with the saffron and reserve. Cook the rice and milk 10 to 15 minutes, stirring constantly and scraping the sides and bottom of the pot. Reduce heat to low and cook, stirring every few minutes, until the milk is reduced to 4 cups. Whenever a scum forms on top, stir it back into the milk. After about 1 hour of slow cooking, when the milk is reduced, remove cardamom pods or add ground cardamom. Stir in the saffron milk, then the sugar and salt and cook, stirring, until dissolved. Stir in the rose water and most of the nuts. Pour into a serving bowl or small individual bowls to cool. When sufficiently thickened, top with remaining nuts and refrigerate. Serve cold.

Coconut Rice Pudding

Serves 8

This pudding can be made two ways. For the quick 20-minute version, use only 1 can of coconut milk. For a creamier version, add a second can after the first is absorbed and continue cooking as directed. Some like to add shredded coconut to coconut rice pudding, but the texture will be creamier without.

> *1 cup short-grain white rice*
> *1 or 2 cans coconut milk (about 14 ounces each)*
> *4 tablespoons raisins*
> *4 tablespoons sugar*
> *$\frac{1}{2}$ teaspoon ground cardamom*
> *$\frac{1}{4}$ teaspoon ground cinnamon*
> *$\frac{1}{4}$ teaspoon ground ginger*
> *$\frac{1}{8}$ teaspoon salt*
> *$\frac{1}{2}$ cup shredded coconut (optional)*
> *3 tablespoons rum (optional)*
> *4 tablespoons shelled, unsalted pistachio nuts*

Bring 3 quarts of water to a boil. Add the rice and boil 15 minutes. Drain through a strainer.

Bring 1 can coconut milk to a low boil. Add raisins, sugar, spices, salt, and shredded coconut, if using. Stir in the boiled rice (and the optional rum, if making the quick version) and cook uncovered until liquid is absorbed. This will take a very few minutes. At this point, your quick coconut rice pudding is done, to be garnished if desired with pistachio nuts toasted as directed below.

For a creamier version, add the second can of coconut milk after the first can has been absorbed. Bring to a boil. Reduce heat to simmer uncovered 25 minutes, stirring gently to prevent sticking and burning on the bottom. Then stir the rum into the pudding to cook another 5 minutes. At the same time, put the pistachio nuts in a 350°F toaster oven or regular oven, to toast for 5 minutes. Cool pudding to room temperature, spoon into individual dishes, and top with the toasted nuts.

Thai Coconut Rice with Mango

Serves 8

This rice pudding is always served with sweet ripe tropical fruit such as mango, which makes all the difference between a plain, rather dense dessert and a made-in-heaven combination. Small portions of the pudding suffice because the coconut milk is so rich.

> *1 cup sticky rice (page 8)*
> *1 14-ounce can coconut milk or 2 cups fresh coconut milk (page 52)*
> *4 tablespoons sugar*
> *$\frac{1}{8}$ teaspoon salt*
> *2 ripe mangoes, peeled and sliced*

Several hours or the night before you plan to serve the pudding, rinse the rice several times in a sieve under cold running water until the water runs clear or almost clear. Put the rice in a bowl with cool water to cover by 1 inch and soak 6 hours or overnight. Then pour off the water through a sieve, rinse the rice again, and drain in the sieve by shaking and raking with your fingers.

Line a steamer with cheesecloth and spread the rice over the cheesecloth. Cover the steamer and steam the rice over gently boiling water 45 to 50 minutes. (For details on steaming rice, see page 18). Twice during the steaming period, lift the cover and quickly sprinkle the rice with 3 tablespoons water. At the end of the steaming period, remove from heat and rest 10 minutes.

While the rice is resting, put the coconut milk in a saucepan and bring to a simmer. Stir in the sugar and salt.

Turn the rice into a bowl and add the warm milk. The mixture will look soupy, but after it rests for 30 minutes you will be able to cut it with a knife. Serve each portion on a small plate with some mango slices.

Philippine-Style Coconut Rice Porridge

Serves 6

Pacific islanders enjoy this Asian equivalent of rice pudding for a snack at any time. It makes a good sweet breakfast and can be cooked the night before, left on the stove, and reheated in the morning.

> ½ cup sticky rice (page 8)
> 4 cups fresh coconut milk (page 52), or 2 (14-ounce) cans,
>   or 1 can coconut milk and 1 can water
> 2 to 4 tablespoons brown sugar or maple syrup, to taste
> ¼ teaspoon salt

Put the rice in a sieve and rinse under running water until the water runs clear. Then put in a bowl with water to cover by 1 inch and soak 2 or more hours or overnight.

Drain rice and put in a heavy-bottomed saucepan with the coconut milk. Bring to a gentle boil. Cover the pot but leave the lid slightly ajar and turn the heat to very low. Cook at a very slow but steady simmer for 1½ hours, stirring occasionally with a wooden spoon to prevent sticking on the bottom. Remove from heat and stir in the sugar or syrup and the salt.

Optional Additions

Sweetened coconut rice porridge needs no enhancement. However, it's also good with any of the following additions:
- Throw in some fresh or dried shredded coconut with the milk.
- Stir in 4 tablespoons of raisins for the last half-hour of cooking.
- When serving, grate some fresh gingerroot over each portion.
- When the porridge is done, roast 4 tablespoons peanuts in a 350°F oven or toaster oven until lightly browned, about 5 minutes. Then crush with a rolling pin and sprinkle over the porridge.

Index